ROMAN REPUBLICAN MONEYERS AND THEIR COINS 81 BCE - 64 BCE

Michael Harlan

MONETA
PUBLICATIONS

Dedication

To my wife Linda whose patient reading and rereading has led only to improvements in my text. This book goes to print in the month of our forty-first wedding anniversary and would never have come to print without her help and encouragement.

Library of Congress Control Number: 2012903810

ISBN 978-0-9654567-0-8

MONETA PUBLICATIONS

Published by Moneta Publications, Citrus Heights, CA 95610

CONTENTS

CONTENTS

PREFACE

When I started this project I felt that it was largely a foray into the unknown. I had chosen the period 63-49 BCE for my book *Roman Republican Moneyers and Their Coins 63 BC-49 BC* (1995) because the moneyers of that period were mostly men well-known in Roman history and there was a great amount of source material to draw on. It was also a period of time when the *cursus honorum* established under the Sullan constitution was being followed by all the aristocrats with one exception, Pompey. This meant that it was easier to find dates for a moneyer's career and thus more accurately date the coins. And a hoard of approximately 5,940 denarii found at Mesagne in Calabria had recently been published by Charles Hersh and Alan Walker [*ANSMN* 29 (1984)] which allowed the first major re-dating of Republican coins since Michael Crawford's two volume work *Roman Republican Coinage*, published in 1974. But the earlier years of Sulla's constitution from 81 BCE to 64 BCE were filled with moneyers who were completely unknown save for the names on their coins. Dating these coins was far more difficult and since interpretation depends on proper dating, the moneyers and their coins presented a daunting, but interesting challenge. How much can one say about unknown moneyers? Quite a bit as it turns out.

In reality, the coins themselves have a lot to say when placed into the proper context and as my study progressed, the coins began to shed light on two particular paths of political propaganda. One theme is the assimilation of the newly enrolled citizens from the Italian *municipia* into the Roman state. It becomes clear why so many of the moneyers are unknown. They were new men, the first of their family line looking to membership in the Senate. Many of the designs on their coins were intended to make them known to their fellow Romans who were just as much in the dark about them as we are. As I noted in the first book's introduction, 'the office of mint magistrate offered a very special opportunity. The moneyer had the right to put a design of his own choosing on the state's money. Each coin offered the chance to introduce the moneyer's name to the public whose votes he would soon seek in his bid for the quaestorship.' The coin is the moneyer's window of opportunity to get his message across and 'the message must be conveyed quickly by symbols readily recognized, images well known, and inscriptions to clarify what was not apparent. The object was self-promotion. We have here something unprecedented: a national coinage with a personal message.'

The second theme is a national message that the individual moneyer now shared with the rest of Italy. That message is that Roman Italy is destined to be the head of the world. We were familiar with this theme in the extant histories, but the coins give us a visual presentation of how that propaganda was passed from hand to hand.

NOTE

In the following chapters all dates given are BCE, unless otherwise stated, and the subject of each chapter is called a moneyer, whether he exercised the function as a mint magistrate or as a higher magistrate or promagistrate under Senate decree. The book is meant to be read without reference to the notes which contain only source references and no further discussion of the material. When I use die numbers, remember that Crawford's estimates are only that, estimates, and contested in many cases, but they do show relative quantities of the coins minted.

Michael Harlan

INTRODUCTION

In this volume, I cover thirty-four moneyers who minted in the period 81 to 64. Added to the thirty moneyers presented in *Roman Republican Moneyers and Their Coins 63 BC-49 BC* this completes a picture of Republican coinage under the Sullan constitution from its beginning in 81 until disrupted by civil war in 49. The basic theories I advanced for the moneyers in the period 63 to 49 apply to the coinage between 81 and 64. But since I have slightly modified my earlier view and since people may not have read the earlier work, I think it best to revisit the discussion of the *cursus honorum*.

Much of the prosopographical evidence on the moneyers comes from a process of reconstruction whose framework depends on reforms in the political process made by Sulla in 81. The course of a Roman political career was marked by stages at which one became eligible to hold a certain office. The process was called the *cursus honorum* or the 'course of offices.' All offices of the *cursus* were unpaid annual positions filled by popular election. These offices were eagerly sought after because of the prestige that the position brought, so it was also the course of honor. The higher one rose in the system, the greater the honor he held and that also attached to his family line.

The first step was the quaestorship of which there were twenty; those elected gained membership in the Senate. Under the Sullan constitution, in order to run for the quaestorship a man had to be at least thirty years old and he had to have sufficient wealth to meet the property qualifications required of a senator. This means that any man holding the quaestorship was at least thirty-one years old at some point during his year of office. The next major step of the *cursus honorum* was the praetorship, of which there were eight. A man had to be at least thirty-nine years old to be a candidate, so any praetor was at least forty years old at some point during his term of office. There were two other offices frequently held at some point during the nine years between the quaestorship and the praetorship. The tribunate of the plebs, of which there were ten, was open only to plebeians, as the office name indicates. Designed as a check on the abuse of power by the patricians, the tribunate of the plebs was not actually a magistracy in the sense of the offices of the *cursus honorum*, but it was an extremely powerful office, because it had the power of veto over legislation and the ability to initiate legislation in the assembly of the people. Since the time of Sulla the office was usually held after the quaestorship, making the minimum age of a tribune thirty-two. A passage from Dio Cassius which refers to a Senate reform of the office under Augustus prior to 13 supports this. Since no one was readily seeking the office any more, the Senate decreed that the tribunes would be appointed by lot from the ex-quaestors not yet forty years old.[1] The legislation probably reflects the normal point in a career for the holding of the tribunate. The second office available before the praetorship was the aedileship, of which there were four, two plebeian and two curule. The minimum age for a candidate was thirty-six, so an aedile was at least thirty-seven years old. Although not a mandatory part of the *cursus*, the office was a stepping stone to the praetorship. The aedileship could be a costly office, since one of its chief duties was the public presentation of annual games. The aediles often spent extravagant amounts of their own money to curry favor with the voting public, expecting that their splendid displays would be well remembered and reap the voters' gratitude in their election bid for the praetorship.

Those who reached the praetorship could look to the ultimate prize of the consulship. The two consulships were open only to those who had held the praetorship. A candidate for the consulship had to be at least forty-two, so any consul was at least forty-three years old. There were restrictions on holding any of the major offices without one year between them, but no restriction on holding the tribunate the year after the quaestorship or the year before the praetorship. Each of the steps raised the individual's and his family's prestige both within the society as a whole and among his peers in the Senate, where the order in which one might speak was determined by how far he had risen in the *cursus*. Membership in the Senate was for life, but a member's wealth and behavior were subject to review by the censors, and should a man be ejected from the Senate for any reason, he had to start the *cursus* again, if he wished to regain his position.

The minimum ages set by the *cursus honorum* provide a valuable means of determining the proper identification of a moneyer and the date of his coinage. For example, if a man was consul in 50, we know that he was at least forty-three years old, which means that he had to have been born by the year 93 and not later. Moreover, if we know of a man who had been an unsuccessful candidate in 51 for the office of consul for the year 50, he too had to have been born by 93. We also know that in order to run for the consulship he had to have already held the praetorship and the quaestorship, even if there is no other historical reference of his ever having held any office. The *cursus* establishes only minimum ages and does not mean that a man could not be older. Cicero prided himself on holding office *in suo anno*, that is, his first year of eligibility. It is because of Cicero's career that we are able to establish the minimum ages for the *cursus* under the Sullan constitution. However, Cicero was from a family which had never held major office. He was a *novus homo*, a new man in politics, and it was a special source of pride to him to win election in his first year of eligibility. To a well-heeled aristocrat election to office was less in doubt and perhaps to win election *in suo anno* was not so important. However, it was election to the quaestorship that brought membership in the Senate where all political power and social prestige resided, and we should expect a noble to seek that office in his first or second year of eligibility, while a 'new man' might take a bit longer to win admission.

Where does the office of mint magistrate, indicated by the inscription IIIVIR on some coins, fit into the career plans of a rising politician? The moneyership was a minor office, a part of the larger *vigintisexviri*, the twenty-six men, consisting of three in charge of the criminal trials, three in charge of minting money, four who took care of the streets in Rome, ten assigned to the courts, two who took care of the roads outside Rome, and four who were sent to Campania. We have little information on these offices under the Republic, but we do get an interesting look at them under Augustus. These positions, reduced to twenty by the elimination of the last six men and now known as the *vigintiviri* under Augustus, had become very difficult to fill because no one wanted the responsibility. The Senate decreed that henceforth 'the *vigintiviri* were to be appointed from the knights.' Dio said that 'thus no one came into the Senate without having held one of the other offices which was able to lead to it.'[2] The offices of the *vigintiviri* were clearly considered to be stepping stones to the Senate, which in Augustus' time were being overstepped by those entering the Senate. The question is, were they mandatory steps or optional? The decree seems to make them mandatory, but that cannot be correct. If these were the only men who could go on to compete for the quaestorship, then their appointment as *vigintiviri* would have amounted to their election as quaestors, since no one else was eligible to run. Moreover, a pool of only twenty men was too small a number from which to draw the twenty quaestors. What we do learn about the *vigintiviri* is that they were knights, that the office was appointed, and that the office was considered a stepping stone to the Senate. Now, can we use this evidence to look back at the offices of the *vigintisexviri* in the period of the Sullan constitution? It may be argued that the Augustan Senate's decree was simply reinstating the practice of the Republic.

The office of mint magistrate offers us our best look at the *vigintisexviri*, since the holder of that office inscribed his name on the coins, while the names of the men who held the other offices of the *vigintisexviri* have been lost in the passage of time. Dio made it clear that 'the office was able to lead to the Senate.' Harold Mattingly felt that Sulla had made the moneyership a 'fixed pre-quaestorian post like other constituent parts of the vigintisexvirate.'[3] We shall see that what we know of the men who held the mint magistracy during the period 81 to 49 confirms that they were indeed knights and that the majority went on to become senators. How were they selected? It seems from the evidence of Cicero's *Pro Cluentio* 39 that the office of triumvir in charge of criminal trials was an elected position as late as the civil wars between Sulla and the Marians. We cannot say with certainty that it remained so after Sulla's reforms. Mattingly infers from Cicero's list of minor magistracies in *De Legibus* 3.3.6 that they were elected, but the passage itself says nothing of the method of selection. In an earlier article, Andrew Burnett argued that since the *Lex Acilia* of 122 did not mention the mint magistrates in its list of elected magistrates, 'it is possible to infer from this that they were not elected.'[4] In any case, the offices of the *vigintisexviri* were never a part of the *cursus honorum*. If an office in the *vigintisexviri* was an elective office which opened a ready path to the Senate, we might have expected Cicero to take it, but he made no mention that he ever held the office. If these offices were appointed by the Senate, then we have a type of nominating process whereby the senators determined the candidates whom they would most like to see eventually elected to their august body. By their selection to the *vigintisexviri*, these candidates for the Senate had an advantage over the other candidates who failed to obtain the endorsement of the Senate. To my mind, the most telling argument for appointment rather than election is what Burnett termed 'a close chronological link between a moneyer and a related consul.'[5]

What was the minimum age for the *vigintisexviri*, assuming that there was a minimum age? If we were to use the currently accepted dating for the coins, and if we review the moneyers' fixed or estimated birth dates, we find that their ages would range from their early twenties to mid-thirties. Since the offices of the *vigintisexviri* were thought to be stepping stones leading to the Senate, the only men who would seek the office were those who would go on to run for the quaestorship. Therefore, we should be looking in the years just before one expects to run for the quaestorship. A knight in his early twenties was still completing his military service with too long a step to take to get into the Senate, and a man in his mid-thirties not yet a senator would be a rather late-blooming aristocrat. The latitude given to the age of the moneyer has been far too wide and, if it is tightened up a bit, we can arrive at more accurate dates and better understand the coins in their historical context. The dating that I offer has been arrived at on the following principle: the position of mint magistrate within the *vigintisexviri* was an office, whether appointed or elected, held by a knight hoping to enter upon a senatorial career, that is a man about thirty years old. Most likely he would be holding the office the same year that he became a candidate for the quaestorship.

All coinage minted under the Sullan constitution is inscribed with the moneyer's name. In some cases the mint magistrate also designated his office with the inscription IIIVIR, triumvir of the mint. However, the total number of coins is far too small to assign one issue to each of the three men and it appears that in many years only one man issued coinage. We cannot say why only one signed the coinage, but it may have been determined by drawing lots, as were so many things in Rome.

The mint magistrate, however, was not the only person who was given authority to mint silver into coin. We have numerous examples of coins issued by higher magistrates: quaestors who marked their coins with a Q, curule aediles who marked their coins with CVR•AED, plebeian aediles who marked their coins AED•PL, praetors who marked their coins with a P or PR, and in one case a special 'curator for minting denarii' who marked his coin CVR⁎FL. In every one of the instances between 81 and 49 where a higher magistrate has inscribed his denarius with his office, there is an S•C, indicating that it was minted by decree of the Senate. However, there are also a large number of coins that have the S•C inscription without any designation of office. It has been generally accepted that the S•C inscription was only used when the needs of the state went beyond the original budgeted amounts and this coinage constituted special allocations made by decree of the Senate. Crawford summed up his assessment of the S•C inscription, 'it thus seems probable, though not absolutely certain, that routine coinage, although authorised by the Senate bore no special mark and that only when an issue was separately authorised during the year was it marked with EX SC.'[6] Crawford assigned to the mint magistrates all the S•C coinage not signed by higher magistrates and this has been generally accepted.

If we consider the evidence we have on the coins themselves for the period between Sulla's reforms in 81 and Caesar's crossing the Rubicon in 49, I believe a fairly simple and consistent explanation for the S•C inscription emerges. First, on many coins we have the inscription IIIVIR, which stands for the office of triumvir of the mint, and when it occurs we do not see the inscription S•C, except in one instance. That coin was minted in 49 by Quintus Sicinius. The inscription Q•SICINIVS appears before the head of Apollo on the obverse of a second coin type with his office IIIVIR behind the head, but on the reverse is the inscription C•COPONIVS on the right edge and PR•S•C on the left edge. Gaius Coponius was a praetor in 49. This is a hybrid coin minted jointly by a mint magistrate and a praetor after Caesar crossed the Rubicon and the S•C inscription is on the side of the coin with the praetor's name. Secondly, from the beginning of the Sullan constitution in 81 until disrupted by civil war in 49, in every case where we have the office of a higher magistrate inscribed on the coin, we also have an S•C inscription. There are a few instances prior to the Sullan constitution when a higher magistrate minted without using the S•C inscription. Publius Furius Crassipes minted as curule aedile and Lucius Manlius Torquatus as proquaestor. But those coins may date to 82 during the civil war or Sulla's dictatorship and may not have been issued by Senate decree. Additionally, the plebeian aediles Marcus Fannius and Lucius Critonius (*ca.* 86) did not use S•C but marked their coin P•A on the reverse for *publico argento* indicating that the coin was struck on the occasion of a public largess under special authorization. There appear to be at least eight such P•A special issues, but the others are not marked with any indication of office.

In *Roman Republican Moneyers and their Coins 63BC-49BC,* I argued that all S•C coins were minted by men who were already senators. But on further consideration I believe that this can be narrowed even more to men who were either quaestors or higher magistrates or promagistrates. Plautius Hypsaeus offers an example of how this would work. He minted as curule aedile in 58 in conjunction with his fellow aedile Scaurus. Those coins are marked AED•CVR and S•C. But Hypsaeus also minted two individual issues that are not marked AED•CVR but still have the S•C inscription. This offers two possibilities. Either he was aedile when he minted those coins and the missing AED•CVR inscription shows that a higher magistrate did not always put his office on the coins; or the AED•CVR inscription is missing because he was not an aedile when he minted those coins, showing that a senator who got special authorization by decree of the Senate to mint coins did not necessarily put his office on the coins. The absence of the non-AED•CVR coins from the Mesagne hoard suggests that they were minted later than 58 and following Hersh and Walker's suggestion, they are now usually dated to 57. To me this evidence suggests that Hypsaeus minted his individual coins the next year as a promagistrate. He was certainly not a mint magistrate.

I believe that S•C coinage offers intrinsic evidence that the man who signed the issue was at least a quaestor, and hence at least thirty-one years old. In other words, S•C coinage was not issued by a mint magistrate. The S•C represents authorization for a higher magistrate or promagistrate to mint money for some special purpose, the most common examples being the purchase of grain or soldiers' pay. The coins themselves then can be an additional prosopographical tool that I have used in the following way. The coins fall into two groups: S•C issues and non-S•C issues. The non-S•C issues are all minted by triumvirs of the mint, who are knights about to enter on a senatorial career and who are about thirty years old, give or take a year. The S•C issues are all minted by men who hold either one of the higher offices or a promagistracy.

The three main points that I use in dating are: 1) a moneyer as a member of the *vigintisexviri* held office as a stepping stone to the Senate and was likely to be a candidate for the quaestorship the same year he was a moneyer; therefore, he was about 30 years old when he minted, 2) at least one mint magistrate issued coinage each year and those coins are not marked with S•C inscriptions, 3) S•C coins and non-S•C coins are to be divided into two different categories, the non-S•C coins represent regular issues minted by a triumvir of the mint; the S•C coins are special issues minted by men who were quaestors or magistrates of higher office or promagistrates. Unlike the mint magistrates, their authorization to mint probably came with the additional responsibility to oversee how it was spent.

Only four of the thirty moneyers whom I treated in *Roman Republican Moneyers and their Coins 63BC-49BC* were unknown from any other source. The ratio is virtually reversed for the moneyers minting between the years 81 and 64, since of the thirty-four men included in this study only eight are known from other sources. Consequently, the dating of this group of men has relied heavily on hoard evidence. Application of the above theories to the hoard evidence for these early years of the Sullan period creates a very different picture from that which has been developed by Crawford's dating.

First, we have to determine what coins belong to the years 81 and later. The Monte Codruzzo hoard is most useful here. The hoard consisted of some 5,000 pieces. Borghesi examined 4,734 coins and they were described by Cavedoni. The hoard contained coins minted by Gaius Annius Luscus, the proconsul sent to Spain in 82 and coins by Gaius Valerius Flaccus, the propraetor in Gaul in 83/82. The latest mint magistrates are P. Crepusius, C. Limetanus, and L. Censorinus who minted both as a college and individually. Crawford dated them to 82. The terminus of the Monte Codruzzo hoard seems fairly well dateable to the year 82, which gives us a good dividing line. The coins in the Monte Codruzzo hoard belong to 82 or before and those not found in the hoard are likely to be later. The thirty-four moneyers treated in this book were all absent from the Monte Codruzzo hoard and, therefore, can reasonably be dated to 81 or later.

Of the issues which Crawford assigned to the first years after the Codruzzo hoard, I do not treat the 'restored issues' of M. Metellus (369), C. Servilius (370), and Q. Maximus (371). Crawford wrote:

> These 'restored' issues borrow the reverse types of nos. 263-5 and are, as it were, struck in memory of the men whose names appear on them, not by these men... I have no doubt that the issues are Sullan...

> they occur for the first time in the San Miniato hoard and thus belong between 82 and 80.[7]

If, as Crawford suggests, these coins were not actually struck by the men whose names are on the coins, they add little to our picture of the moneyers of the period and their political messages. I have also excluded from this study the following coins dated by Crawford to 81: anonymous (373), Q.C.M.P.I. (374), Q (375), EX SC (376), and the aureus by A. Manlius (381), which all appear to be special war issues dateable to 82 or 81. All are outside the mainstream of the new Sullan constitution and it is clear that none were by regular mint magistrates. This leaves a group of thirty-four moneyers for the years 81-64. This number is virtually the same number of moneyers assigned to the period by Hersh and Walker.

There are two notable departures I make from Hersh and Walker's arrangement. I have retained the ten coins by Pomponius Musa and the five non-AED•CVR S•C coins by Plaetorius Cestianus in this period despite their absence from the Mesagne hoard. Hersh and Walker assumed that Pomponius' issue was quite large since it comprised ten different types and they argued that his absence from the Mesagne hoard could only be explained by his minting after the hoard's terminus of 58. They assigned Pomponius to 56. This date now appears in catalogs. I am not convinced that Pomponius Musa's total mintage was ever large. His coins seldom are offered on the market and, when they do appear, command higher prices, which testifies to their rarity. Their appearance in hoards is scanty at best. I opted not to treat him as a moneyer of the 50s in my earlier study. His presence in the 60s becomes necessary in order to have one mint magistrate for each year. But we should also note that, if his mintage was not large, his absence from the Mesagne hoard is not an absolute statement that he did not mint before 58. In fact, I have become more convinced that Pomponius Musa does belong in the 60s and my reasons are given in his chapter.

Also absent from the Mesagne hoard were the five S•C coins by Marcus Plaetorius Cestianus that were not inscribed AED•CVR. Assuming these were later than Mesagne's terminus of 58, Hersh and Walker assigned them to 57. At the time I was not sure about this suggestion either, but that date now appears in most catalogs. Plaetorius had minted as curule aedile in 68 or 67 and for him to mint again a decade later, even after his praetorship, seemed an anomaly, so I opted not to treat those five S•C coins as part of the coinage of the 50s. If we date his non-AED•CVR coins after his aedileship, Plaetorius seems to parallel Hypsaeus. Both men issued as curule aediles and both issued additional S•C coins without designation of office. The willingness to accept a later dating for Hypsaeus' and Plaetorius' coins after a curule aedileship is not only a rejection of Crawford's explanation of S•C coinage as routine coinage by a mint magistrate separately authorized by the Senate during the year, it is also an affirmation that the higher magistrates or promagistrates who minted S•C coins did not always put their office on the coins. If one accepts Hersh and Walker's date of 57 for Plaetorius and Hypsaeus, a year when they were certainly not mint magistrates, we are no longer arguing whether S•C coins were minted by higher magistrates but rather when they were minted. With further study, I think my decision to exclude Plaetorius from the moneyers of the 50s was correct and on the basis of the arguments given in Cestianus' chapter, I have dated his five S•C coins not inscribed AED•CVR to 67, the year following his aedileship, just as Hypsaeus' non-AED•CVR coins are dated to the year following his aedileship.

If we then separate the non-S•C and S•C coins, we are left with eighteen non-S•C moneyers representing the issues of the mint magistrates. This gives us only one moneyer for each of the eighteen years of this period (treating the joint issue by KALENI/CORDI as one year's issue). This sets up a completely different way of assigning the moneyers. Once a year has been assigned, it is removed from the available choices for another non-S•C coin. This allows us to use the hoard evidence in a slightly different way than other commentators have used it.

The hoard of major importance for determining a dividing line within the period 81 to 64 is the Roncofreddo hoard. Found near Savignano in the Romagna in 1756, it consisted of approximately 6,000 denarii and seventeen quinarii which were cataloged by Pietro Borghesi. Cavedoni thought it was buried in the revolt of Spartacus between 73 and 71. Grueber following Count de Salis' arrangement dated its terminus to 75 and this was the date accepted by Crawford. Hersh and Walker in their re-dating moved Lucretius Trio into 74 thereby lowering the terminus, but they offered no reason for this change. The one moneyer in the hoard about whom we have good prosopographical information is Gnaeus Lentulus Marcellinus whose *cursus honorum* dates for his later career suggest a date of 74 for the quaestorship during which he issued the S•C coins inscribed with a Q. Despite the independent evidence of the *cursus honorum,* the Roncofreddo hoard has been dated by Crawford and Grueber to 75 and, therefore, Marcellinus' quaestorship was pushed back to 76. Marcellinus' *cursus* in itself is good reason to rethink the terminus of 75 for Roncofreddo.

I have used the Roncofreddo hoard in the following way. My first working assumption is that there are no gaps within the hoard of the issues by the mint magistrates. The 1,000 coin Frascarolo hoard which contains virtually the same moneyers supports this assumption. There are only ten new non-S•C coins in the Roncofreddo hoard not found in the Monte Codruzzo hoard whose terminus date is 82. Using my argument that coins marked with an S•C are not issued by mint magistrates, those non-S•C coins represent the coins issued by mint magistrates and should be assigned to separate years starting in 81. Assuming that at least one triumvir of the mint issued coins each year, we can find the terminus of Roncofreddo by simply counting. This gives a terminus date of 72 for the hoard. We do not need to know the order of the moneyers to arrive at this date. A date of 72 returns us to Cavedoni's original suggestion that the hoard was buried during Spartacus' revolt.

The Roncofreddo hoard offers a block of ten mint magistrates whose dates can be further placed in relative position to one another using the evidence from other smaller hoards that fall within this period. There is prosopographical evidence for only one of the ten mint magistrates, namely Cassius, and he has been assigned to 76 on the basis of his *cursus*. This offers further definition to the ambiguous hoard evidence. As we proceed beyond the new terminus of 72 for the Roncofreddo hoard, we start with the year 71 for dating the next eight mint magistrates. Since Gaius Postumius is the only additional mint magistrate found in nine hoards whose other moneyers are all found in the Roncofreddo hoard, my system must assign him to the year 71 and, if he can be identified as the candidate for a praetorship in 63, the prosopographical material supports this date. The *cursus* dates of the moneyer Publius Lentulus Spinther who issued S•C coinage as quaestor suggest his coin be dated to 70 and it appears in hoards shortly after Postumius. The lowered dating of the other moneyers opens up new territory for interpretation that has been unexplored because of the traditional dating of these coins to earlier years.

I have already commented on the fact that most of the moneyers of this period are unknown and, because of that, commentaries on the coins have been brief and unsatisfactory. Much of the work on the moneyers in the period 63-49 illuminates the historical references depicted on their coins, but few of the moneyers of the earlier period 81-64 had family histories or personal achievements that they could put before the voters as recommendations for their advancement in the *cursus*. But this should not be surprising since Roman politics had been opened up to a huge new pool of voters and candidates as a result of granting citizenship to the Italian *municipia* in 90. Lily Ross Taylor said that the registration of new voters was not complete until 84 and went on to say, 'The suspension of constitutional forms under the domination of Cinna and Carbo and under the dictatorship of Sulla gave no chance to test the new distribution of voters. That would have to wait until Sulla laid down his dictatorship in 79.'[8]

That so many of the moneyers are unknown is due to the entry of so many new men from the Italian *municipia* into Roman politics after Sulla's reforms. As a result, the character of the coinage changed somewhat in this period. Numerous references to Greek myths began to appear on the coins reflecting traditions that were strong in other parts of Italy away from Rome. The granting of Roman citizenship to the Italian *municipia* also put to rest the contention between Rome and the *municipia* over who was to hold the dominant *imperium* in Italy. That was ceded to Rome when the Italian *municipia* asked for Roman citizenship. But now, the new Roman state composed of Rome and the Italian *municipia* was determined to hold *imperium* over the world.

In the coin designs of the moneyers who held office under Sulla's new constitution, we see the development of these two major themes: the integration of the new voters and their candidates into Roman politics and the assertion by the new Roman state of its right to hold *imperium* over the world.

Acknowledgements for Illustrations

In *Roman Republican Moneyers and Their Coins 63 BC-49 BC*, the obverse and reverse images were used separately and kept at denarius size. In this volume, I decided to use enlarged images to better illustrate the coins and to keep obverse and reverse together as they are in catalogs. I have used several images in some cases because it is not always possible to find the whole design on one coin. I wish to thank the following companies for allowing me to reproduce illustrations from their catalogs. I have noted in the chapters where each individual coin came from, but sometimes the same coin has appeared in different auctions at different companies. I only cited one auction.

A. Tkalec AG
Classical Numismatic Group, Inc.
Freeman and Sear
Gemini Numismatic Auctions, LLC
Gorny & Mosch Giessener Müzhandlung
Numismatica Ars Classica
The British Museum

Chapter 1

AULUS POSTUMIUS ALBINUS 81 BCE

In late 82, the battle at the Colline Gate made Sulla the victor in Rome's civil war and the *interrex* Lucius Valerius Flaccus, who later became Sulla's *magister equitum*, secured Sulla's election to the dictatorship. Sulla was also given complete immunity from prosecution for his subsequent reforms and he immediately set out to eliminate his personal enemies by publishing their names on proscription lists, offering rich rewards for their heads. Early in 81, he also undertook a reform of the constitution that was designed to put power into the hands of the Senate. The number of the Senate was raised from 300 to 600 and the power of the tribunate of the plebs, the people's advocate, was limited. He also established the new *cursus honorum* that determined the path of a magistrate within the Senate. This new constitution remained in place from 81 until disrupted by the next civil war between Pompey and Caesar that began in 49. Aulus Postumius Albinus represents the first generation of the new candidates hoping to advance under Sulla's new constitution.

The moneyer who signed his name A•POST•A•F S•N•ALBIN, Aulus Postumius Albinus, son of Aulus, grandson of Spurius is unknown, but his patronymic leads us to identify him as the son of the earlier moneyer Aulus Postumius, son of Spurius, who together with Gaius Publicius Malleolus and Lucius Caecilius Metellus held the mint magistracy (*ca.* 96). While it was common for a moneyer to include his father's name in his own identification, Grueber noted that this is only the second time that a moneyer added the name of his grandfather. In this case, it suggests that he was the grandson of Spurius Postumius, the consul of 110. Although our moneyer has been lost to history save for his name on the two coin types he minted, his was an illustrious and highly respected family that had made significant contributions to the Roman state.

A relative dating of Postumius' two coin types is easily established by their absence from the large Monte Codruzzo hoard which consisted of some 5,000 coins.[1] Aulus Postumius Albinus' coins must be dated after the terminus of the Monte Codruzzo hoard. The latest regular issues in the hoard were the joint and individual issues by the triumvirs of the mint L. Marcius Censorinus, P. Crepusius, and C. Mamilius Limetanus dated by Crawford to 82. The Bellicello, Capalbio, and Carrara hoards add only Postumius as a new mint magistrate to those already found in Monte Codruzzo. This indicates that he was the next mint magistrate to issue coins after the college of Censorinus, Crepusius, and Limetanus which gives us a date of 81. A chance archaeological discovery in the ruins of Norba, whose destruction in 81 is well documented, adds additional support for this date.

Classical Numismatic Group, Inc. Triton VIII Lot 866

> Diana is on the obverse. The moneyer inscribed his name A•POST•A•F S•N•ALBIN on the reverse.

Sulla's narrow victory at the Colline Gate on 1 November 82 finally broke the back of the Marian opposition. The Samnite army which had hoped to relieve the younger Marius and his forces besieged in Praeneste failed in its attempt to capture Rome. The heads of the slain generals carried to Praeneste on spears announced the news to the beleaguered Marius. The townspeople of Praeneste despaired of continuing the struggle and decided to surrender. Marius was foiled in an attempt to escape and committed suicide. Upon Praeneste's surrender to Sulla's general Lucretius Ofella, the senators who had held commands under Marius were arrested. Some were executed by Ofella and others were cast into prison, only to be executed on Sulla's arrival. Sulla then separated the other captives into three groups. He pardoned the Romans, but shot down every last man of the 12,000 Praenestians and their Samnite allies.[2] With this example before them, the town of Norba, still in Marian hands, continued its resistance to Sulla's forces. However, when Aemilius Lepidus was let into the city at night through treachery, the citizens in their terror and despair went into a frenzy of self-slaughter. They set their town on fire, burning it to the ground so that no plunder could be found.[3]

Amidst the ruins and rubble of ancient Norba, archaeologists recovered one specimen of the coins newly minted by Aulus Postumius Albinus. The terminus date of the site offered Crawford corroborating evidence for dating Postumius to the year 81. Crawford wrote,

> The evidence of the Bellicello and Capalbio hoards tends to place this issue, that of A. Postumius Albinus, as the first moneyer's issue after

> those of the college of 82, thus early in 81; the finds in the excavations at Norba confirm this placing. The city was destroyed soon after the capture of Praeneste, thus early in 81, and was uninhabited in the time of Pliny; neither the temple of Juno nor the temple of Diana nor the site as a whole produced any coin later than a hardly worn denarius of A. Postumius Albinus.[4]

Sulla's victory stifled the last gasp of the rebel Italians who contested Rome's right to dominance over the Italian peninsula and brought to fulfillment the almost five century old prophecy which is commemorated on one of the coins minted by Aulus Postumius. On the obverse Postumius depicted a draped bust of Diana, clearly identified by the bow and quiver over her shoulder. Above Diana's head is the skull of a cow. This device specifically ties the obverse to the sacrificial scene on the reverse, recalling a legend connected with Diana's temple on the Aventine whose founding was traditionally attributed to the king Servius Tullius. Influenced by the famous temple of Artemis at Ephesus, which was built with the cooperation of a number of Asian cities, Servius lobbied for such a temple in Italy and finally prevailed on the Latin communities to cooperate with the Romans in building a common temple on the Aventine hill. By building it in Rome, Livy said that this was an admission by the Latins that the long struggle for supremacy was over and that they had accepted Rome as the capital, the *caput rerum* 'the head of things.'

There remained, however, one Sabine citizen who thought he saw a chance for his people to gain supremacy without the risks of war. On one of the Sabine farms there was a heifer of marvelous size and beauty, but most conspicuous for her horns. To the Romans her unusual horns marked this heifer out as a prodigy. The prophets foretold that *imperium* would reside in whatever city the man came from who sacrificed the heifer to Diana. So the Sabine led the heifer to Diana's shrine and stood before the altar. Aware of the prophecy, the Roman priest weighed the momentous consequences. 'Stranger,' he said, 'are you preparing to make an impure sacrifice to Diana? Will you not first purify yourself in a living river?' Not wanting to do anything wrong in the eyes of the goddess, the Sabine went down into the valley to the Tiber to purify himself. Our moneyer has depicted the scene at the point when the Roman priest has been left alone with the heifer standing before the lighted altar located on the rocks of the Aventine. He has started the sacrifice by sprinkling her head with holy water; and so it came to be that it was a Roman who sacrificed the heifer to Diana.[5] For generations thereafter the heifer's skull with its wondrous horns was seen hanging in the vestibule of the temple of Diana on the Aventine. Since it was customary in her other temples to hang stag heads, the cow skull here identifies this unique scene. Unfortunately, those wondrous horns depicted on Postumius' bovine led Crawford to misidentify the heifer as a bull and this description continues to be repeated in some modern catalogs.

Classical Numismatic Group, Inc. Triton XIV Lot 577

Above the head of Diana is the cow skull placed in her temple on the Aventine after the heifer was sacrificed by the Roman priest.

The tradition as preserved by Livy does not identify the priest by name; the emphasis was on the man's nationality, not his individual identity. But we know from Plutarch, who cited Juba as his source, that there were other versions of the story giving the names of the parties. The Sabine was Antro Coratius and the priest who sent him to purify himself was a Cornelius and the Roman who actually sacrificed the heifer was Tullius himself.[6]

The great battle at Lake Regillus, dated to 499 by one tradition and to 496 by another, was the first major battle fought between Rome and Italians over *imperium* following the sacrifice. This battle threatened the very existence of the new Roman Republic since it was an all-out attempt by the Latins and Etruscans to restore the exiled Tarquins to the throne. The Roman forces led by the dictator Aulus Postumius Albus were particularly hard pressed by the Latins until Postumius rallied the Roman cavalry and routed the Latins under the command of Sextus Tarquinius on the left wing. Their camp was taken and their leaders killed. In the rout that followed, out of an army of 40,000 infantry and 3,000 cavalry, less than 10,000 Latins returned home.[7]

Modern scholars argue that their crushing defeat at Lake Regillus forced the Latins to admit the supremacy of Rome and led to the building of the temple of Diana on the Aventine. The sacrifice of the heifer is taken as little more than a charming piece of folklore. From an historic position the modern research may well be correct, but the Roman annalistic tradition placed both the building of the temple of Diana and the sacrifice of the heifer in the time of the king Servius Tullius. None of the ancient sources dispute this and it is in this ancient tradition that we must assess Postumius' message to his contemporaries. The devices of the cow skull on the obverse, the rocky setting of the Aventine, the wondrous horns of the heifer, and the lone figure of the priest about to make the sacrifice relate specifically to the ancient sacrifice of the heifer to Diana on the Aventine which vouchsafed the eventual Roman rise to dominance. The battle of Lake Regillus which established the fame and nobility of the *gens* Postumia was but the first in a long line of battles and wars which would lead to Rome's *imperium* over all of Italy and beyond. The final conflicts over *imperium* in Italy were to come in the lifetime of our moneyer Aulus Postumius some four hundred years after Lake Regillus.

Ten years before this coin was minted, the Social War had been kindled by the smoldering resentment among the allies who argued that Rome could never have won her dominant position without their help, yet they did not enjoy the legal status of even the lowest Roman citizen. No longer content with their unequal position, they demanded Roman citizenship, a status unthinkable among the fiercely independent Italians living during the reign of Servius Tullius. This evolution in thought took centuries and was the greatest admission that Rome was the *caput rerum*, the head of things. But neither the established Roman aristocracy nor the citizen body of almost 400,000 enfranchised Romans was willing to share its privileged position. The allies' demands were constantly rebuffed. When their main patron in Rome, Livius Drusus, was murdered by an unknown assassin, the allies despaired of reaching a political solution. The people of Asculum precipitated armed rebellion with their murder of the praetor Servilius in late 91. The Marsi, Picentines, Paeligni, Vestini, Frentani, Marrucini, Hirpini, and the Samnites raised the standard of rebellion and the revolt spread to Lucania and Apulia.

The rebels chose the city of Corfinium as their rival capital, renamed it Italica, and began to mint their own money to pay troops. They quickly marshaled 150,000 soldiers, redoubtable warriors who had long been trained in the Roman style of fighting. The rebels also had control of the seas and their hopes were high that they might expect help from abroad. Bitter and bloody battles were waged throughout northern Italy and Campania. To prevent the spread of rebellion to the Latin and Etruscan cities, the *lex Julia* of 90 granted Roman citizenship to the Italian cities and provided for their reorganization as self-governing *municipia* rather than independent states. It is uncertain whether it applied only to those not currently in revolt or if it also, as seems probable, was offered to those who would lay down their arms. The law also allowed generals in the field to grant citizenship to individuals who served the Romans in battle. The *lex Julia* effectively slowed the tide of revolt, granting the allies the very issue for which they had lobbied before resorting to war. By the end of 89, most of the fighting was over. These concessions won over the moderate group who had always hoped to obtain their rights by legal means, leaving the battlefield to those more independence loving Italians who still dreamed of winning the *imperium* for their own people. The intensity of the passion that burned in those who maintained the struggle can be seen in the final casualty toll given by Velleius Paterculus who said that more than 300,000 Italian youths were killed.[8]

The die-hard Samnite and Lucanian rebels represented the last vestiges of Italian independence. When factious fighting broke out between the Marians and the Sullans, the Samnites and Lucanians allied themselves with the Marians from whom they won certain concessions. They bitterly opposed Sulla when he returned from the war with Mithridates, knowing that he would not honor the Marian concessions. Their battle cry before the Colline Gate, calling for the destruction of Rome, betrayed the depth of their hostility. Sulla's victory steeled him in his determination to eliminate those who refused to be assimilated. He butchered them as unarmed prisoners in the Villa Publica, slaughtered them at Praeneste, allowed them to destroy themselves at Norba, and then hunted down the survivors by placing them on the proscription lists. The very last vestiges of Italian independence had by now either been exchanged for Roman citizenship or were in the process of being so brutally suppressed that they were never to rise again.

But the spread of Roman *imperium* over four centuries had not stopped at the shores of Italy and as the empire had grown so too had the concept of *caput rerum*. Rome was no longer content to be the capital of just Italy. She would be the *caput orbis terrarum*, the head of the world, and that ancient prophecy that promised *imperium* to the people who sacrificed the heifer to Diana was now interpreted to mean that the Roman state would hold *imperium* over the whole world. Aulus Postumius' coin was not simply a commemoration of the ancient sacrifice on the Aventine that prophesied Roman *imperium*, it was a celebration of its fulfillment in Italy in his own lifetime. All of Italy had become Roman; now Roman Italy would become the head of the world.

But there remained one active bastion of Marian resistance to Roman *imperium* in Spain, where Sertorius, who had been given the governorship when the Marians were in power, refused to obey the Senate in Rome and had established an independent state and a refuge for the defeated Marians fleeing from Italy. By reducing the taxes and discontinuing the Roman practice of billeting troops in the cities, he had easily won over the Spaniards long oppressed by the greed and insolence of the Roman officials. Toward the end of 82 Sulla sent an army under the proconsul Gaius Annius to force a passage through the Pyrenees into Spain in order to dislodge Sertorius.

Roman concern over Spain is evidenced by the larger of Postumius' two issues. On an estimated 198 obverse dies he depicted a female head wearing a veil with the inscription HISPAN behind her head clearly identifying her as Hispania. On the reverse is a togate Roman magistrate standing between a legionary eagle and the fasces. Our moneyer has again insinuated his name into the design inviting us to assume some kind of family connection with the Spanish province, and so the magistrate has been identified as the praetor Lucius Postumius Albinus who had gone to Further Spain in 180 and had his term prorogued into 179. He fought two major battles with the Vaccaei, killing a reported 35,000. When he returned to Rome in 178, he celebrated a triumph over the Lusitanians and others in the same area and carried 20,000 pounds of silver in procession.[9]

Classical Numismatic Group, Inc. Triton VIII Lot 867

The head of Hispania on the obverse is identified by the inscription HISPAN. The moneyer's name on the reverse is read beginning on the left side of the eagle standard with A and on the other side of the pole with AL (ligature) BINI then POST•A•F in the exergue and S•N read from bottom up on the other side.

If the magistrate on the coin is the victorious praetor, his century old triumph over the Lusitanians was especially relevant in 81, for it was among the Lusitanians where Sertorius found the greatest support. They even reignited the war by inviting him back to Spain in 80 after he had been driven out by Annius and they remained his most loyal allies throughout the war.[10]

While it is possible to see a family reference in the reverse design, we should note that our moneyer chose not to be specific. He identified Hispania on the obverse by inscription, but not the magistrate on the reverse. That unnamed togate magistrate flanked by the fasces and the legionary eagle is a symbol of Roman *imperium*. Postumius' coin shows that Spain, represented by Hispania on the obverse, must also recognize Roman *imperium* and embrace Rome as the head of things just as Italy had done.

Chapter 2

GAIUS MARIUS CAPITO 81/80 BCE

The coin minted by the unknown moneyer Gaius Marius Capito, son of Gaius, was not found in the Bellicello or the Capalbio hoards which did contain Postumius' issue dated to 81. Marius' coin was found in the large Carrara hoard, which contained no mint magistrate later than Postumius. On this hoard evidence, Crawford's date of 81 is the best year in which to place Marius.

Marius issued only one coin type, depicting on the obverse the draped bust of Ceres whose head is bound with a wreath of grain. On the reverse is a plowman who holds a prod in his right hand and a staff in his left hand while guiding a yoke of oxen. From the control numbers extending from I to CLI we see that Marius used 151 sets of dies. Crawford recorded the 125 dies known when he published. The Mesagne hoard contained one previously unknown variety bearing the number LXXXII with the symbol of a tripod. This gives hope that more discoveries may fill in the other blanks.

Classical Numismatic Group, Inc. 87 Lot 931

This coin is an example from the first series up to number XXIIII. The inscription C•MARI•C•F•CAPIT is around the head and the number II follows the name near the chin. The number II is over the oxen on the reverse and the exergue is blank.

The way Marius used his control symbols divides the issue into three sections. On the first twenty-four die pairs, the numbers I to XXIIII appear along the edge of the coin's obverse with the name C•MARI•C•F•CAPIT. The same obverse number is repeated on the reverse over the oxen. No specimen XXV is recorded so we do not know if it ended the first series or started the second or was skipped. On numbers XXVI to XXXII a control symbol was added in the exergue of the reverse. On the numbers XXXIII to CLI the moneyer's *cognomen* CAPIT remains on the obverse and the symbol in the exergue of the reverse is moved to the obverse while C•MARI•C•F has been shifted to the exergue of the reverse.

Numismatica Ars Classica Auction 40 Lot 464

This die set used the number XXVII. On the reverse it has a turtle as the symbol in the exergue below the S•C.

The change of major importance to note in Marius' issue is that the coins marked I to XXIIII are non-S•C coins, but the remaining numbers XXVI to CLI are all inscribed S•C. The consecutive number sequence of the dies, however, makes it clear that this was a continuous issue. Why did Marius only start using the S•C inscription with the second series? Crawford in his discussion of the S•C inscription argued that the routine coinage, although authorized by the Senate, bore no S•C inscriptions and it seemed probable 'that only when an issue was separately authorised during the year was it marked with an EX SC.'[1] Marius' issue would seem to support Crawford's theory that the S•C inscription on a coin indicates money that was required beyond that originally budgeted for the year, and when the mint magistrate received special authorization to mint more, he added the S•C inscription. I agree that S•C issues were separately authorized issues, but I think that a moneyer who issued S•C coinage was not a mint magistrate, but rather a quaestor, or a higher magistrate in the *cursus honorum,* or a senator in a prorogued or special office, and he minted under special Senate authorization.

The continuity of type and the consecutive numbering sequence suggest that the entire issue was used for the same purpose right from the beginning. So, why were they not marked with the S•C from the beginning? No other moneyer split the same homogeneous issue into S•C and non-S•C coins. In this, Marius was unique, but then, the year in which he minted was unique, and I believe that something else was happening in this year of 81.

The consuls of the year 82 perished fighting Sulla, Marius at Praeneste, Carbo in Sicily, and no consuls had been elected for 81. Lucius Valerius

Flaccus was chosen *interrex* in order to hold the consular elections. Sulla sent him a letter ordering him to put before the people Sulla's own opinion that it was necessary to revive the old office of dictator, unused now for 120 years. Sulla also expressed the opinion that the dictatorship should not be for just the normal fixed period of six months, but for as long as it took to set the state back on solid footing. He made no bones about it, he expected this dictator to be himself. With few options before them, Sulla was chosen dictator for as long as he himself deemed necessary.[2] A decree was passed giving him immunity for all his past acts and he was given the power of life and death decisions, the power to confiscate property, to settle colonies, to found new cities, or demolish old cities. He was given power to make laws and was entrusted with the most important task of establishing a new constitution for the Republic.[3]

Classical Numismatic Group, Inc. 202 Lot 132

This example of the third type in the series has the moneyer's *cognomen* CAPIT behind the head of Ceres on the obverse with a prawn beneath her chin. The number XXXVIIII is on both the obverse and reverse. The inscription in the exergue is C•MARI•C•F with S•C beneath.

Marius' coins have usually been dated to the year of Sulla's dictatorship when the decisions of government were in Sulla's hands, not the Senate's.[4] Marius was probably a higher magistrate with a special commission from Sulla to mint money serving Sulla's needs. If Marius began minting in 81, his authorization came from the dictator himself, not from the Senate. Sulla's new constitution was in place in 80 when Sulla became consul and Marius' later addition of the S•C inscription at the point of the twenty-fifth die would then reflect the return to a more normal constitutional process. But Sulla was still in charge as both consul and dictator and we must assume that any Senate decree authorizing Marius to continue minting was requested or sanctioned by Sulla and the money continued to serve Sulla's purpose.

But what might that purpose have been? Crawford's interpretation offers nothing at all here. To him the obverse design of Ceres, goddess of grain, and the plowman on the reverse simply complement one another, although, he said, the reason for Marius Capito's devotion to Ceres is obscure. However, if the coinage was intended to serve Sulla's purposes, there need be no connection whatsoever between Marius and Ceres. The most readily detected message of the type is that seen by Grueber who said that Ceres' head coupled with the plowman on the reverse referred to the foundation of a colony.[5] This too was seen by Babelon who attributed the coin to the younger Marius, the consul of 82, and suggested that the coin referred to the colony of Eporedia founded by his adoptive father Gaius Marius in Cisalpine Gaul about 100. But the re-dating of the coin to a time when the younger Marius was dead and Sulla was in command of Rome eliminated this possibility. Crawford did not believe that there was any reference to Sulla's colonies.

Marius' type is distinctly different from the many S•C coins issued during the civil war. Their themes were militaristic; Marius' is pacific. The plowman behind his oxen turning over the earth, planting the grain represented by Ceres on the obverse is a scene of a peaceful countryside. Gone are arms and armies, only bucolic serenity is to be found here. The terrible civil war had come to an end in Italy and the Sullan soldiers were returning to civilian life. The coin depicts the dream of the veteran soldier who expected on his discharge final payment for his service and a gift of land to farm. And this is exactly what Sulla provided for his loyal armies, ruthlessly extracting it from their defeated foe.

After the terrible destruction of the cities of Praeneste and Norba, Sulla's generals went throughout Italy establishing garrisons in the suspected areas. In Rome Sulla addressed an assembly of the people telling them what to expect, praising his own successes, and inspiring terror with more menacing statements. He ended his speech saying that he would bring about the most beneficial changes, if they would obey him. However, he would spare none of his enemies. The proscriptions followed. Lists of names were posted and rewards offered for the murders of forty senators and 1,600 knights who had attached themselves to the Marian side.[6] There was also a great deal of slaughter, exile, and property confiscation among the Italians who had obeyed the Marian generals. Penalties were laid upon whole towns. Some had their walls destroyed or they were crushed with heavy fines, but particularly harsh was the confiscation of their land and property which was divided up among the Sullan soldiers who were established in colonies among them.[7] Sulla had twenty-three legions to discharge. Appian said that there were 120,000 veterans throughout Italy who received land and gifts from Sulla.[8] The list of colonies is not fully known, but soldiers were settled at Arretium, Clusium, Faesulae, Interamnia, Nola, Pompeii, and Praeneste. Appian noted that since these soldiers could not be secure in their holdings unless Sulla's constitution remained on a solid footing, they were the staunchest supporters of Sulla himself while alive and of his constitution after his death.

Given Sulla's absolute control over the Roman state in 81, we might well expect to see Sullan programs or propaganda reflected in the design of Marius' coin. Marius' type not only depicts the expectations of the veterans who were to receive land, but also expounds the benefits to be found in the return to peace, masking in bucolic tranquility the terrible exactions that procured the soldiers' rewards. Besides the land given to the veterans in those new colonies established among the Italians, Sulla also had to pay his troops their back wages and maintain them until they were discharged. This special S•C issue may well represent some of that money distributed to the soldiers and the design on the coin also may be heralding the expected grants of land.

The name C•MARI•C•F•CAPIT stamped on these coins given to the soldiers as payment could not fail to conjure up the ghosts of Sulla's hated Marian foes, Gaius Marius, who was seven times consul, and his adopted son of the same name who had most recently perished at Praeneste and whose severed head Sulla had displayed in Rome. Crawford noted how our moneyer distanced himself from the defeated Marii by including his *cognomen* Capito, but the Marian name still stood out too clearly in the minds of the Romans not to evoke these very recent recollections of Sulla's foes. We must assume that the moneyer Gaius Marius Capito had sided with Sulla and was now reaping his rewards. He probably minted the first series as a higher magistrate or promagistrate under the dictator's authority then continued minting the S•C coins under Senate authority. Marius' very name on this coin is a message that Sulla bore no hatred against the Marian family name, only those opposed to his program. Symbolically the name Marius on this coin may have suggested that it was time for all Marians to come into Sulla's camp. Even so we cannot but wonder if this moneyer was not chosen by Sulla himself for the irony implicit in the name. The spoils of war bearing the name of a moneyer similar to the defeated enemy leader's name were counted into the hands of the victorious soldiers.

In the larger sense, the bucolic theme of the coin symbolized the promise Sulla had made to the people when he said that he would bring about the most beneficial changes if they would obey him. The coin depicted peace; prosperity would follow. But during the course of the year in which the coin first circulated, an incident occurred that would offer the populace a whole new light in which to interpret the reverse design, for Sulla soon gave an unforgettable lesson to those who chose to disobey him. Did the plowman on the coin inspire him or did the incident inspire the design of the coin?

Lucretius Ofella, relying on his recent fame as the man who had besieged Praeneste and who had sent the younger Marius' head to Sulla, decided to campaign for the consulship despite not having held the previous magistracies now required under the new Sullan constitution. At first Sulla tried to prevent him, but Lucretius persisted and even came into the Forum to appeal to the crowd. Sulla was then sitting on a raised platform near the temple of Castor and Pollux and he sent one of his centurions to Lucretius. The centurion summarily cut Lucretius down as Sulla watched. People grabbed the centurion and dragged him back to Sulla, who quieted the commotion when he said what had happened was done on his orders.[9]

> 'Know, citizens, and hear it from me, that I killed Lucretius for his disobedience toward me.' He then told them a parable. There once was a plowman who was bitten by fleas while he was plowing. He stopped twice to shake them out, but when they bit him again, he burned the shirt, in order that they not be a frequent interruption to his work. Sulla ended by telling the people, 'And I advise those who have been defeated twice not to stand in need of fire the third time.'[10]

Freeman & Sear Mail Bid Sale 12 Lot 366

The number XXXXIII die has a ship prow beneath the chin.

Chapter 3

L. VOL STRABO 80 BCE

The coin issued by the moneyer L•VOL•L•F•STRAB is missing from all the smaller hoards of this period except the Montiano hoard whose latest issues were the S•C coins by Marius, Procilius, and Naevius. Crawford dated Montiano's terminus to 79 with the issue by Naevius. He wrote that Strabo's coin was 'slightly, but not greatly, worn; this fact and the style of the issue suggest 81 as its date.'[1] Strabo's coin is a non-S•C issue which indicates that he was a regular mint magistrate. Since there are only enough non-S•C coins in my arrangement to allow one regular moneyer per year, I must date Strabo to a year following Postumius Albinus who is already assigned to 81. It seems best to date Strabo to 80. This allows time to produce some slight wear on his coin before it was buried in 79.

A. Tkalec AG Auction May 2005 Lot 166

> Jupiter with laurel in his hair is on the obverse, but has changed into the bull on the reverse as the thunderbolt near the bull reminds us. Using ligatures the moneyer has inscribed his name in the exergue as L•VOL•L•F•STRAB.

This mint magistrate L•VOL•L•F•STRAB so abbreviated his family name that we cannot be certain today to which *gens* he belonged. Even the VOL is a ligature. The leading possibilities are the Volteia, the Volcatia, or the Volumnia. He is cataloged under Volteius (or Volumnius) in Sear. Crawford decided on the Volumnia *gens* since we have an inscription recording a certain Lucius Volumnius, son of Lucius, who served on the military council of the consul Gnaeus Pompeius Strabo during the Social War. He may be the Lucius Volumnius who was a senator in 50. I am inclined to accept the identification of the moneyer as a Volumnius, but there is really no way to proclaim it with certainty since the *cognomen* was not preserved on the inscription, nor is anything else known of the life and career of the senator. It is best then to leave this moneyer as unknown, a state of knowledge probably shared by most of his own contemporaries.

Strabo depicted the laureate head of Jupiter on the obverse of his coin. On the reverse is a bull running off with the maiden Europa mounted on his back. A winged thunderbolt behind the bull reminds us that the bull's true identity is the same Jupiter seen on the obverse. The type was clearly meant to recall Europa's rape by Jupiter which was a popular Greek myth.

The best surviving account in literature comes from the Alexandrian Greek poet Moschus. Europa was the daughter of Phoenix, king of Tyre. The fateful day of her abduction began with a troubling dream. She saw two women fighting over who should possess her. One woman was dressed in the familiar clothes of her homeland in Asia, the other was a foreigner dressed in different clothing. The one claimed her by birth, the other by right, saying that Jupiter had given Europa to her. Shaken by her dream, she jumped from her bed and prayed that nothing bad come of it. That morning she went to the seashore with a number of her companions to enjoy the beach and to gather flowers. Jupiter, overcome with lust for Europa, devised a plan to spirit her away from her companions. He changed himself into a bull. His short horns bespoke a gentle nature and his body was so beautiful that the girls were not afraid of his presence. The divine beast knelt at Europa's feet and beckoned with his neck for her to climb onto his back. Unsuspecting of any guile, she did his bidding. The bull then turned and made for the sea, his feet merely gliding over the waves as he left the shore. Europa turned back and stretched out her hands to her companions to no avail. She knew now that this was no ordinary bull. The sea was calmed and a procession accompanied the disguised Jupiter. Dolphins jumped for joy, the Nereids on their sea animals surfaced and rode beside him as an escort, while his brother Neptune cleared the path through the waves. The Tritons blew on their seashells sounding the marriage hymn. Europa held onto one of the bull's horns with one hand and with the other hand she caught up the folds of her long purple robe to keep it dry and the robe billowed over her shoulder like a sail. Europa's trip ended in Crete where she bore to Jupiter three sons, Minos, Rhadamanthys, and Sarpedon. And finally she came to understand what her dream meant. The woman fighting over her who was dressed in the familiar clothes of her homeland represented the continent of Asia, and the woman in the strange clothing was the continent of Europe, of which Crete is part. Europe would take possession of her and she would give her name to the continent.

In the early artistic depictions of the scene, Europa's garment does not billow and she instead rests one hand on the bull's back to balance herself rather than catch up her garment. A metope from a mid-sixth century temple at Selinus in Sicily depicts Europa riding sidesaddle looking forward, holding the horn of the bull who turns his head to be viewed frontally. Two dolphins swim beneath the bull's feet. The representation on an Etruscan hydria from Caere shows Europa in a similar style riding sidesaddle and grasping the bull's neck. One dolphin leaps to the front of the bull, one leaps behind him, and two fish swim below his feet. In the later depictions as seen on Strabo's coin and as described in Ovid's later poetry, Europa sits sidesaddle and holds her robe billowing in the wind.[2]

Numismatica Ars Classica Auction 54 Lot 213

Europa is seated sidesaddle on the bull and grasps her billowing robe which is frequently called a veil in the catalogs, but clearly it is not connected to her head and the poet Moschus says she gathered up her robe to keep it dry. An ivy leaf is on the ground line under the bull.

It is impossible to say whether poetry inspired art or vice versa, but the billowing robe remained a popular way to depict Europa. While the billowing robe is typical of the scene, the ivy leaf Strabo put below the bull seems strangely out of place where artists usually depict some type of fish or dolphin to indicate the passage over the sea. Crawford noted that the significance of the ivy leaf has remained obscure, 'though it should be remembered that Europa sometimes appears as a vegetation power.'[3] However, Europa is not the only girl depicted riding a bull on ancient vases. Maenads also ride bulls and without the sea animals or the thunderbolt it is not always easy to tell if the girl on the bull is Europa or a maenad. In fact, there is a mosaic from the Roman Imperial period in the Archaeological Museum of Sparta that shows a half-naked girl sitting sidesaddle on a bull running to the right. Her legs are turned toward the back of the bull, her torso is frontal, her left hand rests on the neck of the bull and she looks slightly to the right. In her right hand she holds an ivy leaf. She has been identified as Europa, but is more likely a maenad since the ivy is sacred to Dionysus and just such confusion may have led to the ivy on Strabo's coin.

As charming as the story is, what was the point of putting this Greek myth on Roman coinage? The Europa myth recounted the origin of the Minoan dynasty of Crete and as such it was quite foreign to Rome. In filling the office of mint magistrate, we expect that Strabo was about to begin his *cursus* under Sulla's new constitution, and if it was a moneyer's hope to make himself better known to his countrymen through his coinage, what was Strabo telling his countrymen with this Greek myth? Grueber wrote that no satisfactory explanation has been found. Crawford said that Europa appears on the reverse only to complement Jupiter on the obverse. But any number of mythical women who were Jupiter's paramours could have appeared on the reverse to complement the obverse. Why did Strabo choose Europa?

A common modern way to interpret such Greek themes has been to look outside Italy for the inspiration, to explain the themes as inspired by contacts made with the Eastern Greek world by family members either in their capacity as soldiers or businessmen. But we do not have to look outside Italy. The Greek myths were well known in Italy as the vase paintings and artworks show. In fact, a contemporary statue of Europa sitting on the bull was one of the great art treasures of Tarentum[4] and this directs our attention to local Italian traditions. The geographer Strabo said the whole area of the Tarentine gulf and the heel of Italy were settled by Cretans prior to the arrival of the Spartan colonists. Minos had led an expedition to Sicily where he died. After this unexpected end to his endeavor, his followers tried to return home but were driven off course and landed near Tarentum where they settled. Strabo said that all the people in the area as far as Daunia were called Iapygians from their leader Iapyx, a son of Daedalus by a Cretan woman.[5]

While Europa might have little relevance to Rome, there was a considerable population in Italy who cherished Cretan heritage with a sense of pride and we know such pride survived even into the empire for Suetonius tells us that the emperor Galba made claim to Cretan lineage, asserting that his family was descended from Jupiter and Pasiphae, Minos' wife.[6] The key to Strabo's pairing of Jupiter and Europa with his coin type is to be found in just such claims.

If we look to a coin issued only two years before by Gaius Mamilius Limetanus, we can understand Strabo's message. On Mamilius' reverse Ulysses is depicted returning home to Ithica where he was met and recognized by his faithful dog Argus. On the obverse is the god Mercury whom Ulysses claimed as an ancestor. We might find this Greek type as obscure and difficult to interpret as Strabo's coin if we did not already know that the *gens* Mamilia claimed descent from Ulysses and Circe, which meant the Mamilii could ultimately trace their line to the god Mercury.[7]

The Mamilia family tradition survived in literature; the traditions of most Roman families are lost. We know nothing about the moneyer L•VOL•L•F•STRAB, but on the analogy of Mamilius' coin we can assume that he was making the same type of claim regarding his lineage, tracing his line to Jupiter and Europa. Let us use Galba's claims and Mamilius' coin as signposts pointing the way to the interpretation of Strabo's coin. Strabo's claims to Cretan lineage and divine ancestry survive only in the representation on this coin. It may go against our grain to attribute divine descent to mere mortals, but in pagan antiquity it was conventional.

A. Tkalec AG Auction May 2005 Lot 159

This coin by Gaius Mamilius Limetanus minted about two years before Strabo's informs the Romans of his family's illustrious ancestry traced back to the Greek hero Ulysses and through him to the god Mercury on the obverse.

The nobility of one's ancestor was of paramount advantage to a Roman contending for public office. Cicero noted that things were not the same for new men from the *municipia* and the 'men who are born from a noble line, on whom all the favors of the people are bestowed even in their sleep.'[8] A famous family name was all the recommendation some voters needed as Cicero pointed out to Calpurnius Piso, 'even those who have never seen you entrusted that office to your name.'[9] Even if the voters did not know much about L•VOL•L•F•STRAB, he might expect that his fellow citizens should prefer him in the polls over some less distinguished competitor, for his coin did boast a very good pedigree.

Chapter 4

LUCIUS PROCILIUS 80 BCE

The identity of the moneyer who signed his name L•PROCILI•F is uncertain. Although the name of his father preceding the F is omitted from all the coins, it is reasonably assumed to be Lucius. The family name Procilia is not commonly found and no members of the *gens* are attested in the Senate before 56. There was a Procilius, an historian, mentioned by Cicero in a letter dated to December 60, but it is uncertain if he was the same man as the senator whose comments about Gabinius' requests for a *supplicatio* were mentioned by Cicero in a letter to his brother Quintus in May 56.[1] Early scholarship further assumed that this Procilius was a tribune of the plebs, hence Grueber identified our moneyer as the tribune of the plebs of 56. Lily Ross Taylor's refutation eliminated the assumption that the senator Procilius held a tribunate in 56.[2] A certain Procilius appears again, presumably the same senator, in two of Cicero's letters to Atticus dated to July 54. It seems that this Procilius was tried and convicted for murdering a father of a family in his own home.[3] If our moneyer was this murderous senator, it would appear, on the evidence of his coin, which is an S•C issue, that he had entered the Senate about twenty five years beforehand and quite possibly was either one of the new senators selected by Sulla to fill up his expanded Senate or one of the first quaestors elected under the new Sullan constitution.

The dating of Procilius' coin is determined by hoard evidence. No coins from this large issue which Crawford estimated at a combined total of 254 reverse dies were found in the 3,500 coin Carrara hoard whose latest mint magistrate was Aulus Postumius and latest S•C issue was Gaius Marius, both dated to 81/80. A date after 81 is then reasonable for Procilius. Two of his coins were found in the Montiano hoard with Strabo and Naevius and his coin was also in the San Miniato al Tedesco hoard which did not contain Naevius. This suggests that Procilius minted with Strabo but before Naevius. Crawford's date of 80 appears to be the best year in which to place Procilius and his S•C issues would appear to supplement the very small mintage by Strabo. This seems to me better than having Procilius share a year with the other large S•C issue by Naevius. Procilius' large S•C issue possibly represents special money voted by the Senate to continue the Sullan programs.

Procilius depicted Juno Sospita, the chief deity of Lanuvium, on two different coin types. On unserrated flans he depicted a standing Juno on the reverse holding a figure-eight shield in her left hand and hurling a spear with her right. On her head she wears a goat-skin cap and on her feet are shoes with upturned toes, all details matching the description of the goddess given by Cicero in *De Natura Deorum* 1.82. Procilius has surely depicted the cult statue of the goddess here. At her feet is a serpent that alludes to a sacred ritual performed at Lanuvium. On the coin's obverse he depicted the laureate head of Jupiter, Juno's husband. He too had a temple at Lanuvium where he was called Jupiter Bonus, but nothing more is known of his rites or image. Procilius' Jupiter head is the same as that seen on Strabo's coin and probably represents Jupiter Capitolinus in Rome.

A. Tkalec AG Auction May 2005 Lot 167

Procilius' Jupiter is the same head we saw on Strabo's Europa coin. Juno Sospita on the reverse holds a figure-eight shield and spear. She wears a goat-skin cap and upturned shoes. A snake is at her feet. The moneyer's name L•PROCILI is written to the left of the goddess from the top down and F stands separately on the outside edge.

That Procilius minted two coin types, one on unserrated flans, the other on serrated, is strange, but not unprecedented. In 82 the mint triumvirate of Publius Crepusius, Gaius Mamilius Limetanus, and Lucius Censorinus jointly issued unserrated coins, but each also had an individual issue and Mamilius alone serrated his. Such inconsistency does seem to indicate that serration was not done as mint policy or by decree, but was rather an individual preference of the moneyer. Each moneyer was personally responsible for returning the proper number of coins from the bullion issued to him and I speculated in my earlier work on Roscius Fabatus that serration was a control method used to discourage theft among the mint slaves. Such saw-toothed coins look difficult or dangerous to swallow.

The town of Lanuvium had been given citizenship in 338 in return for sharing the goddess with the Romans. In 197 before a battle with the Insubres in Gaul, the consul Gaius Cornelius Cethegus vowed a temple to Juno Sospita if the enemy should be routed that day. The soldiers shouted that he would see the fulfillment of his prayer and a great victory followed for which Cornelius celebrated a triumph. He dedicated the temple to Juno when he was censor in 194.[4] Even though Juno Sospita now had a temple in Rome, the consuls still made a yearly trip to Lanuvium to propitiate the goddess in her hometown.[5]

A. Tkalec AG Auction May 2005 Lot 168

Procilius' second obverse type, struck on serrated flans, gives us a close-up of the goddess' head in her goat-skin cap, while on the reverse the goddess is virtually in the same standing pose, but driving a two-horse chariot. The snake is seen under the horses. His name inscribed L•PROCILI•F is in the exergue.

After a century, Juno's Roman temple was in bad repair. In 90, Caecilia Metella, the daughter of Balearicus, reported to the Senate that she had a dream in which she saw the goddess fleeing from her temple and only with great difficulty was she able to recall her. Juno was outraged because her precincts were being befouled and defiled by the sordid and obscene way married women were using their bodies in her temple. A dog had even recently littered right at the feet of her cult statue. Prayers of supplication were made and the Senate voted to restore the temple to its original splendor.[6]

We might argue that Procilius was making reference to the recently restored temple of Juno Sospita in Rome. However, his design also included the erect serpent on the reverses of both coins. The serpent was not actually connected with the temple worship of Juno Sospita. Separate rites and ceremonies placated this serpent whose steep and rocky grotto was located near Juno's temple in Lanuvium. It is the serpent which best confirms that Procilius' coins make a local reference to Lanuvium. The one thing that the coins enable us to say with a great degree of confidence about our moneyer Lucius Procilius is that he came from the town of Lanuvium, for that is quite simply the message that his coins convey to his fellow countrymen.

Procilius' designs not only show his hometown pride but also remind the Roman people of Lanuvium's important contribution to the greatness of the

Roman state, an importance recently reaffirmed by the Senate. The commemoration of one's hometown contributions, rather than one's family contributions, is understandable from a moneyer whose *gens* is virtually unknown in Roman history. It is no coincidence that references to traditions outside Rome occur more frequently following the end of the Social War which brought the enfranchisement of the Italians in the *municipia*. The last census before the Social War taken in 115/114 recorded 394,336 Roman citizens.[7] The first census figure after the Social War taken in 86/85 recorded 463,000.[8] The process of assimilation was to proceed rapidly under Sulla's constitution. By 70/69 the number had swollen to 910,000.[9] Cicero, himself a 'new man' from the *minicipium* of Arpinum, expressed the feelings of the new Italian majority of Roman citizens.

> I believe that all the townsmen of the *municipia* have two fatherlands, one of nature, one of citizenship. That famous Cato, though he was born at Tusculum, was accepted into the Roman state, and so although Tusculan in origin, he was Roman in citizenship, and had one fatherland of place and one of law... The Republic which bears the name of the whole state must come first in our affection, on whose behalf we ought to be ready to die, to whom we ought to give our whole self, in whom we ought to invest all we have, and as it were, to consecrate ourselves. But the fatherland of one's birth is no less sweet than that which adopted us.[10]

In the period before the Social War the traditions of local *municipia* had little appeal to the Roman voters and little benefit for candidates in Roman elections. But following the war, such themes had greater appeal to the huge block of newly enfranchised Italians anxious to fill the Senate and curule offices with men of similar background who would protect and promote their newly won rights and privileges. The moneyer L•VOL•L•F•STRAB had used the Cretan theme of Europa, which had greater relevance in southern Italy than in Rome, just the year before. We will see that in the following years other moneyers found the hometown reference useful in promoting themselves with the new Roman electorate.

Chapter 5

GAIUS POBLICIUS 79 BCE

The moneyer who signed his name C•POBLICI•Q•F is unknown, so we must again rely on hoard evidence for his dating. Crawford estimated that Poblicius used 104 reverse dies.[1] Since this rather large issue is missing from the Montiano hoard, which contained one coin from the very small issue by the mint magistrate Strabo, its absence from Montiano is most likely due to Poblicius minting after Strabo. Poblicius, however, was the only additional non-S•C moneyer after Postumius Albinus, dated to 81, in the San Miniato al Tedesco and Rizzi hoards, but Strabo's coin was missing from these hoards. Strabo's absence, however, may be explained by its rarity. The Montiano hoard indicates that Poblicius should follow Strabo and be assigned to the year 79.

Although Gaius Poblicius is unknown, his coin tells us that he was the son of Quintus. A Quintus Poblicius was praetor in 68 or 67, and it is quite possible that he was an older brother, but then, we have no additional family information on Quintus either. The *gens* Poblicia was not new in Roman politics and the family name was already connected with public works. The curule aediles Lucius and Marcus Poblicius Malleolus built the Clivus Poblicius, the road up the Aventine, and they also built the temple of Flora and instituted the games of Flora in 241. Two other members of the Poblicii Malleoli named Gaius issued coinage which Crawford dated to 118 and 96. These earlier moneyers from the Poblicii have given us a telling difference between themselves and this moneyer C•POBLICI•Q•F. The Poblicii Malleoli did not inscribe their *nomen* on the coins, using instead only the abbreviations MALL or MALLE for their *cognomen* Malleolus, indicating that the Poblicii Malleoli were better known by their *cognomen* than by their *nomen*. On the other hand, our moneyer spelled out his *nomen* in full and added no *cognomen*. That this Gaius Poblicius was not of the Malleoli line seems likely from the way he inscribed his name. Moreover, the Malleoli used the names Gaius, Marcus, and Lucius; our moneyer's branch of the family used Gaius and Quintus.

Poblicius' coin also differs from the more traditional military themes found on the coins of the Malleoli. His reverse design depicting Hercules strangling the Nemean lion has a distinctly Greek look. It is a scene frequently found in Greek art and on Greek coinage, but not Roman. Although the head of

Hercules had appeared on Roman coins, no moneyer had yet chosen to depict the god actually engaged in one of his twelve labors.

Classical Numismatic Group, Inc. Triton VI Lot 685

Hercules wrestles the Nemean lion on the reverse. The quiver filled with ineffective arrows is to the left side and the club is discarded at his feet. The intensity of the struggle is even evident in his facial features. A control letter is above the lion's head and the moneyer's name is to the back of Hercules.

The fight with the Nemean lion was the first and most famous of Hercules' labors and the story was well known. This savage lion, whose hide was invincible to metal, was sent upon the men and fields of Nemea by Juno as a curse on the sons of Phoroneus. The lion ranged at will and wreaked wide-spread slaughter. One version of the story of Hercules' encounter with the lion is found in the works of the Alexandrian poet Theocritus.

Taking his bow and club newly fashioned from the olive wood of Mount Helicon, Hercules set out on his hunt for the lion. He searched high and low, but found nothing until evening when the lion, still licking his chops and dripping blood from his wet mane, was returning to his cave. Hercules hid behind a large bush and waited for the lion to pass. He then let loose an arrow, but it could not pierce the hide. The lion turned and bared his teeth. Another arrow bounced off his chest. As Hercules was drawing a third arrow, the beast spotted him and drew himself into position to pounce. Hercules prepared to defend himself by covering his quiver with his cloak and holding it before him. With his other arm he wielded a stout club. The lion sprang. The upraised club came down upon his head, dropping him in mid air. Landing on all four feet, the lion stood wobbling and dazed. Hercules then threw down the quiver and club and grabbed the lion's neck in a strangle hold. He attacked from behind lest he be clawed. Straddling the lion, he heaved him up and the lion fell back into his arms dead.[2]

Both art and literature found a number of ways to describe the way Hercules overcame the Nemean lion. The oldest representations show him tackling the lion from behind and seizing him around the neck. Other early works depict him as a pancratiast engaged with the lion, wrestling full length on the ground. But the most common depiction from the fifth century on, in both Greek and Etruscan art, was the upright wrestling hold. It was not thought that the beast was overcome by force so much as 'by skill and the tricks of the palaistra.'[3] The object of the wrestling match was to throw one's opponent. The lion, treated almost as a human, is shown in one of the grips that led to the throw. One favorite hold is Hercules grasping one forepaw with his right hand and wrapping his left arm around the neck of the lion whose paw pushes on his shoulder. In another hold, he grasps the head under his arm, linking his hands together around the neck. There are a few representations that show the lion already thrown down on the ground.

On Poblicius' coin, Hercules' quiver and club lay discarded on the ground and Hercules is naked as was typical of Greek athletes. Poblicius has adopted the most popular artistic rendition which shows the lion supporting himself with one hind leg and clawing at Hercules' thigh with his other leg, while using his teeth to break the deadly neck hold. All this was to no avail, for Hercules strangled the lion and skinned him using the lion's own claws. The lion skin that he wore in his subsequent labors became Hercules' most recognizable attribute.

Grueber noted that the design of Hercules strangling the Nemean lion had appeared earlier on coinage from the Greek city states of Neapolis, Tarentum, and Heraclea, 'but as it does not seem possible to associate the design in any way with the personal history of the moneyer's family, it may refer to the recent victory of Sulla over the Marian party.'[4] However, if we follow the faint tracks left on Roman history by an ancient member of the *gens* Poblicia, they lead us, as it were, to the very cave of the Nemean lion.

During the reign of Tullus Hostilius, the third king of Rome, the Romans destroyed their parent city of Alba Longa and moved all the families to Rome. Rome then claimed leadership over the thirty cities of the Latin League which had been colonies or subjects of Alba Longa. King Tullus sent ambassadors to the cities to put forward the Roman claim, but the cities were unwilling to yield to Roman authority. The league instead chose Ancus Poblicius from Cora and Spusius Vecilius from Lavinium as leaders invested with full authority to make war or peace with Rome. They chose to fight. There was little enthusiasm on either side for a full-scale war. After making a few foraging raids into each other's territory, the hostilities came to an end with no major calamities and the brief war left no bitterness.[5] This is the earliest historical mention of any Poblicius and it is significant that the family traditions preserved this distant ancestor's part in such a minor event and traced him to the town of Cora. Ancus Poblicius was obviously a leading citizen of Cora in the seventh century.

Gemini Numismatic Auctions, LLC Auction VIII Lot 192

The obverse female head wearing a Phrygian helmet with two feathers has long hair falling down her neck. The inscription ROMA behind her head makes it clear that she is Roma.

The town of Cora was founded by Coras, who was one of three Greek brothers who migrated to Italy from Greece and first settled the city of Tibur, which was named after the oldest brother. Tradition made these brothers contemporaries of Aeneas. Virgil said Coras and his brother Catillus were joint captains who led troops from Tibur to fight against Aeneas. The brothers were grandsons of the famous seer Amphiaraus of Argos.[6] The valley of Nemea was on the road between Argos and Corinth and the site of the lion's cave in Mount Tretus was still being pointed out to travelers on the road even in Imperial times.[7] In addition to coming from the vicinity where Hercules killed the lion, another even more obscure tradition from the lost poem of Asius made Hercules' mother Alcmena a daughter of Amphiaraus and Eriphyle.[8] So besides coming from the region of Greece where Hercules strangled the lion, some writers alleged a family connection to Hercules for Coras and his brothers. If Poblicius traced his origin back to the towns of Cora and Tibur and from there back to Argos, and possible kinship with Hercules, his coin design is readily understandable and is, indeed, a family reference. We should note that one of the most famous temples to Hercules in Italy was in Tibur and these traditions about the town's founders must have been well known locally.

The town of Cora and Ancus Poblicius' position of importance and influence in the Latin League may also hold the key to understanding the goddess Roma depicted in a Phrygian helmet on the obverse of Poblicius' coin. The helmet is decorated with two plumes. Mars was depicted in helmets similarly decorated with plumes, but this head is clearly female. An earring dangles below the helmet and long hair falls down her neck. Crawford said that the Phrygian helmet was no more than an artistic variant, but even Poblicius recognized that the style he chose was so different from the conventional helmet in which moneyers, even the Poblicii Malleoli, depicted Roma that he placed the inscription ROMA behind her head to make sure that the proper identification was made. It may be more than just an artistic variant. The Phrygian helmet is clearly a reference to Rome's Trojan heritage. Other traditions tell of Cora's colonization by the Trojan descendents of Aeneas living at Alba Longa just as was the case with so many other cities of the Latin League.[9] Pliny noted that the Corani claimed descent from Dardanus the founder of Troy.[10] A significant number of the voters in the districts closest to Rome would recognize much of their own heritage in this blend of Trojan and Greek culture. This coin type epitomizes the pride many of the newly enfranchised Italians had in their own ancient roots in Italian soil. Poblicius was one of their own, a man who would most likely continue to promote and support the policies the new citizens wanted Rome to follow.

Classical Numismatic Group, Inc. 76 Lot 1204

Chapter 6

GAIUS NAEVIUS BALBUS 79 BCE

The moneyer Gaius Naevius Balbus is unknown. The *cognomen* Balbus was first attested for the *gens* Naevia in 168 when a Lucius Naevius Balbus served as one of five commissioners sent to investigate and settle a boundary dispute between Pisa and the colony of Luna.[1] The only other Naevius Balbus known to us is our moneyer whose name survives in the inscription C•NAE•BALB on this coin. Speculation that this Naevius was the Sullan cavalry officer who reached Rome in time to stop the Samnites' advance on the Colline Gate cannot be confirmed since Plutarch only called him Balbus, a *cognomen* common to too many men.

Naevius' coin was not found among the 1178 coins of the San Miniato al Tedesco hoard whose latest mint magistrate was Gaius Poblicius. His coin did appear in the Amaseno, Montiano, and Rizzi hoards which also had no mint magistrates later than Gaius Poblicius. This hoard evidence suggests that Naevius' coin dates to the same year in which Poblicius minted, that is 79.

Classical Numismatic Group, Inc. 174 Lot 185

Naevius put his name on the reverse under the triga driven by a winged Victory. The letter O is the control mark on the obverse below the chin.

The coins themselves give us two small pieces of information. They are inscribed S•C, indicating that they were issued by decree of the Senate, and their control marks show that the issue was quite large. These control marks are in separate series. First Naevius used the letters of the Roman alphabet on the obverse, some letters having more than one die. Then he put the control marks on the reverse, first using Roman letters and when he ran out of letters, he used

Roman numerals from I to CCXXX. Crawford estimated a total of 311 reverse dies were used.

What required such a large amount of coinage in the year 79? The most ready answer is the war with Sertorius in Spain. The type depicting Victory in a chariot is military in nature and parallels the issues of Gaius Annius who was sent against Sertorius at the end of 82. We have S•C coinage bearing Annius' name with his title of proconsul and the names of his quaestors for the years 82 and 81. On the coins signed by the quaestor L. Fabius Hispaniensis, Victory drives a quadriga. On those signed by Gaius Tarquitius, Victory is in a biga.

Classical Numismatic Group, Inc. Triton VI Lot 675

Classical Numismatic Group, Inc. Triton VIII Lot 861

These S•C coins by Gaius Tarquitius and L. Fabius Hispaniensis, identified as Gaius Annius' quaestors by the Q on the reverse, were minted to pay the troops in the Sertorian War.

Sertorius was driven out of Spain by Annius in 81, but returned in 80 at the invitation of the Lusitanians. He won over more Spanish tribes and consolidated his base that year. Although the praetor Fufidius did suffer a reverse, there was little military action in 80. In 79 the proconsul Quintus Caecilius Metellus Pius was sent to Spain with a large additional army. He took over a war that had grown more threatening because of the failures of the earlier commanders. Metellus was to remain in Spain until the war's end in 72. From a small out-of-context fragment of Sallust's *Histories* which reads, '*quae pecunia ad Hispaniense bellum Metello facta erat*,' 'money which had been made for Metellus for the Spanish war,'[2] we know that at some time between

79 and 72 money was specially minted for Metellus to pay his troops. In what issue of coinage are we to find this money?

Grueber found the money referenced in Sallust's quote in the coinage minted by Metellus inscribed Q•C•M•P•I and he assigned the coins to the years 79-77. But since these coins were found in the Carrara hoard which has no other coins later than Aulus Postumius and Gaius Marius, Crawford assigned the Q•C•M•P•I coins to 81.[3] Crawford identified the 'money made for Metellus for the Spanish war' as the S•C coinage issued by Gnaeus Cornelius Lentulus Marcellinus inscribed CN•LEN•Q and LENTCVR×FL, which he assigned to the years 76-75.[4] However, we will see in Marcellinus' chapter that in the years 76 and 75 the armies in Spain were hard pressed for pay and provisions, which we would not expect to be the case if there was a large issue of S•C coinage specially minted for paying the soldiers in Spain. I propose that 'the money made for Metellus for the Spanish war' is to be found in two separate S•C issues, one by Naevius minted in 79 and one minted the next year by Tiberius Claudius. Naevius and Claudius probably minted as Metellus' quaestors just as L. Fabius Hispaniensis and Gaius Tarquitius minted as Annius' quaestors.

The deity on Naevius' obverse is uncertain. Grueber identified her as Juno since a similar diademed head identified by inscription as Juno Moneta is found on L. Plaetorius' coin, also an S•C issue. Crawford made a comparison with the earlier coins by Gaius Norbanus (Crawford 357) and Lucius Cornelius Sulla (Crawford 359) and identified the head as Venus. The appearance of Venus may be seen as an allusion to the recent victory of the Sullans at the Colline Gate which took place near the temple of Venus Erycina.

Classical Numismatic Group, Inc. Triton VIII Lot 873

On the reverse, Victory drives a three-horse chariot which is a rare depiction on Republican coins. This special triga was used in one of the chariot races held during the *Ludi Romani*. The control number LXX is above the horses.

The reverse of the coin depicts Victory, naked to the waist, driving a three-horse chariot, holding the reins with both hands. This is the second and last time that a triga appears on Republican coinage. Grueber's commentary cites a passage of Dionysius of Halicarnassus which Borghesi used to show that the Romans borrowed this type of war chariot from the Greeks.[5] What Dionysius actually said was that the triga, used long ago by Homeric heroes, was completely out of fashion with the Greeks. Its current use in Rome in the first century was only found in the celebration of the *Ludi Romani*, a religious and ceremonial survival of the games originally held by the dictator Aulus Postumius to commemorate the victory at Lake Regillus. Dionysius wrote,

> In the chariot races two very ancient practices have been preserved by the Romans down to my time, performed just as they were ordained from the beginning. The first concerns the three-horse chariot, which the Greeks no longer use, being an ancient heroic practice which Homer portrayed the Greeks using in battles. A third horse, joined to the team only by a trace, runs alongside the two horses yoked together in the usual way.[6]

Naevius' coin has the look of a typical military issue predicting the expected Roman victory, but there is a subtle difference. This particular three horse chariot was only used in the celebration of the *Ludi Romani* which commemorated the Roman victory at Lake Regillus. Naevius' imagery is intended to recall that ancient victory which established Roman *imperium*, echoing the *caput rerum* theme found on the coinage of Aulus Postumius Albinus. Victory driving the three-horse chariot shows that all efforts to dispute Roman rule were fated to end in Roman victory. The prophecy would be fulfilled and Rome would be the head of the world.

Classical Numismatic Group, Inc. Triton VI Lot 687

On this variant Naevius put the control letter M on the reverse of the coin.

Chapter 7

LUCIUS PAPIUS 78 BCE

Since the moneyer Lucius Papius is unknown, we must again look to hoard evidence to date his coin. Papius' coin was not found in the San Miniato al Tedesco, the Rizzi, or the Central Italy hoards which contained Poblicius. Papius appears then to follow Poblicius in the mint magistracy. He did appear as the latest mint magistrate in the Fragagnano hoard which contained the S•C issue of Naevius Balbus and in the Spoleto hoard which contained the S•C issues of Naevius and Claudius. This relative time frame is consistent with Papius holding the mint magistracy after Poblicius and I date Papius to 78.

Although this moneyer is unknown, his family name had already appeared on coinage just over a decade beforehand. During the Social War, Gaius Papius Mutilus, the infamous Samnite rebel who was to inflict such heavy casualties on the Romans, issued coinage in the name of the rebel state of Italia depicting the Italian bull goring the Roman wolf with his name 'c paapi' in Oscan letters in the exergue. Our moneyer was anxious to find a different association for his name. The desire to distinguish himself from the notorious Samnite Papii may account for Lucius Papius' choice of type.

Classical Numismatic Group, Inc. 61 Lot 1390

The moneyer's name L•PAPI is on the reverse. The head of Juno Sospita on the obverse suggests that Lucius Papius came from the town of Lanuvium where the cult of Juno Sospita originated. This die pair has the control marks of a scepter on the obverse and a radiate crown on the reverse under the gryphon.

With the goat-skin capped head of Juno Sospita on the obverse, we see Procilius' earlier theme repeated and readily recognize Papius' connection with the town of Lanuvium. We know from non-numismatic sources that a branch of the *gens* Papia did live in Lanuvium. Titus Annius Milo, the praetor of 55 who later murdered Publius Clodius, was a Papius by birth. Although adopted by his maternal grandfather Annius, Milo maintained his connection with Lanuvium where he held the local office of dictator. In January 52, he was on his way home to perform the rites of Juno Sospita when he and Clodius crossed paths on the Appian Way and a brawl ensued in which Clodius was killed. Nothing, however, is known of Milo's Papian family, but Lily Ross Taylor noted that since Cicero makes no reference to Milo's ancestors in the peroration of Milo's defense, they were probably not distinguished.[1]

Classical Numismatic Group, Inc. 61 Lot 1392

This die set uses a tanner's knife on the obverse and a scraper on the reverse as control marks.

Our moneyer Lucius Papius may be the first of his line entering into Roman politics. Excluding Milo who was adopted into another family, the only Papius known to have been a senator during the Republic was Gaius Papius, a tribune of the plebs who secured the passage of the *lex Papia de peregrines* in 65.[2] Another Lucius Papius with the *cognomen* Celsus minted coinage under Caesar about 45. A later notice of this family line is found in a dedicatory inscription discovered near Narona in Dalmacia that commemorated Augustus' capture of Sicily from Sextus Pompey in 36. It was set up by a Gaius Papius Celsus and a Marcus Papius Kanus, *fratres*.[3] Whether *fratres* meant brothers or cousins is uncertain. It would appear that the Gaius/Lucius line used the *cognomen* Celsus which suggests that our moneyer's *cognomen* was Celsus. He quite possibly was the father of the Caesarian moneyer. The later associations of the family name with Caesar and Augustus also hint at the family's *populares* political sentiments.

Like the other moneyers of this period Papius serrated his flans and used control marks to keep track of production. However, he developed an unusual series of control marks which are of great interest to collectors and antiquarians. He used one symbol on the obverse and a different one on the reverse. Each pair of symbols is related to one another and has only one set of dies. Crawford cited 211 pairs. However, one coin bears the numeral CCXLVI instead of a symbol, which indicates that there may have been as many as 246 pairs. One coin with the new combination of helmet with long visor on the obverse and *petasus* on the reverse was found in the Mesagne hoard.[4] Attempts to find greater meaning in the symbols is exceedingly speculative and Crawford is probably correct in saying, 'the control-symbols are no more than a random selection of pairs of everyday objects.'[5] Lucius Roscius Fabatus who later imitated Papius' coin developed a whole different series of paired control marks. The intent was to keep track of production and control loss among the slaves who used the dies.

Classical Numismatic Group, Inc. 73 Lot 790

> The control mark on the obverse of this die set is a dolium, a wide-mouthed jar frequently used for holding wine. On the reverse is a hydria, a water jug. Romans and Greeks mixed their wine with water.

Juno Sospita whom Papius depicted on the obverse has already been treated in Procilius' chapter. On the reverse Papius depicted a gryphon leaping to the right. A description of this fantastic beast is found in Aelian's *On the Nature of Animals*:

> The gryphon, I hear, is a four-legged Indian animal like the lion and it has especially strong claws most nearly resembling the lion. They say that it is winged and the color of the feathers along the back is black and the front feathers are red, while the wings are neither such color but white. Ctesias narrates that its neck is variegated with dark blue feathers. It has an eagle-like beak and head just like artisans paint and shape them. He says that its eyes are like flames. It makes its nest in the mountains. Full grown gryphons are impossible to capture, but the young are captured. The Bactrians, who are neighbors of the Indians, say that the gryphons are guardians of gold there, and they say that they dig it from the ground and weave nests from it and the Indians take what falls off. But the Indians say that gryphons are not guardians of the gold, for they have no need of gold... but the Indians themselves come to collect the gold and the gryphons are afraid for their own offspring and attack those who approach.[6]

Classical Numismatic Group, Inc. Triton VI Lot 689

This die set uses the forepart of a lion and the forepart of a bull.

Crawford wrote that ‘the gryphon is perhaps regarded as connected with Juno Sospita, though the evidence is not good.’[7] Grueber had earlier noted, ‘In her militant character Juno Sospita was analogous to Juno Martialis, who, on Greek statues is sometimes represented wearing a diadem, from which issue gryphons.’[8] The real point of connection between Juno and the gryphon, however, is not found in the martial aspect of the goddess, but in her title, which defines her nature. Sospita means savior or guardian. The gryphon which guards its nest and attacks those who come near epitomizes the protective nature of the goddess who, in her martial dress, is ever prepared for battle against those threatening harm to her people.

Classical Numismatic Group, Inc. 88 Lot 1159

This die set has an amphora on both the obverse and the reverse.

A. Tkalec AG Auction May 2006 Lot 115

This die set has a column base on the obverse and a capital on the reverse.

Chapter 8

TIBERIUS CLAUDIUS NERO 78 BCE

The hoard evidence for the coin by the moneyer Tiberius Claudius indicates a date contemporary with or one year later than Naevius Balbus. His coin was not found with Naevius' in the Amaseno, Montiano, and Rizzi hoards. He did appear with Naevius in the eighty-six coin Central Italy hoard and with Naevius and the mint magistrate Papius in the 146 coin Spoleto hoard. Crawford associated Naevius and Claudius with Papius to make a college of three moneyers for 79. Grueber dated Naevius to 81 and Claudius to 80. Separate years seem more likely to me for these two large S•C issues and it is consistent with the hoard evidence to put Claudius in the year of Papius' mint magistracy which I dated to 78 in the previous chapter.

On the reverse of his coin, Claudius depicted a fully clothed Victory in a biga holding a palm branch and the reins of the horses in her left hand. A wreath is in her right hand. Claudius maintained a continuity of type and fabric with the coins minted by Naevius and Annius' two quaestors. All four moneyers minted serrated denarii marked with the inscription S•C and all four depicted Victory driving a chariot. We know that Annius' coins were produced to pay troops in Spain and I suggested in Naevius' previous chapter that both Naevius' and Claudius' S•C coinages represent money minted for Metellus for the Spanish war.

Two series of control marks on the reverse show that Claudius' coinage was a large issue: the first series used numbers from I to CLXV, the second used the letter A coupled with numbers I to CLXXXII. The large number of dies used indicates a mintage close in size to the S•C issues of Naevius, which was also minted in two separate series. Similarity of theme, size of mintage, S•C designation, and the division into two separate series suggests that both issues were minted for the same purpose.

Our moneyer signed his name TI•CLAVD•TI•F AP•N without *cognomen*. The *praenomen* Tiberius was used by only two branches of the Claudii, the patrician Nerones and the plebeian Aselli. Our moneyer is identified as Tiberius Claudius Nero who served under Pompey in the pirate war in 67. His area of command was the Spanish waters as far as the Pillars of Hercules.[1] He may well have been a praetor before 67 when he was chosen as one of Pompey's legates in the pirate war, for Plutarch said that Pompey chose his legates from a pool of men who had either held command of armies or had been praetors.[2] Furthermore, a praetorship sometime before the year 63 can reasonably be assumed since he was high enough in the speaking order of the Senate to be one of the senators to give an opinion on what to do with the five Catilinarian conspirators arrested by Cicero in 63.[3] If Claudius had already been a praetor by the time he became Pompey's legate in 67, he would have been about 31 years old in 78. I have argued that the S•C coinage was minted by quaestors or higher magistrates or promagistrates rather than mint magistrates, and the evidence indicates that it was possible for Claudius to have held his quaestorship by 78 if he was a praetor by 67. While we have no other information on Claudius' life, his main claim to fame from our perspective today is that he was the grandfather of the emperor Tiberius.

Classical Numismatic Group, Inc. Triton VI Lot 688

Diana is on the obverse and Victory drives a biga on the reverse while holding a wreath in her right hand and a palm branch and the reins in her left hand. The number CXIII is below the horses.

The goddess Diana graces the obverse of Claudius' coin. Grueber said that she was a reference to the Sabine origin of the *gens* Claudia, citing Varro's *De Ling. Lat.* 5.74 as evidence.[4] Crawford doubted that Diana could be a reference to the Sabine origin of the Claudii, dismissing Varro's belief in Diana's Sabine origin as wrong.[5] The Sabine origin of the Claudii is not in question, and to debate a Sabine origin for Diana sheds no light on this moneyer. The style of design shows that the inspiration for Claudius' rendering of Diana came from the coin of Aulus Postumius minted in 81. The goddess is depicted in the very same style on both coins: her hair is tied in a knot on top of her head and the unmistakable attributes of bow and quiver are over her shoulder making the identity of the goddess certain. Claudius' coin continues the theme of *caput orbis terrarum* so clearly expressed by Postumius. Diana, whose appearance on Roman coinage during the 70s was far more common than any other decade of Republican coinage, was emblematic of the extension of Roman *imperium*.

Classical Numismatic Group, Inc. 61 Lot 1389

On this reverse die from the second series, the control mark beneath the horses is an A with the number II.

These Roman claims to *imperium* divinely sanctioned by the goddess Diana did not go unanswered by Sertorius. His response is to be seen in a cleverly manipulated ploy designed to beguile his followers. Shortly after his arrival in Spain, Sertorius received a female fawn as a present from a native Spaniard. At first Sertorius paid her little attention. She grew up tame and willingly came to Sertorius' call, accompanying him on walks and displaying no fear of crowds. Little by little Sertorius created the impression that the fawn was sacred. He declared her to be a gift from Diana and said that the fawn had the power to reveal secrets to him. Whenever he received secret intelligence, he gave it out that the fawn had spoken to him in his sleep and alerted him. Whenever he was brought news of a victory by one of his generals, he hid the messenger until he could have his fawn make an appearance crowned with garlands, as if ready to celebrate a victory. He would then encourage his soldiers to rejoice and to make sacrifices to the gods for they could expect the arrival of good news soon.[6]

Sertorius continued to exploit this device for years. Plutarch tells us that Sertorius once was deprived of this wonderful avenue of influence with the natives when the deer had disappeared for a period of time shortly after Pompey's arrival. By chance, some men roaming about the country recognized the doe, caught her, and returned her to Sertorius, who promised them a large reward to keep quiet about the capture. A few days later Sertorius appeared in public, cheerfully declaring to the Spanish chieftains that the gods had foretold great good fortune to him in a dream. He mounted his tribunal and began conducting business. Then his men released the deer. She bounded onto his tribunal, laid her head in his lap, and licked his hand. Sertorius with tears in his eyes stroked her head. Those present were stunned at first, but then broke into cheers and applause and escorted Sertorius to his home. Plutarch says that they were convinced that he was loved by the gods and that he had supernatural powers, which assured them and filled them with hope for the future.[7] If

Naevius' and Claudius' coins do represent the money made for Metellus for the Spanish war, they give us a better appreciation of the subtle ways the propaganda war was waged. Both sides exploited Diana. Sertorius' flair for the dramatic was far more impressive and colorful, but Rome's destiny, vouchsafed by Diana with the sacrifice of the heifer and advanced by Roman arms and money, assured Roman *imperium* and Rome's position as the head of the world.

Chapter 9

GAIUS EGNATIUS MAXSUMUS 77 BCE

Except for the inscription C•EGNATIVS•CN•F CN•N on the reverse of his coins and MAXSVMVS on the obverse, Gaius Egnatius Maxsumus is unknown. So once again we have no prosopographical evidence to use in dating his coins. Using hoard evidence, Crawford felt that the coins must date between 78 and 75, noting that the 'shared approach to choice of types associates the issues of C. Egnatius Maxsumus and L. Farsuleius Mensor, beyond this certainty is unattainable.'[1] He finally settled on Grueber's date of 75. Hersh and Walker also believed Egnatius and Farsuleius minted in the same year, but in their revision of the dating they used the evidence of the San Mango hoard to move Egnatius ahead of the moneyers that Crawford had dated to the years 78 through 76, that is, Volteius, Cassius, Rustius, and Lucretius. They dated Egnatius to 76. But Rutilius and Satrienus, whom they dated to 77, were not in the San Mango hoard either. The San Mango hoard contained a single example of Egnatius' coin with Cupid's bust which Crawford estimated at thirty-three reverse dies, a much smaller issue than either Rutilius or Satrienus. I would place Egnatius ahead of these men as well, immediately following on Poblicius and Papius who are the latest mint magistrates in the San Mango hoard before Egnatius. Besides the evidence of the San Mango hoard, I believe that the fabric of the coins suggests a date earlier than 75. Egnatius issued three different designs, one serrated and two unserrated, indicating a transition from the practice of serration used by the moneyers before him to the unserrated coins issued by the subsequent moneyers. If Egnatius represents the transition to regular flans, his mint magistracy falls after Papius and before the non-serrating moneyers. In my arrangement this puts the coins in 77.

Grueber wrote that the *gens* Egnatia was of Samnite origin and did not appear to have come to Rome until after the Social War.[2] The name Egnatius, like the name Papius, was certain to evoke immediate associations with the recent Social War, for Marius Egnatius was conspicuous as one of the leaders of the Samnites and was famous for two defeats he inflicted on the Roman forces. He captured Venafrum by treachery and slaughtered two Roman cohorts there.[3] The next year he inflicted even greater casualties. While Sextus Caesar was leading an army of 30,000 infantry and 5,000 cavalry through a deep and rocky ravine, Egnatius attacked and drove him back to a river where he destroyed a large part of his force.[4] These brave actions undertaken on behalf of the liberties of the Italian peoples showed how truly Marius Egnatius lived up to the family tradition of resistance to Rome displayed two centuries before by Gellius Egnatius who had been one of the Samnite leaders in the great Third Samnite War begun in 298.

However, more recent scholarship gives us reason to believe that our moneyer Gaius Egnatius did not have close ties with the rebellious Samnite Egnatii. We have the name of a certain Gnaeus Egnatius, C. F. Ste., who was already a member of the Senate as early as 175-160. He was from the Stellatina tribe which suggested to L. R. Taylor that he may have been from Capena, which was in the Stellatina tribe and close to the *municipium* of Falerii where the names of Egnatii are found on four inscriptions.[5] The filiations of the early senator and our moneyer do show that the preferred *praenomina* were Gnaeus and Gaius. A Gnaeus Egnatius was mentioned as a senator in 66 by Cicero.[6] Our moneyer may be a brother of this senator and the grandson of the early senator Cn. Egnatius. That may be the reason his coin has his filiations extended to his grandfather. It is likely that he was from a family with at least a century old citizenship, not from the newly enfranchised. This separates him from any close relationship with the Samnite Marius Egnatius, and calls into question Grueber's suggestion that his types, which associate Jupiter, Venus, Cupid, and Libertas crowned by Victory, denote the freedom which the Samnite nation obtained after the Social War and refers to the new friendly relations between Rome and Samnium. In all of Italy, friendly and amicable relations between Rome and Samnium were most improbable. Under Sulla Samnium was so ruthlessly and systematically suppressed that, after being the fiercest foe to Roman expansion for centuries, it now all but ceased to exist.

Egnatius minted three different types and the date of 77 gives us the best political context for appreciating Egnatius' emphasis on Libertas repeated on all three types. The return to peace achieved by the crushing defeat of the Marian forces in Italy was overseen by the ruthless dictatorship of Sulla in 81. Traditional Roman liberty was forfeited to one man while he undertook the reconstruction of government. His solutions, rendered in such an uncompromising manner, were not intended to please every faction. The grain dole was discontinued, many Italians who had fought for Marius were dispossessed of their homes, the civil rights of the sons and grandsons of the proscribed were forfeit, and the courts were transferred from the knights to the Senate. The powers of the tribunes of the plebs were curtailed and the tribunate was made a dead-end office. No one who held it was permitted to go on to the praetorship or consulship. Any man of ability who wished to advance in the *cursus honorum* would not hold the tribunate. In 80 Sulla together with his kinsman Metellus Pius held the first consulship under the new constitution in order to guide its initial steps. In 79 he completely withdrew from office and allowed his new creation to function on its own terms without him. After Sulla withdrew from power, those most grievously oppressed by the losses caused by his reforms began to polarize in 78 behind the consul Marcus Aemilius Lepidus, the only leader of serious opposition to raise his voice in Italy against the new constitution.

Sulla headed off an immediate confrontation and succeeded in moderating any groundswell of revolt by making Lepidus swear an oath not to disturb the constitution while consul. But upon Sulla's death later that year, Lepidus opposed his fellow consul Catulus' effort to quiet unrest in Etruria and again began to encourage the hopes of the dispossessed. He further increased the chances of anarchy by refusing to hold the elections for the next year. At the end of the year, feeling that he was released from his oath, Lepidus began to menace Rome with his army and to demand another consulship contrary to the laws of the new constitution. A speech by Lepidus which survives from Sallust's *Histories*, although it was delivered before Sulla's death, preserves the sentiments which fueled the revolt in 77.

> Why then does he [Sulla] walk about with such a crowd and in such high spirit? Because success is a wonderful pretext for crime, but with the situation reversed he would be as despised as he is now feared. Or is it for the appearance of concord and peace which are the names he gives to his wickedness and the murder of his country? And he declares that there is no other way that the Republic can survive and that there be an end to war unless the plebs are driven from their fields, the citizens most cruelly plundered, and justice and the jurisdiction over everything, which used to belong to the Roman people, now rest with him. If this is what you understand peace and order to be, applaud this greatest cause of disturbance and destruction to the Republic, nod your head in assent to the laws imposed upon you, accept your peace with slavery, and hand down to posterity an example how the Republic is oppressed at the cost of its own blood. For me, although in reaching this highest office enough has been attained for the name of my ancestors, for my own dignity, and even for my own protection, nevertheless it was not my plan to look only to my private ends. Liberty fraught with danger seemed better than a quiet servitude. If you agree, Romans, present yourselves, and with the aid of the gods, follow your consul Marcus Aemilius, your author and leader in recovering liberty.[7]

Lepidus' speech is redolent with the theme that Sulla's settlement had brought peace but at the cost of liberty. How could Roman citizens be so complacent? Lepidus complained, 'Peace and quiet combined with liberty, which many good men would rather have than labor with honors, no longer exists. In these times one must either be a slave or be the master, either be in fear or inspire fear.'

Whether Lepidus truly felt a deep sympathy for those upon whom Sulla's settlement fell the hardest or simply saw in them the raw material to be used in securing his own preeminence was a suspect point among his fellow aristocrats. After all, he had earlier prosecuted the war against the Marians most zealously on behalf of Sulla. In the mop-up operations, he took the town of Norba by treachery and watched it burn to the ground. Later during the proscriptions, he profited handsomely by buying up the property of the condemned. In a speech delivered before the Senate in January 77, Lucius Marcius Philippus contended that the recovery of liberty was only the pretext Lepidus was using to disrupt the present state of peace for his own ends.

> My greatest wish, Senators, would be that the Republic be at peace, or if in danger, that it be defended by its most resolute men, and finally that depraved undertakings bring ruin to those who devised them. But to the contrary, everything has been thrown into commotion by sedition, even instigated by those who more properly should have prevented it. The final straw is that the good and wise must now do what the worst and the most foolish have decreed. For war and arms, although hated by you, nevertheless, because they are pleasing to Lepidus, must be taken up.[8]

Philippus repeatedly asserted that Lepidus 'has his army for the purpose of suppressing liberty.' Exhorting the Senate to oppose Lepidus' sedition he pleaded, 'If liberty and truth are more pleasing to you, pass decrees worthy of your name and strengthen the natural disposition of our brave men.' Both sides were using Libertas to rally troops to their cause; the one called for recovering Libertas it claimed had been lost, the other for preserving Libertas it claimed had been restored with the return to peace.

Egnatius' coins seem to echo the claims of the Sullans that peace brought liberty. He issued three different types. Since Venus and/or Cupid appear in combination with Libertas on all three, it is reasonable to assume uniformity of theme. Venus can reasonably be seen as a Sullan reference, for a great deal of Sulla's success in his battles against both Mithridates and the Marians had been attributed to her. Venus took on martial characteristics under Sulla who even dedicated an axe to her with the inscription, 'The dictator Sulla dedicated this to you, Venus, for he saw you in a dream armed with the weapons of Mars marshaling the army and waging war.'[9] A coin type issued earlier (*ca.* 84/83) by Sulla in both gold and silver depicted the bust of Venus. To the right the small figure of Cupid holds a palm branch, glorying in the victories his mother has given Sulla.

Numismatica Ars Classica Auction 29 Lot 338

Sulla's coin (*ca.* 84/83) has the diademed bust of Venus with Cupid standing to the right holding a palm branch.

Egnatius' first type is a serrated denarius depicting the bust of Venus draped and wearing a diadem. The head and wing of her son Cupid appear just over her right shoulder. On the reverse, Libertas rides in a chariot drawn by two walking horses. The pileus, the cap of Liberty, behind her back makes her identification certain. Above the horses a flying figure commonly identified as Victory, although Cupid cannot be ruled out, is about to crown her. This triumphant return of Libertas who is greeted with a victory wreath is imagery quite different from Lepidus' picture of Libertas lamented as lost.

Numismatica Ars Classica Auction 29 Lot 344

Libertas is on the obverse with a small winged Cupid over her shoulder. Libertas drives a biga on the reverse. A flying Victory is about to crown her.

On a second type, Cupid has the whole obverse to himself. A wing with delineated feathers sprouts from his back. His identifying attributes are the bow and quiver over his shoulder. Venus is nowhere to be found on this coin. It seems that the small figure who first appeared behind Venus' shoulder now has come to the fore and claims the dominant position on the coin. This is strange.

The chief association the ancient world made with Cupid was sexual love and that was his normal association with his mother Venus, who had always been most widely worshipped as the goddess of love. The military guise in which Sulla had cloaked Venus was anomalous to the traditional Venus and Cupid. We see Venus' nature best illustrated by the contemporary poet Lucretius in a passage where he asks Venus to secure a respite from war.

> For the meantime, make the fierce works of war
> on all the sea and land come to rest and grow quiet.
> For you alone are able to delight mankind with tranquil
> peace, since the fierce works of war are ruled
> by Mars mighty in arms, who often lays himself back
> in your lap, overcome by the eternal wound of love,
> and so bending back his shapely neck and looking up at
> you he feeds his greedy eyes with love, longing for you,
> goddess, and the breath of reclining Mars lingers
> on your lips. Enfold this supine Mars with your divine body,
> and with tender words pouring sweetly from your lips,
> beloved goddess, beseech placid peace for the Romans.[10]

Classical Numismatic Group, Inc. Triton IX Lot 1292

> The bust of Cupid with his bow and quiver is on the obverse. Such a non-warlike god suggests the enjoyment of peace now possible with the return of liberty to the Roman people.

In Catullus' love poetry, Cupid and Venus are constantly paired as the patrons of all sensual love and they have maintained the same symbolism even today for people who no longer worship them as gods. The bust of Cupid so prominently placed on the obverse of Egnatius' coin, depicted with his cherub-like features and armed with a bow whose arrows only wound one's heart with passion and desire, but never kill, is symbolic of peace and the pleasures it brings.

On the reverse side of Cupid's bust, Egnatius depicted a temple shared by two deities. The style of drapery distinguishes the figure on the left holding a staff in the right hand as male and the one on the right as female. Their identifying attributes are found in the tympanum, the triangular pediment of the temple. Above the male figure is a thunderbolt, the attribute of Jupiter, and the pileus is over the female Libertas.

Numismatica Ars Classica Auction 54 Lot 219

> On the reverse is the temple of Jupiter Libertas. Originally just the temple of Libertas when built in 246, the two figures, Jupiter on the left with the thunderbolt above him in the tympanum and Libertas on the right with the pileus above her in the tympanum, reflect the bipartite nature of the temple in Egnatius' time.

The temple of Libertas was built on the Aventine in 246 by the plebeian aediles Tiberius Sempronius Gracchus and Gaius Fundanius. The money came from fines. The main contributor was Claudia, the sister of the consul of 249, Publius Claudius Pulcher. On an occasion when she found it hard to make her way through the crowded streets of Rome she exclaimed that she wished her brother was still alive to lose another fleet for the Romans for that would thin out the population a little. That insensitive comment cost her 25,000 asses.[11]

The son of the aedile of 246, also named Tiberius Sempronius Gracchus, later decorated the temple with a painting which commemorated the battle he won against Hanno near Beneventum in 214. A large number of slaves had been promised their freedom if they distinguished themselves in battle. Gracchus so thoroughly defeated Hanno that he magnanimously granted freedom to all the slaves who had been enrolled in the army, even though some 4,000 had proven less than helpful. The painting he commissioned commemorated the happy aftermath of victory when the people of Beneventum laid out tables of food for the victorious soldiers who had saved them. The slaves now freedmen wearing the caps of liberty or white woolen bands were seen everywhere merrily taking part in the feast.[12]

In the course of time the temple came to be better known as the temple of Jupiter Libertas. The original connection between the two deities may be found in the belief that Libertas was the daughter of Jupiter and Juno.[13] Egnatius' depiction of the temple shows its true bipartite nature at that time.

On the third type, Libertas dominates the obverse. Her draped bust wearing a diadem is again identified by the pileus placed behind her. On the reverse, two figures stand together between rudders stood upright on ship prows so as to frame them like columns of a temple. The figure on the right holds either a staff or a spear and has her gown cinched below her breasts. She is clearly Venus because the small figure of Cupid again appears behind her right shoulder. We realize now how important Cupid is to Egnatius' theme, because it is Cupid who allows us to identify Venus with certainty. He is used as an attribute, appearing there as if to remind Venus of her softer nature. Venus who had been symbolic of the Sullan victories had now become symbolic of the Sullan peace.

Classical Numismatic Group, Inc. Triton VIII Lot 876

Libertas identified by the pileus behind her head is on the obverse. On the reverse, two figures are framed by rudders stood upright on ship prows. Venus is on the right identified by the Cupid over her right shoulder. The other figure is also female and usually identified as Roma because of the spear and sword she holds.

The other figure on the left is more difficult to identify, but it too appears to be a female. She wears a helmet and holds a spear in her right hand and a sword in the left. She is most commonly identified as Roma. In an interesting and symbolic gesture her left leg extends from her gown at the knee and she rests her foot on the head of a wolf. This perhaps is the cleverest imagery used to support the claims of the first two types that peace has restored Libertas to her proper place. Before the battle of the Colline Gate, which took place near Venus' temple outside the Colline Gate, the Samnite general Telesinus called for the destruction of the city of Rome, calling it the forest which harbored the wolves who destroyed Italian liberty. Roma's foot resting on the wolf's head suggests the suppression of that ravager of liberty. The oars lifted from the water and stood upright on the ship prows represent the newly installed peace on land and sea won by the Sullan victories. The oars stand architecturally like the columns of the temple framing Venus and Roma. Secure within this protective temple of peace, Roma now suppresses those impulses of the predatory wolf which ravaged the liberty of the Italians. Roma has changed.

Numismatica Ars Classica Auction 59 Lot 777

This reverse die offers a clearer image of the Roma figure with her left leg on the wolf's head.

The propaganda of Lepidus' revolt in 77 provides the best context in which to understand the themes of Egnatius' coins. Both sides bandied about the watchwords of peace and liberty. Lepidus' claim that to accept the Sullan peace was to accept slavery and his claim that peace and quiet coupled with liberty no longer existed were countered by the simple imagery on Egnatius' coins depicting Venus and Cupid, the representatives of the Sullan peace, coupled with Libertas.

Chapter 10

LUCIUS FARSULEIUS MENSOR 77 BCE

Not only is the moneyer Lucius Farsuleius Mensor unknown, the *gens* Farsuleia is unknown. His S•C issue indicates to me that he was at least a quaestor at the time he minted, but prosopographical evidence is lacking and the hoard evidence used for dating Farsuleius' coin is most ambiguous. His appearance in the Roncofreddo hoard gives us only a terminus date of 72. His absence from the Fragagnano and Spoleto hoards and his unserrated flan indicate a date after Papius' moneyership of 78. Except for the Capreni hoard, Farsuleius is missing from most smaller hoards that might help further narrow his date. The evidence of the Capreni hoard, which contained the coins of Rutilius and Satrienus, but not those of Volteius, Cassius, or Lucretius led Hersh and Walker to date Farsuleius immediately after Rutilius and Satrienus, and before Volteius, Cassius, and Lucretius. Crawford, on the other hand, discounted the Capreni evidence. He used the Kerassia hoard which contained Cassius and Volteius, but no Rutilius, Satrienus, Farsuleius, Egnatius, or Lucretius, and dated Cassius and Volteius before all the others. Crawford omitted from his table the Capreni and San Mango hoards used by Hersh and Walker; Hersh and Walker's table omitted the Kerassia and Bompas hoards used by Crawford. The real problem is that all the smaller hoards leave gaps in whatever order you arrange the moneyers.

At this point commentators turn to comparison of style and type. The appearance of Libertas on the obverse of Farsuleius' coin provides a thematic and stylistic linkage with the coinage of Egnatius. Both have busts of Libertas on the obverse done in the same style, draped and diademed, and identified with the pileus behind the head. Libertas appears on no other coinage of this decade. The consensus of opinion remains that Egnatius and Farsuleius should be paired because of similarity of theme and style.[1] If the San Mango hoard puts Egnatius into the year 77 after Papius, then Farsuleius should also date to 77 with Egnatius.

On the coin's reverse, a helmeted figure driving a chariot reins in two horses rearing their front legs. The figure is viewed by us frontally as it turns to the right and stretches out a hand to help an unarmed togate figure into the chariot. The helmeted figure was identified by Grueber as either simply a warrior or as the goddess Roma. Eckhel saw the armed figure as Roma, or the Genius of the Roman People, inviting the Genius of Italy into the chariot. He interpreted it as a reference to the acceptance of the Italians into Roman citizenship.[2] Crawford insisted that the helmeted figure is clearly male and should be identified as Mars. A scorpion appears below the horses on one series of coins and Scorpio was the astrological house of Mars. Although the figures on the coin's reverse are not identified by inscription or attributes and remain difficult to identify, a reasonable interpretation does not demand precise identification.

Numismatica Ars Classica Auction 33 Lot 255

A helmeted figure carrying a spear offers the right hand to an unarmed togate figure to help him into the chariot. Neither figure is identified by inscription but the scene suggests reconciliation. A scorpion is below the horses.

The contrast between armed and unarmed figures dominates on Farsuleius' coin. Crawford perceived the reverse type as suggesting 'the notion of peace and reconciliation between soldier and civilian and perhaps alludes sympathetically to a second objective of some politicians in the 70s, the assimilation of the new citizens enfranchised after the Social War.'[3] Whether the figures represent Rome and Italy or soldier and civilian, the notion of peace and reconciliation can be seen in the joined hands of the two figures. The same idea will be seen again on the reverse of the joint issue by Calenus and Cordius, where an armed Roma, identified by inscription, clasps the hand of an unarmed Italia, identified by inscription. Farsuleius and Egnatius both expressed the same Sullan sentiments about peace and liberty.

Lepidus' revolt in 77, discussed in the previous chapter, was not only a likely source of inspiration for Egnatius' and Farsuleius' theme of Libertas, it also produced a Senate decree which may well have authorized the striking of this special coinage in order to pay the troops who fought against Lepidus. In January 77, Marcus Philippus urged the Senate to pass its emergency decree.

> If liberty and truth are more pleasing to you, pass decrees worthy of your name and strengthen the natural disposition of our brave men. A new army is present, to this add the colonies of veterans, all the nobility, the best leaders. Good fortune follows the better side. These forces which have been collected despite our negligence will soon slip away. Therefore, I propose that, since Marcus Lepidus in defiance of the authority of the Senate has raised an army in his own private interests and together with the worst enemies of the Republic is leading it against the city, let Appius Claudius the *interrex* together with Quintus Catulus the proconsul and the other military commanders see to the defense of the city and take care that the Republic comes to no harm.[4]

The Senate enacted its emergency decree. The proconsul Catulus remained in Rome to defend the city. Pompey was sent north into Cisalpine Gaul which Lepidus controlled together with his proconsular province Transalpine Gaul. Lepidus' legate Marcus Junius Brutus was actively recruiting forces for him in the province and the Senate feared that Lepidus would soon receive massive reinforcements. Pompey, however, quickly subdued Brutus and with his subsequent execution, the threat from Cisalpine Gaul was gone. Deprived of these reinforcements, Lepidus decided that he had to march against Rome before Pompey returned. He won an initial battle at the Mulvian Bridge, but met defeat in the Campus Martius. He retreated to Cosa and from there sailed with his remaining forces to Sardinia, where he died a defeated and broken man. Perperna took over command of the army and transported it to Spain, joining Sertorius who offered the one remaining sanctuary for disaffected rebels still intent on resisting the Sullan settlement.[5]

If Farsuleius' coinage was issued under the emergency decree in order to pay the soldiers in Pompey's and Catulus' armies, the appearance of Libertas on the obverse may have been meant to remind the soldiers what was at stake. It was Lepidus who presented the threat to both peace and liberty.

Farsuleius issued only the one coin type, but it is clear from the control marks that it was issued in two distinct series. One series used control numbers from I to LXXIII on the obverse and the symbol of the scorpion on the reverse. (Crawford noted numbers only to LXXII, but LXXIII appears on a coin in NFA catalog XXVII, no. 448.) A second series was more than one and a half times the size of the other. The control marks from I to CXX are on the reverse in place of the scorpion. The control marks indicate the use of 193 different dies which must have produced a rather large number of denarii. The amounts of money minted by Farsuleius in this special issue would seem to be far in excess of what was needed to deal with Lepidus, who was overcome quite quickly. However, subsequent events may explain the need for a second series.

Classical Numismatic Group, Inc. 79 Lot 919

The figure on the obverse is identified as Libertas by the pileus behind her head. This reverse die has number VII under the horses in a series that is attested up to LXXIII.

When the forces of discord had been driven out, Italy no longer needed Pompey's army. Catulus ordered him to dismiss his soldiers, but Pompey, looking to be appointed to the command of an army to reinforce Quintus Metellus Pius in the war against Sertorius, refused to dismiss his troops and kept offering excuses.[6] He could well point out that Lepidus' revolt was not at an end but had merely transferred location and joined itself to Sertorius. Metellus had not been able to subdue Sertorius in two years of fighting and his military expertise, once quite respectable, was less lustrous now that he was getting on in age. Pompey's menacing presence in the vicinity of Rome rattled the Senate's nerves. The senators finally saw the wisdom of Lucius Philippus' proposal to send Pompey to Spain with the status and power of a consul even though he was not yet a senator.

Pompey was later to claim that the Senate bestowed upon him only the mere name of commander and that he raised and equipped an army in forty days on his own. But given the conditions under which he extorted his appointment, we cannot believe that he dismissed his experienced army after he got what he wanted. The soldiers who supported his demands for a Spanish command surely expected to go to Spain with him. The forces he raised during those forty days must have been reinforcements and these must have been the troops Pompey paid for with his own funds. Pompey had to fight his way into Spain, since Gaul, which had shown a significant amount of support for Lepidus, offered resistance to his passage. He was forced to spend most of the campaigning season of 77 reducing Gallic cities between the Alps and the border of Further Spain and did not arrive in Spain until 76.

One series of Farsuleius' coins may then represent money minted to pay the troops while they were used to repulse Lepidus. The other series may represent the additional expenses of keeping the troops under arms while Pompey led his army to Spain. When Pompey wrote to the Senate at the end of 75 begging for more money he said that the Senate had barely provided one year's expenses out of the last three years[7] and Farsuleius' coinage of 77 most likely represents that funding.

A. Tkalec AG Auction May 2005 Lot 182

Chapter 11

LUCIUS CASSIUS LONGINUS 76 BCE

The moneyer signing his name L•CASSI•Q•F has been identified as Lucius Cassius Longinus, one of the six candidates for the consulship of 63.[1] His candidacy indicates that Lucius Cassius had already been praetor by 65. Asconius mentioned that a Publius Cassius was the praetor in charge of the *maiestas* trial of Cornelius in 66. Publius, however, was not a common *praenomen* for the Cassii and it appears that Asconius was simply wrong here, so the praetor in charge of the trial has been identified as Lucius Cassius Longinus and his praetorship is dated to 66.[2] The family of the Cassii Longini was one of the noblest houses in Rome and the branch of our moneyer's family line is traced in the following stemma.[3]

```
                    Q. Cassius Longinus
                        tr. mil. 252
                             |
                    L. Cassius Longinus
                             |
                    Q. Cassius Longinus
                        consul 164
                             |
                    L. Cassius Longinus
                             |
L. Cassius Longinus ——— Q. Cassius Longinus
     tr. pl. 104                  |
                         L. Cassius Longinus
                         IIIVIR 76, praetor 66
```

The hoard evidence for dating Cassius' coin is poor. He appeared in the Roncofreddo hoard which gives us a terminus of 72. He appears in only two other small hoards that offer any help in a relative placement of his mint magistracy in the 70s. The first is the forty-seven coin Kerassia hoard where he appears with Volteius. The large issues by Rutilius and Satrienus were not found in the Kerassia hoard, suggesting only that Cassius minted before them. The second hoard to offer evidence is the 120 coin Hev-Szamos hoard which has a disputed terminus date. Grueber felt that Cassius and Volteius were the latest moneyers in the Hev-Szamos hoard and dated them to 78. But this hoard also contained one KALENI/CORDI coin, which Grueber considered to be a later insertion by the hoard's finder. Sydenham agreed with Grueber.[4] Since none of the nine moneyers who minted between Volteius and KALENI/CORDI were found in the Hev-Szamos hoard and since many of them were very common issues, I too accept Grueber's assumption that Volteius and Cassius mark the real terminus of the Hev-Szamos hoard.

Fortunately, in Cassius' case we have prosopographical evidence to support us in a more precise placement of Cassius' moneyership than can be obtained from the hoard evidence. Cassius' praetorship in 66 gives 106 as his latest year of birth. Lucius Cassius was then eligible for the quaestorship of 75 and since his issue is not an S•C coin we should expect that he held the mint magistracy at least the year before his quaestorship. It is not likely that the date of Cassius' mint magistracy should be moved forward given his other *cursus honorum* dates and his family's nobility, and, since the coin is not serrated, the fabric argues against moving it back into a year when the moneyers were serrating the flans. It would appear Cassius minted after Egnatius and Farsuleius discontinued the practice. Egnatius was the latest moneyer in the San Mango hoard, and since Cassius was not in that hoard, a date of 76 for his coin accords well with the scant hoard evidence and with his *cursus honorum* dates.

The small size of Cassius' issue, estimated by Crawford at thirty-six reverse dies, also accords well with what we know of the financial condition of the treasury in 76. After years of rather large mintages produced by a combination of regular and S•C issues, the treasury was feeling the strain. In a speech delivered in 75, the consul Gaius Cotta complained that he had come into the consulship at a time when the revenues of the Roman state had been reduced and made uncertain by wars and could barely sustain just a part of the state's expenditure.[5] The consuls of 75 inherited this situation from the previous year so we should expect a reduced mintage for the year 76. The low die estimate for Cassius' coin is in line with the depleted resource situation described by Cotta. I assign no S•C issues to the year 76 leaving Cassius' issue as the only money newly minted that year.

What appears to us to be the simplest of coin designs was for Roman citizens one of the most evocative images stamped on the coinage of this period. Cassius depicted the heads of Liber and Libera. Liber, on the obverse, is identified by the ivy wreath on his head and the thyrsus over his shoulder, attributes proper to the Greek god Dionysus, also known as Bacchus. Liber's assimilation with the Greek god Dionysus causes some confusion. Dionysus was the son of Semele and Jupiter, but Liber, who was originally an ancient Roman agricultural god, was the son of the goddess Ceres. In Latin, Liber's name meant simply 'son' and his sister's name Libera meant 'daughter.' Libera is the deity on the reverse whose head is wreathed with grape leaves and grape cluster. Their mother Ceres, the goddess of grain, was readily identified with the Greek Demeter whose daughter Persephone always remained best known to the Greek world as Kore, or simply 'daughter.' This mother and daughter pair was widely worshipped in the Greek world, but a son was not part of the Greek myth. Consequently, in the Roman triad of Ceres, Liber, and Libera, the boy Liber had no close Greek equivalent. The grape leaves and grape cluster which his sister wears in her hair hint at the logic that led the Romans to identify her brother Liber with Dionysus, the Greek god of wine. That the Romans equated Liber with Dionysus was evidenced in his own temple by a famous painting of Dionysus by the Greek artist Aristeides that was deposited there following the sack of Corinth in 146. Soldiers had been using it as a dicing board before it was rescued and displayed in the temple where it hung until it was destroyed by the fire that consumed the temple in 31.[6]

A. Tkalec AG Auction May 2005 Lot 177

The god Liber is on the obverse. He has an ivy wreath on his head and a thyrsus over his shoulder. A strand of hair falls loosely down his neck. These attributes are typical of Bacchus with whom Liber became associated.

The temple of Ceres, Liber, and Libera was originally vowed by Aulus Postumius just before the battle of Lake Regillus. Postumius had become concerned over the scarcity of provisions and he consulted the priests who had charge of the Sibylline books. They ordered him to propitiate Ceres, Liber, and Libera. Following his vow to build them a temple, Rome was filled with more food than ever in both grain and fruit and even imported provisions increased.[7] After the Roman victory in the battle of Lake Regillus, the Senate decreed that the temple be built from the spoils. It was not completed until 493 when it was dedicated by the consul Spurius Cassius.[8]

The primary association which our moneyer expected the Romans to make between the name L•CASSI•Q•F and the images of Liber and Libera on his coin is that a Cassius dedicated the temple of Ceres, Liber, and Libera. But in calling to mind the consulship of Spurius Cassius, he also expected his countrymen to recall that the year of the temple's dedication was the same year in which the first secession of the plebs came to an end with the creation of the tribunate of the plebs.

Classical Numismatic Group, Inc. 79 Lot 925

> The goddess Libera is on the reverse. She has grape leaves in her hair and a grape cluster hanging between two leaves at her ear. The moneyer's name L•CASSI•Q•F is behind the head.

The plebs burdened with debt and constant military service felt that their liberties were being trampled by the unrelenting demands of the nobles. They had withdrawn in the previous year 494 to the Sacred Mount some three miles (4.8 km) from Rome and refused to return to the city or to man the army until they had some kind of protection against the arbitrary commands of the consuls. The Senate sent a group of ten consular envoys to negotiate a compromise. As a safeguard to their liberty, the plebs demanded that they be allowed to elect officials who would be invested with no other power than to protect those plebeians who suffered any injury or violence and to prevent them from being deprived of their rights. The Senate agreed and the first tribunes of the plebs were elected in Spurius Cassius' consulship of 493.[9] As a further protection, another law was passed making the office inviolable and sacred. Should anyone attack a tribune he was to be accursed and his property was to be consecrated to Ceres. The temple became the repository for the fines levied on those who would assault the protectors of the people's liberty.[10] The plebeian aediles were also created at this time to serve as assistants to the tribunes and they were headquartered in the temple of Ceres. In 449 when the consuls Horatius and Valerius started the practice of delivering the decrees of the Senate to the plebeian aediles for the inspection of the tribunes, the temple became the repository for senatorial decrees. Previously they had been suppressed or falsified as it pleased the consuls.[11]

From its very beginning the temple of Ceres, Liber, and Libera was associated with the liberty of the plebs. A secondary meaning of the names Liber and Libera became significant. As an adjective the word means 'free.' By depicting Liber and Libera rather than Ceres, by whose name the temple was commonly called, Cassius has stressed the temple's association with freedom and has picked up the theme of Libertas so heavily worked in the political rhetoric generated by Lepidus' revolt and disseminated in the coinage of Egnatius and Farsuleius the year before.

The tribunate and the protection it provided for the liberty of the Roman citizen was a major bone of political contention in the 70s. It had been stripped of much of its power by the reforms of Sulla in 81 and had been made into a dead-end office. Velleius Paterculus said that Sulla, having taken away the right of the tribunes to initiate legislation, had left the office *imago sine re* 'a shadow without substance.'[12] The restoration of the tribunate to its pre-Sullan position was one of Lepidus' promises in his failed rebellion. The clamor for its restoration did not die down after Lepidus was defeated. A speech by the tribune Macer in 73 shows that the rhetoric of the period continued to characterize the plebs' present condition as slavery.

> Citizens, if you did not understand what a difference there is between the rights left to you by your ancestors and this slavery imposed on you by Sulla, I would have to make a long speech and instruct you on account of what injuries and how often the plebs took up arms and seceded from the patricians and how they obtained the tribunes of the plebs as protectors of their rights.[13]

With the images of Liber and Libera whose very names carried the sweet sound of liberty, Cassius brought up the subject of the tribunate and the enslavement of the plebs in a far more subtle way than Lepidus' armed rebellion. He reminded the people that the name Cassius was to be closely associated with their winning those safeguards of their liberties. His coin design served as his pledge to support legislation that would restore the liberties of the people.

Cassius' coin gives us an insight into the man's character and early politics. Lucius Cassius saw how the clamor for the tribunate in 493 resembled that of his own time and it would seem that he chose his ancient ancestor Spurius Cassius as his political mentor. Spurius Cassius was legendary and most Romans knew his story. Depending on one's viewpoint, he was seen either as one of the most notorious villains or as one of the great champions of the people in the early Republic.

Spurius Cassius was the first man to hold three consulships, 502, 493, and 486, and to celebrate two triumphs in 502 and 486. Puffed up by success, he became pompous and aspired to greater power. He sought to win over the plebs. The day after his second triumph, he called an assembly and addressed the people. First he gave an account of his accomplishments: how, in his first consulship, he had defeated the Sabines, who were laying claim to supremacy, and made them subject to Rome; how, in his second consulship, he resolved the secession of the plebs and conferred equal citizenship rights on the Latins so that they no longer regarded Rome as a rival but as their fatherland; and how, in his third consulship, he won over the Volscians as friends and got the Hernicans to voluntarily submit. He asked the people to pay him heed as one who had always had great concern for the commonwealth and who would soon bestow numerous benefits on them, surpassing all others who had been acclaimed for befriending and saving the plebs. He dismissed the assembly and the next day convened the Senate where he proposed to divide among the people the land conquered in war which, although nominally public land, was presently held by patricians. He further proposed that the public treasury should repay to the people the price that they had been compelled to pay for grain which had been sent to Rome from Sicily by Gelon as a present to the Roman people.

There was a great uproar in the Senate and they charged him with attempting to stir up sedition. His colleague Proculus Verginius vehemently opposed him. Both consuls continued to give speeches before the people, but Cassius lost ground when the tribunes of the plebs finally sided with the nobles. What eventually told against him was his proposal that the Latins and the Hernicans share in the division of the land. The plebs felt that that would make their own share too small. A proposal was made by the tribune Gaius Rabuleius that Cassius drop this part of his bill and Verginius declared that he could accept that and would not oppose the people's desire to divide the land. Cassius was not willing to withdraw his original proposal and set about to secure it by force and violence. He sent for Latins and Hernicans to come to Rome to support his proposal. Alarmed by the number of strangers flooding the streets of Rome, Verginius declared that non-residents were to leave the city; Cassius countermanded that order. Meanwhile, Senate debate eventually produced a bill that called for a board of the ten oldest ex-consuls to determine the boundaries of the public land and declare how much was to be rented out and how much divided. This put the wrangling to an end.

The next year the quaestors Caeso Fabius and Lucius Valerius Publicola denounced Cassius, charging him with aiming at monarchy. On the day appointed for him to respond to the charges, the quaestors called an assembly and laid out their case. They pointed out that the people themselves knew full well of the proposals Cassius had made, but there was a more sinister intent hidden from public view. They produced witnesses and evidence that

Cassius had obtained money and arms from the Latins and Hernicans and had conspired with them to use violence. Cassius' well prepared defense accompanied by the tears of three sons fell flat. He was condemned and sentenced to death. He was led up the Tarpeian Rock overlooking the Forum and with the citizen body looking on he was hurled over. His house was razed to the ground and his goods confiscated and dedicated in various temples, but especially in that of Ceres, Liber, and Libera. Some tried to extend the punishment down his family line, proposing to kill his three sons. This suggestion was rejected and it remained a Roman custom to exempt sons from the punishment of the father's crimes.[14] The most notable exception was Sulla's disenfranchisement of the sons and grandsons of those whom he had proscribed. This too had been one of the wrongs Lepidus promised to right in his insurrection in 77 and something to which Cassius might be expected to be sensitive. It remained the last issue of Sulla's settlement to be corrected and was not resolved until Caesar took control in 49.

Following Spurius Cassius' condemnation and death, the aristocracy grew more contemptuous of the plebs. The Senate did not carry out its decree. Livy wrote that popular resentment against Cassius was short-lived since the idea of land reform was popular. Soon the plebs began to accuse themselves of a great blunder in condemning their guardian.[15]

Although he had little confidence in its veracity, Livy preserved an alternate version of Spurius Cassius' failed plot. According to that story, Spurius' plans were discovered by his own father who put him on trial in his own house and found him guilty. As punishment, his father had Spurius scourged and then he put his own son to death. Afterwards he made a gift of his son's property to Ceres. A statue inscribed '*ex Cassia familia datum,*' 'a gift from the Cassia family,' still stood in the temple when this coin was minted.[16] It would seem that the *gens* Cassia itself, anxious to maintain its traditional role as defenders of the people's liberty, promulgated this version. Traditional family values would not abide any return to monarchy or diminution of the people's rights and liberty, even by its own members.

Our moneyer's coin type with its emphasis on liberty places him squarely within that family tradition, but within Lucius Cassius' veins flowed the blood of that famous Spurius and over the course of the next thirteen years the same character flaw was to develop and play itself out in similar fashion. Following his defeat in the consular elections of 64, our moneyer sought to achieve his political goals through violence. Throwing in with Catiline, he became one of the most villainous leaders in the conspiracy to overthrow the government. Whether Lucius Cassius really had the best interests of the plebs at heart any more than Spurius Cassius was suspect, for Lucius Cassius had requested the privilege of directing the arson fires which were intended to spread chaos throughout Rome. Such destructive fires would have most severely affected the urban poor. The plot was detected by Cicero in its planning stages and measures were taken to prevent arson and to acquire the evidence on which to arrest the conspirators. A trap was laid. Envoys from the Gallic tribe of the Allobroges, in Rome to seek relief from their heavy public and private debt, had been approached by the conspirators to join them in their revolt. Having considered their options, the envoys disclosed everything to the Senate. Cicero recommended that they pretend to go along with the plot and that they demand of Lentulus, Cethegus, Statilius, and Cassius a written and signed oath which could be taken back to their people. Lentulus, Cethegus, and Statilius suspected nothing and executed their oaths. Each letter was sealed with the man's signet ring. Cassius, however, signed nothing, saying that he himself would soon be going to Gaul, and he did leave the city before the envoys. By arrangement, the Allobroges were apprehended at the Mulvian Bridge outside Rome and the sealed letters handed over. On this evidence the other three were convicted and executed. Lucius Cassius had made good his escape and was condemned *in absentia*. We do not know if he was ever captured.

Chapter 12

MARCUS VOLTEIUS 75 BCE

The moneyer Marcus Volteius is unknown. With no prosopographical evidence available, we must once again turn to hoard evidence to establish a date for Marcus Volteius' moneyership. Crawford arrived at a date of 78 for Volteius and Cassius using the Kerassia and Bompas hoards.[1] As discussed in Cassius' chapter, Grueber felt that Cassius and Volteius were the latest moneyers in the Hev-Szamos hoard and he too dated both of them to 78. Hersh and Walker reinterpreted the dating using the Alba di Massa and Capreni hoards, which led them to date Volteius after Rutilius and Satrienus rather than before as in Crawford's arrangement. They assigned both Volteius and Cassius to the year 75.[2]

The common assumption derived from the hoard evidence is that Volteius and Cassius belong closely together, either in the same or consecutive years. In my arrangement, I must place them in separate years. Cassius' coin is the only one of the period on which we can use prosopographical evidence and in the previous chapter I dated it to 76. His issue is small and since Cassius was found in the Kerassia and Hev-Szamos hoards with only the addition of Volteius and not the rather large issues of Rutilius and Satrienus, I am inclined to date Volteius right after Cassius and before Rutilius and Satrienus. To me, it is easier to excuse the absence of Cassius' rarer coin from the Alba di Massa, Capreni, and Bompas hoards rather than to explain the absence of the large issues by Rutilius and Satrienus from the Kerassia and the Hev-Szamos hoards which do contain Cassius' coin. Although I interpret the hoard evidence differently from the other commentators, I have arrived, nonetheless, at Hersh and Walker's date of 75.

Volteius issued five different types, each one depicting a different god or goddess. Taken individually none is significant, but considered as a series, Mommsen detected a common theme. Each of Volteius' five deities had annual celebrations of games held in their honor. Mommsen interpreted the five different coin designs as referring to the major games celebrated in the Roman calendar: the *Ludi Megalenses*, the *Ludi Ceriales,* the *Ludi Apollinares*, the *Ludi Romani,* and the *Ludi Plebeii.*[3]

Ludi Megalenses

The *Ludi Megalenses* held between 4 and 10 April were the first games of the calendar year. Volteius represented these games with the depiction of a male head wearing a Phrygian helmet on the obverse and the goddess Cybele driving a cart drawn by a pair of lions on the reverse. Cybele, also known as the Great Mother, was a Phrygian goddess whose frenzied rituals were quite foreign to Roman sensitivities. A passage giving an enlightening description and philosophical analysis of her rites is found in Lucretius' poem *On the Nature of Things*.

> The ancient learned Greek poets sang that the goddess
> drives a chariot drawn by a pair of yoked lions...
> they yoked wild beasts, because no matter how
> wild offspring may be, they ought to be tamed and
> softened by the gentle care of parents,
> they ringed the top of her head with a mural crown
> because, protected by goodly strongholds, she sustains
> cities. Distinguished now by such insignia, the image
> of the divine mother is borne throughout many lands
> exciting dread. Various peoples following the ancient
> custom of their rites call this goddess the Idaean
> Mother and give her crowds of Phrygians as attendants,
> because they claim it was first from those regions that
> fruits began to be produced throughout the world.
> They assign eunuch priests to her because they wish
> to signify that those who violate the divine power of
> the Mother and are found ungrateful to their fathers
> ought to be considered unworthy to bring forth living
> progeny into the light of day. Around her image, hollow
> cymbals and tightly stretched drums resound under
> palms, and horns with their hoarse voice make menacing
> sound, and the hollow flute stirs souls with its
> Phrygian melody. They carry before her weapons, signs
> of frenzied madness, which are able to fill the
> ungrateful souls and impious hearts of the crowd with
> dread of the divine power of the goddess.
> Therefore, when first she is drawn through great
> cities, she mutely blesses mortals with unspoken
> benediction. Her followers strew the whole line of
> procession with bronze and silver coins, enriching her
> with generous alms, and they shower her with rose
> petals covering both the Mother and the retinue of her
> attendants. Then the armed band, which the Greeks call
> by the name the Phrygian Curetes, joust between groups

> as the fancy strikes and dance in rhythm, rejoicing in the shedding of their own blood, shaking the terrifying crests of their helmets with the nodding of their heads. They recall the Dictaean Curetes who are said to have once hidden the infant cries of Jupiter in Crete, when armed boys in nimble dance beat bronze on bronze in rhythm around an infant boy, lest Saturn snatching him up crush him with his jaws and give an eternal wound to his mother's heart.[4]

The Phrygian followers of Idaean Cybele were called Corybantes, but in Latin literature they were frequently confused with the Curetes who concealed infant Jupiter's cries on Mount Ida in Crete.[5] It may be one of these Corybantes who appears to be represented on the obverse of Volteius' coin, but more likely it is Attis, the young consort of Cybele. He is usually depicted in Phrygian trousers fastened with toggles down the front and a laureate Phrygian cap. His act of self-castration is the reason why Cybele's priests were eunuchs and why in Rome Cybele's worship remained distinctly Greek in character and was maintained by Greek priests. Romans were prohibited by decree of the Senate from taking part in the priestly service of the goddess. Even the name of the games remained Greek, derived from *Megale Mater* meaning Great Mother.[6] The goddess did not become part of the Roman pantheon until 204. In that year the Sibylline Books were consulted because, according to Livy, it had rained stones more than usual that year. In the books a prophecy was found that if the Romans ever wished to drive out a foreign enemy who had invaded Italy, they would be successful if they should bring Cybele, the Idaean Mother of the Gods, from Pessinus to Rome.[7]

Classical Numismatic Group, Inc. Inventory no.734470

The obverse head is most likely Attis, the consort of Cybele famous for his act of self-castration. He is usually depicted as a sensuous youth dressed in Phrygian clothing; note the long wavy hair under the Phrygian cap. Classical Numismatic Group noted that the duck symbol behind the head on this die is very unusual.

Rome might well have expected the goddess to be willing to help. When Aeneas transferred the remains of smoldering Troy to Italian soil, the goddess almost followed the Trojan ships then, but since she felt that fate did not yet call for her intervention on Italian soil, she stayed behind in her beloved Phrygian haunts.[8] After nine centuries, the Romans needed her help in order to drive out the Carthaginians. The Sibyl advised the Romans, 'The Mother is absent: I bid you, Roman, seek the Mother. When she comes, she must be received by chaste hands.'[9]

By happy coincidence, Attalus of Pergamum had recently become an ally of Rome because of their common dispute with Philip. The Romans sought his help in obtaining the sacred stone at Pessinus which the natives believed represented the goddess. In order to stress the importance and dignity of this mission, an embassy of five men and five quinqueremes were dispatched by the Senate to bring the goddess from Pessinus to Italy.[10] When they obtained the stone, one ambassador returned to Rome with advance word, while the others with proper pomp and ceremony conveyed the sacred stone back to Rome in a ship specially built and painted for the occasion. Back in Rome the Senate had to determine whose chaste hands were to receive the goddess on her arrival. Publius Cornelius Scipio Nasica, son of Gnaeus, was the man chosen. On word of the ship's approach, he went down to the port of Ostia accompanied by the married women of Rome. When the ship reached the mouth of the Tiber, Scipio sailed out to meet it and received the sacred stone from the priests. He conveyed it ashore and placed it into the hands of the married women who passed the goddess along from hand to hand. All the people had come out to witness the goddess' arrival and escort her into the city. Censers burning incense had been placed in doorways along the path of the procession that wound its way to the temple of Victory on the Palatine. Here the people crowded in with gifts. The day of her installation was 4 April 204 and games were held in her honor for the first time.[11] The specific contests of the first games were not recorded, but scenic games were added for the first time by the curule aediles A. Atilius Serranus and L. Scribonius Libo in 194.[12] A day of racing closed the ceremonies.

At some point in the development of the games, the re-enactment of the goddess' reception into Rome became part of the ceremonies. The version presented during the games was somewhat more mystical than that recorded in Livy's history. Ovid prefaced his narration of this version saying, 'My story is strange, but I say that it is attested on the stage.'[13]

When the ship bearing the sacred stone arrived at Ostia, it stuck fast in the muddy shallows and could go no farther. Men tugged mightily on ropes, but failed to move the ship. Was this a portent that the goddess did not wish to come ashore? The men were shaken. But a certain Claudia Quinta, who though of good family, was widely rumored to be of loose virtue, stepped forward from the crowd and took up the pure water from the river letting it drip over her head three times. On bended knee, she addressed the goddess beseeching her to prove her virtue by delivering herself into Claudia's chaste hands. She then drew on the rope with only the slightest effort and the goddess' ship followed. The people let out a cry of joy and the ship was drawn up the Tiber and secured for the night. On the next day, they offered a heifer in sacrifice and took the sacred stone off the ship. At the confluence of the Almo and the Tiber, Cybele's purple robed priest washed the sacred stone and the goddess' sacred things. Her attendants howled and there was a din of flutes and drums. The goddess entered into the city through the Capene Gate seated in a wagon drawn by oxen and Claudia, her chastity vindicated, led the procession. Scipio Nasica finally received the goddess at the end of the procession and she was installed in the temple of Victory. Not until 191 did she receive her own temple.

Classical Numismatic Group, Inc. 61 Lot 1399

Attis is on the obverse with an axe behind his head. On the reverse Cybele drives her cart drawn by lions. The moneyer's name M•VOLTEI•M•F is in the exergue.

Volteius' coin depicts Cybele in her typical Greek aspect rather than as the sacred stone that was brought to Rome. She wears a mural crown and drives a cart pulled by a pair of lions, beasts once common to Phrygia.

Ludi Ceriales

After a break of only one day, the games of Ceres, the goddess of grain, followed immediately on the heels of the *Ludi Megalenses*, extending from 12 to 19 April. The celebration was first attested in 202 when Livy stated that the dictator held the games in place of the plebeian aediles.[14] Clearly, the games had been established earlier. On a coin minted in 57, the moneyer Gaius Memmius claimed that 'the aedile Memmius was the first to celebrate the games of Ceres.' Broughton dated the aedile Memmius to the year 211, but certainty is impossible. If the plebeian aediles were the first to hold the games of Ceres, they could date as far back as 493 when the office of plebeian aedile was created and the temple of Ceres dedicated.

Classical Numismatic Group, Inc. 79 Lot 923

Ceres is on the reverse in a low chariot drawn by a pair of serpents. She holds two torches in her hands as she searches for her abducted daughter. A rudder is the symbol behind her.

No record of the games exists in similar detail to that which we find for the *Ludi Megalenses*. The precise memories may have been lost and in the *Fasti* Ovid cleverly avoided giving the history of the games saying, 'Next are the games of Ceres. There is no need to give the reason. The gifts and merits of the goddess are obvious on their own.'[15] Ovid did recount the well-known story of the abduction of Ceres' daughter Proserpina by Pluto and the world-wide search made by Ceres to recover her. The story, which explains the yearly cycle of food production, was an ancient Greek myth adopted by the Romans when they assimilated the Greek Demeter with their native Ceres. Ovid told how Ceres used two pine trees as torches to light her path[16] and how she left her home of Sicily flying over the waves in a winged chariot drawn by two yoked serpents.[17] Holding two torches in her hands and riding in a low chariot drawn by snakes is Volteius' depiction of Ceres on the reverse of his coin. A reenactment of this story was probably a part of the ceremonies of the games. The people dressed in special white garments to attend her rites and torches were passed out to the populace as they entered the Circus.[18]

The appearance on the coin's obverse of the Roman god Liber, who had no part in the Greek myth of Demeter and Kore, reminds us that the Roman rites of Ceres are not to be confused with Demeter and Kore's secret mysteries celebrated at Eleusis. The ivy wreathed head of Liber, just as on Cassius' coin discussed in the previous chapter, was intended to recall the dedication of the temple of Ceres, Liber, and Libera built at the foot of the Aventine near the Circus Maximus where the games of Ceres were held. The temple was dedicated in 493 on 19 April, which in Republican times was the closing day of the festival. It is possible that the first games of Ceres were held on that day.

Classical Numismatic Group, Inc. Triton IX Lot 1291

The obverse head crowned with an ivy wreath is Liber. It recalls the dedication of the temple of Ceres, Liber, and Libera near the Circus Maximus where the games of Ceres were held. A plumb-bob is the symbol behind Ceres on the reverse.

On the final day of the games, they conducted a special ceremony rooted in Italian tradition.[19] Foxes were set loose in the Circus with burning torches tied to their backs. They ran wildly about until they perished from the flames. This rite represented ritual punishment on their species for an alleged crime against Ceres committed many years before by one unfortunate fox. In the Italian city of Carseoli, a twelve-year-old boy had caught the clever fox that had been stealing the family's chickens. He wrapped her in straw and hay and set her on fire. The fox struggled free from his grip and wherever she fled set fire to the fields of ripe grain, the very embodiment of Ceres herself. The breezes whipped up the flames and the fire devoured the grain. Wildfires were always to be dreaded in the harvest season and the sacrifice of the foxes at Ceres' games was to make amends for past transgressions and to ward off any fresh recurrence. When this rite was over, chariot racing closed the ceremonies.

Ludi Apollinares

The next games in the Roman calendar were celebrated between 28 April and 4 May in honor of Flora, the goddess of fruit crops. Volteius issued no coin to commemorate these games. After the first three sets of games coming so closely together, the next games did not occur until July when the games of Apollo were celebrated between the 6th and 13th. Coins commemorating these games had been issued about fifteen years before by the moneyer Lucius Calpurnius Piso Frugi whose ancestor had a part in establishing the games as a permanent part of the religious calendar. Piso Frugi depicted the head of Apollo on the obverse and on the reverse a horse with a naked rider represented the races that closed the ceremonies.

Classical Numismatic Group, Inc. Inventory no. 812123

This coin minted by Lucius Calpurnius Piso Frugi (*ca.* 90) commemorated his family's role in establishing the games of Apollo who is on the obverse.

Piso's coins were in wide circulation when Volteius minted. Volteius, like Piso Frugi, depicted Apollo on the obverse, although in a different style. Piso's Apollo has laurel in his hair with five flowing curls of hair falling below. Volteius' Apollo is also laureate but has only two flowing strands of hair down the neck. On his reverse, Volteius chose not to emphasize the contests that were part of the games as Piso did, but to recall the events which established the games.

Having survived the devastating and demoralizing defeat of their forces at Cannae in 216, the Romans three years later still found it difficult to remove the Carthaginian thorn from their side. In 213, a prophecy by the seer Marcius was found that promised Apollo's aid in driving out this foreign foe if the Roman people would hold games in his honor. The matter was referred to the *decemviri sacris faciundis* who consulted the Sibylline Books and confirmed the prophecy. The games were first celebrated in 212 after the Senate issued a decree that the funds for the games should come both from the public treasury and private subscription, that the urban praetor preside over the games, and that the *decemviri* make sacrifices in Greek fashion.[20] The tripod on the coin's reverse recalls the part that the *decemviri* played in establishing the games.

The tripod is well recognized as a sacred symbol of Apollo and the snake winding around one leg recalls the serpent of Pythia, but Volteius seems to have represented one of the tripods which were kept by the *decemviri* as part of the sacred objects used in their worship of Apollo. A specific mention of these tripods is found in Servius' commentaries on the *Aeneid.* He recounted the story of Icadius, the son of Apollo and the nymph Lycia, who was shipwrecked and saved from drowning by a dolphin who took him onto his back. Icadius reached land near Mount Parnassus and set up altars to his father and the place came to be called Delphi from the dolphin. From this incident, the dolphin became sacred to Apollo. Servius said that a proof of this is that on the tripods of the *quindecemviri* dolphins are placed on the rim.[21] (The number of the *decemviri* had been raised to fifteen at some point after 82.) On the rim of the left side of the tripod, Volteius has a figure which appears to be a leaping dolphin. Volteius also inscribed the letters S•C and D•T beside the legs of the tripod. In earlier interpretations of the inscription, the S•C and D•T were taken to mean *Senatus consulto de thesauro* indicating that this particular issue, unlike the other four that are not marked S•C, was a special issue authorized by the Senate on the occasion of the current celebration of the games and the silver came from the public treasury.[22]

Gemini Numismatic Auctions, LLC Auction II Lot 226

The laureate head of Apollo on the obverse of Volteius' coin is done in a style quite different from Piso Frugi's. On the reverse Volteius' inscription S•C D•T recalls that the games of Apollo were paid to the god by decree of the Senate. The tripod indicates the role that Apollo's prophecy played in establishing the games.

Crawford realized that the inscription referred to the circumstances under which the very first games were held in 212. He offered an interpretation of S•C D•T as *s(tips) c(ollata) d(ei) t(hesauro)*, 'offerings collected for the treasury of the god.'[23] Such a rendering stresses the private contributions which supplemented the public funds. However, the inscription S•C is so common on coins meaning 'by decree of the Senate' that it is hard to see how most Romans would have taken it as anything else, especially since it is separated from the D•T. To fill out the inscription as *S(enatus) c(onsulto) d(eo) t(ributum)* or 'paid to the god by decree of the Senate' quite simply describes the way the games came about in 212. The tripod of the *quindecemviri* recalls the part prophecy played in initiating the games and the inscription beside its legs attests to the Senate's response to the prophecies.

Ludi Romani

The regular celebration of the Roman Games can be traced back to 366 when the curule aediles were created to present the *Ludi Maximi* in place of the plebeian aediles who refused to hold the games. Clearly, their tradition dates back even further and it seems probable that these games originated as the payment of vows made on behalf of the state by the consuls or the kings. Dionysius of Halicarnassus traced the first presentation back to the payment of a vow made by Aulus Postumius before the battle of Lake Regillus.[24] Livy referred to these games which Postumius vowed to Jupiter as *Ludi Magni.*[25] It seems the games got bigger over the years and went from the *Ludi Magni* to the *Ludi Maximi*. By the time Volteius minted, the games were also called the *Ludi Romani* and extended from 5 to 19 September.

Dionysius of Halicarnassus who witnessed the games in the late first century wrote a description of the ceremonies for his Greek audience and it has survived for us. The principal magistrates initiated the festival by conducting a procession of the gods from the Capitol through the Forum to the Circus Maximus. The sons of knights who were approaching manhood led the procession on horseback in squadrons and those boys who would serve in the infantry followed on foot in companies. They were followed by charioteers and behind them came the contestants, naked except for their loins. Bands of dancers arranged in three divisions of men, youths, and boys followed the contestants accompanied by flute-players and lyre-players. The dancers were dressed in crimson tunics girded by bronze belts, with swords hanging at their sides and carrying short spears. On their heads were bronze helmets adorned with crests and plumes. Each group had one leader for the warlike movements and rapid rhythms. Behind the dancers came others impersonating satyrs wearing goatskins and on their heads were manes which stood upright. Others who represented Sileni wore shaggy tunics and mantles of flowers. The group of satyrs mimicked and mocked the serious dances of the other groups and inspired laughter among the spectators. Lyre and flute players followed and then came men carrying censers filled with perfumes and frankincense which were burned along the whole line of march and there were also men carrying the sacred silver and gold vessels of the gods and of the state. Then finally came the images of the gods carried on men's shoulders, not just the twelve Olympians, but also numerous other gods and demigods. After the procession, the consuls and priests sacrificed oxen.[26] The first days of the festival were occupied with dramatic presentations. This tradition started at the *Ludi Romani* in 240 when Livius Andronicus, translating from Greek originals, presented the first regular comedy and tragedy.[27] Their popularity led to such plays becoming a regular part of all five games and the number of days for their presentations increased over time.

The design of Volteius' coin with the head of Jupiter on the obverse and his Capitoline temple on the reverse focuses on the central part of the festival which occurred on the 13th, when the *Epulum Jovis*, the feast of Jupiter, was held. This was one of the most spectacular scenes in Roman religion. It began with a sacrifice, and then the huge public feast was laid out. The Capitoline triad Jupiter, Juno, and Minerva were present in visible form, for the images of the gods were decked out in their best attire and seated on their couches. The priesthood of *septemviri epulones* created in 196 had special charge of the ceremony.

Classical Numismatic Group, Inc. 79 Lot 922

Volteius commemorated the *Ludi Romani* on this coin. The laureate head of Jupiter Capitolinus is on the obverse and his Capitoline temple is on the reverse. The four columns indicate the tripartite nature of the temple shared by Jupiter, Juno, and Minerva. Jupiter occupied the center cella and his thunderbolt is in the pediment.

The 13th was also the birthday of the great temple of Jupiter Optimus Maximus on the Capitol, the most significant temple of ancient Rome. Tacitus called it the 'seat of Jupiter, founded by our ancestors under propitious auspices as a pledge of our *imperium.*'[28] The first King Tarquin began its construction in payment of a vow he had made to Jupiter, Juno, and Minerva when he was fighting the Sabines. He undertook extensive site preparation on the Capitoline where the ground was steep and uneven, requiring massive retaining walls and huge amounts of fill dirt. After four years of work, the ground was finally ready for construction, but Tarquin died before he could lay the foundation.[29] The actual construction of the temple was undertaken by Tarquin the Proud. During the course of the excavations for the foundation, the diggers found a human head with features intact. The seers interpreted this to unambiguously portend that this spot was to be the citadel of *imperium* and the *caput rerum*.[30]

Tarquin the Proud was driven from power before he could finish and dedicate the temple. This privilege fell to a magistrate of the newly born Republic, the suffect consul of 509 Marcus Horatius Pulvillus.[31] After centuries of glory, the temple burned to the ground on 6 July 83. Its reconstruction was undertaken by Sulla, but he died in 78 before it could be completed. This is the one point at which the ancient authors noted that Sulla's good fortune failed him. Lutatius Catulus, consul 78, won the glory of continuing the restoration.

This was still ongoing and far from completion when Volteius' representation appeared on the reverse of this coin. A problem exists with Volteius' depiction. Dionysius of Halicarnassus said, 'The temple constructed in our fathers' time after the conflagration was built on the same foundation, differing from the ancient temple only in the costliness of the materials, having a triple row of columns on the front portion facing south and a single row on the sides.'[32] We know that Catulus did not change the original size of the temple, but the restored temple depicted on a later coin by Petillius had six columns across the front not the four seen on this coin. Crawford says that the unfinished state of construction excuses Volteius for not necessarily accurately reflecting the reconstructed appearance of the temple. But we might ask, if Volteius did not reflect the new reconstruction, did he reflect the old temple? After only eight years, people could not have forgotten how many columns the temple of Jupiter once had across the front. Surely Volteius himself had seen the temple and could remember it. Did Volteius not care about accuracy, or were there originally only four front columns? Probably not. The temple was about sixty-one and one-half meters long and fifty-seven meters wide.[33] If there were originally only four columns, the space between each column would have been nineteen meters, an unreasonably long open span for the architrave. Even with six columns the spacing would be about eleven and one-half meters on center. By way of comparison, the Parthenon built of stone was sixty-nine and one-half meters long and almost thirty-one meters wide with eight columns across the front. Since the reconstructed temple of Jupiter Capitolinus matched the original size, it is most likely that the temple seen on Petillius' coin reproduced the ancient temple's design.

Rather than try to precisely depict the new temple, whose columns may not have been set in place when he minted, Volteius seems to have chosen to emphasize the tripartite nature of the temple of Jupiter Capitolinus. In typical Etruscan style, the temple was divided into three cellas, the larger central one occupied by Jupiter, the one on the left belonged to Minerva, the one on the right to Juno. Volteius depicted this feature of the temple by using four columns to divide the space into three sections and his uneven spacing of the columns makes the central cella the largest. The representation of the doors to the separate cellas can be seen between the columns. Such a representation, true to the nature of the temple but not to the details of the completed reconstruction, would have been best suited to a time when Catulus had not yet erected the columns at the entrance. He did not dedicate the temple until 69 and even then its embellishment was not complete. The incentive for accuracy in column numbers would have been much more compelling further along in the reconstruction process. Dating Volteius' moneyership to the year 75 still leaves six more years of construction until the temple was dedicated.

Classical Numismatic Group, Inc. Triton XII Lot 515

In 43 Petillius minted a coin with the head of Jupiter Capitolinus on the obverse and on the reverse Jupiter's rebuilt and richly decorated Capitoline temple with six columns across the front and three garlands hanging between the columns.

The Circus games that occupied the last five days of the *Ludi Romani* were also described by Dionysius of Halicarnassus. First there were races of four-horse chariots, two-horse chariots, and unyoked horses. There were also the special races using the three-horse chariot, which we saw depicted on the coin by Naevius Balbus. After the chariot races, the runners, boxers, and wrestlers entered the Circus and contended for prizes.[34]

Ludi Plebeii

The next games in the Roman calendar were the games of Victory instituted in 81 by Sulla to commemorate his victory at the Colline Gate. These games extended from 26 October to 1 November. A coin by the moneyer Nonius Sufenas depicting a seated Roma being crowned by Victory made the claim that Sextus Nonius Sufenas was the first to hold the games. Volteius minted no coin to commemorate these games. His fifth type has the lion-skin covered head of Hercules on the obverse and the Erymanthian boar on the reverse. This type has been identified as commemorating the *Ludi Plebeii*. Grueber stated that the Plebeian Games were held in honor of Hercules as patron of contests in the *palaestra* and musical contests.[35] A reference in Pseudo-Asconius said that the games were instituted either in commemoration of the freedom of the plebs after the banishment of the kings in 509 or after the Secession of the Plebs in 493.[36] The name of the games suggests an event specific to the traditions of the plebeians. The commemoration of the secession of the plebs and the rights they won thereby may well have been at the heart of the celebration. Originally the games were probably held on only one day, but by the end of the Republic they extended from 4 to 17 November. The time of year coincides with the traditional ending of the secession of the plebs.

The first historic mention of the games was in the year 216 when Livy noted that they had to be held three times by the plebeian aediles.[37] Since the *Ludi Plebeii* were held in the Circus Flaminius built in the Campus Martius by the censor Gaius Flaminius in 220, it is thought that the yearly celebrations of the games date from 220.

Despite Grueber's statement, no ancient references state to whom the *Ludi Plebeii* were sacred. Hercules may well have had a part in the games as he did in the *Ludi Romani*, but there are suggestions that the *Ludi Plebeii* may have been sacred to Jupiter, because another *epulum* for Jupiter occurred during the games on the 13th, and this day may have been the nucleus of the festival.[38] In the absence of written testimony, Volteius' coin is the only piece of ancient evidence to support the supposition that the games were held in honor of Hercules. However, if the *Ludi Plebeii* were sacred to Jupiter, Volteius needed a type which would differentiate between the *Ludi Romani* and the *Ludi Plebeii*. For this Hercules was a useful device since he had a special relationship with the Circus Flaminius where the *Ludi Plebeii* were held.

Classical Numismatic Group, Inc. Triton XII Lot 681

The lion skin covered head of Hercules is on the obverse. He is associated with the celebration of the *Ludi Plebeii* since the temple of Hercules Magnus Custos ad Circum was near the Circus Flaminius where the games were held.

As the patron of athletic contests, it was proper that temples of Hercules be erected close to gymnasiums, amphitheaters, and circuses.[39] There were temples of Hercules near both the Circus Maximus where the *Ludi Romani* were held and the Circus Flaminius where the *Ludi Plebeii* were held. The temple near the Circus Maximus was dedicated to Hercules Invictus; the one at the Circus Flaminius was called Hercules Magnus Custos ad Circum, Hercules the Great Guardian at the Circus. From Ovid we learn that this temple had been built there on the advice of the Sibyl of Cumae.

> The other part of the Circus is under the protection
> of Hercules the Guardian which office the god holds

> thanks to the Euboean oracle. The date of his
> installation is the day before the Nones. If you
> inquire of the inscription, Sulla approved the work.[40]

It seems that the inscription Ovid mentioned refers to a restoration of the temple by Sulla completed only a short time before this coin was minted. The site was identified by Lanciani on the ancient Severan map of Rome, the *Forma Urbis Romae,* as the round temple near the Circus Flaminius. He felt that the site of Hercules Magnus Custos was confirmed when the cult statue of Hercules was found in excavations made in 1864.

As mentioned earlier, Hercules' temples were properly sited near circuses and gymnasiums, but we need more than this to connect Volteius' coin with the temple of Hercules Magnus Custos ad Circum and the *Ludi Plebeii*. Is it coincidental that of Hercules' twelve labors the least interesting tale of the Erymanthian boar, whose image is on the reverse of Volteius' coin, is the only one which can be connected to the Sibyl of Cumae who was responsible for the construction of the temple of Hercules Magnus Custos?

This fierce boar coming down from the mountain Erymanthus had been ravaging the territory of Psophis in the Peloponnese. Hercules was sent to capture it alive. The trick, on the one hand, was to avoid its terrifying tusks, which could rip a man open and yet, on the other hand, to avoid killing it or the labor would be unfulfilled. Hercules had to keep a balance between the two extremes. He succeeded by chasing the boar from its thickets and exhausting it in relentless pursuit. He finally drove it into deep snow and trapped it.[41] He returned home to Mycenae carrying it over his shoulders and when Eurystheus saw him coming he was so terrified that he hid in a huge bronze vessel. This scene is frequently reproduced on Greek vases.

Freeman and Sear Auction 14 Lot 360

How can this Greek myth be connected with the Sibyl of Cumae in Italy? Strangely enough, and as unbelievable as it sounded to the Greek travel writer Pausanius who reported it, the tusks of the Erymanthian boar were preserved in the sanctuary of Apollo at Cumae.[42] The temple of Hercules Magnus Custos ad Circum was built on the prompting of the Sibyl of Cumae.

Now that we have examined the five games commemorated by Volteius, we can ask this question: were these five coin types originally conceived as a series or did they just develop over the course of the year? As a planned series, we might expect an almost equal number of coins to be minted for each type, but the reverse die estimates given by Crawford show that there is a wide difference in mintage: Cybele, sixty-eight; Ceres, sixty-eight; Apollo, seven; Romani, seventy-eight; Plebeii, twenty-two. Moreover, there is no consistency in the way Volteius used his control marks. Two types have control marks while three have none. On the coins of Cybele, he used a series of symbols and Greek numbers. The Ceres type shares some of the same symbols, but has no numbers. These two types also share a similar reverse design depicting the respective goddesses riding in bigae drawn by their sacred animals. We also note that about the same number of dies was used in the production of both types. This suggests a certain continuity in conception and production for the Cybele and Ceres types. That Volteius did not use any control marks on the other three issues suggests that they were minted at a different point in the year when he was in a different state of mind and saw no need to use control symbols. It is an interesting piece of speculation to suggest that since the games of Cybele and Ceres were the first games of the year, their coins may have been issued first. Their minting may have used all the bullion originally budgeted. When new financial needs required additional minting, the other types followed later in the year. Volteius continued with the same theme by issuing new coins commemorating the games then being held in the season when he minted the coins.

Crawford suggested that Volteius' series of coins was minted 'presumably to convey a promise of *largitiones* in the future.'[43] Moneyers did claim family connections with the establishment of certain games and promises of continued largess were implied, but there is no connection to be found between the Volteii and any of the games commemorated, nor did any Volteii hold any of the magistracies which were responsible for their presentation. The only other appearance of the family name Volteius in Republican history is a Lucius Volteius who was on the staff of Caecilius Metellus when he served as governor of Sicily in 70. No single noble family in Rome, let alone the unknown Volteii, could make claims on five of the major festivals. Moreover, Volteius was not in a position to perform on any promises of largess. The commemoration of five different games by a man whose family name must have been virtually unknown at Rome suggests a theme common to the state as a whole rather than family tradition.

If the theme is not related to the *gens* Volteia or promises of largess, we should look to the politics of the times in which the coins were minted. The year 75 was one of great difficulty and uncertainty for Romans. Grain shortages had produced hostile sentiments among the people and after civil discord, in which the consuls were attacked, the consul Gaius Cotta put on mourning clothes and addressed the people.[44]

> You have made us consuls, Romans, at a time when the Republic is most entangled in difficulties both at home and in war. Our commanders in Spain are asking for pay, soldiers, arms, and grain -- and circumstances force this since with the defection of our allies and with the flight of Sertorius through the mountains, they are not able to come to battle nor to provide their needs -- armies are maintained in Asia and Cilicia because of the excessive power of Mithridates, Macedonia is full of enemies, as is the coastline of Italy and the provinces, since for the time being our revenues, reduced and made uncertain by wars, barely sustain a part of our expense.

Cotta offered to consecrate himself to the gods following the ancient custom, sacrificing his life on behalf of the country. He closed his speech saying,

> By your own name, Romans, and by the glory of your ancestors, endure adversity and take thought of the Republic! Supreme power brings great anxiety and many heavy labors which you refuse in vain and, in vain, you seek the opulence of peace when all the provinces, kingdoms, seas, and lands are battered or devastated by wars.

Cotta's lament over the cash shortage that the Senate faced early in 75 was carried over from the previous year and may be reflected in the small mintage by Cassius. But what of Volteius' five issues which together used an estimated 243 reverse dies? How does this square with Cotta's speech? During the course of the year, the Senate set about to find cash and by the end of the year two major sources were found, making future prospects considerably brighter. One source was ready at hand. Twenty years beforehand, Apion the king of Cyrene died leaving his kingdom to Rome. Having paid it little attention this whole time, the Senate decided in 75 to exploit its resources. Publius Cornelius Marcellinus was sent on a special mission with the title *quaestor pro praetore.* This title was the same title that was later given to Cato in 58 when he was sent to Cypress to convert Ptolemy's treasure to cash and bring it back to the treasury in Rome. Marcellinus' mission presumably was to raise cash from Apion's untapped resources. This is usually dated to 74, but Stewart Oost has shown that Appian figured his history in Olympian years, that is, summer to summer, and his reference to Cyrene falls within 75/74.

Marcellinus probably left for Cyrene in the second half of 75.[45] It is possible that these resources were silphium. Pliny recorded that thirty pounds of silphium had been sent to Rome in 93 as a gift, but when Caesar broke open the treasury in 49 he found 1,500 pounds of silphium stockpiled within.[46] The five different types minted by Volteius may represent separate mintings as funds came available from these additional sources of revenue during the course of the year. At the end of the year or early the next year, there came another windfall. Nicomedes the king of Bithynia died childless and in his will he too bequeathed his kingdom to Rome.[47] By the end of 75 and beginning of 74, Rome's cash shortage was over. We will see that the Senate was able to provide bullion for large issues, both S•C and regular, in the next three years.

If Volteius' coinage is to be dated to 75, his theme reflects the anxious mood of the Senate and people described in Cotta's speech. Volteius' commemoration of the games has an underlying theme that the health of the nation depended on its relationship with the gods. Most of the games were originally instituted in troubled times. Their initial celebrations brought the promised and desired results so that the Romans overcame their difficulties. The annual performance of the games served to maintain that beneficial relationship with the gods. Volteius' coinage affirms the special protective relationship that Rome enjoyed with its gods and expressed a continued confidence that everything would be all right.

Chapter 13

LUCIUS RUTILIUS FLACCUS 74 BCE

The moneyer Lucius Rutilius Flaccus is unknown, which leaves us only hoard evidence as a dating tool. Rutilius used an estimated 213 reverse dies and his large issue was not found in the Kerassia or Hev-Szamos hoards whose latest coins were by Cassius and Volteius. The coin was in the Bompas hoard, which contained one coin by Volteius, and in the Capreni hoard, which had no coins by Cassius or Volteius but one coin by Farsuleius. All this evidence has been interpreted differently by each commentator creating different relative arrangements for the various moneyers. Even so, Grueber, Crawford, and Hersh and Walker have all arrived at the same date of 77 for Rutilius and Satrienus, who appeared with Rutilius in the Capreni hoard. Using the Kerassia and Hev Szamos hoards, I date Rutilius and Satrienus after Volteius, whom I have dated to 75. Since I can only have one mint magistrate per year in my arrangement, I must date Rutilius and Satrienus to two separate years; Rutilius minted in 74 and Satrienus in 73.

Classical Numismatic Group, Inc. Triton VI Lot 693

The moneyer inscribed his name FLAC behind the head of Roma and L•RVTILI is on the reverse in the exergue. Victory drives a biga on the reverse. She is holding a wreath and is naked to the waist with her gown held forward over the reins.

The Roma head on the obverse, which was commonly found on the earliest coins of the Republic, is used here for the last time. On the reverse Victory drives a biga. She is naked to the waist and her gown is pulled forward making an S-shape as it crosses her waist and drapes over the reins. She holds a wreath in her right hand. The coin's design seemingly offers little insight into either the moneyer or the message, except perhaps to say that Lucius Rutilius Flaccus had little imagination. The only thing to distinguish this coin from any of the similar issues of the previous century is the moneyer's name. Crawford's entire commentary on the coin reads, 'The moneyer is presumably the man attested as Senator in 72 (Cicero, Cluent. 182).'[1] Cicero's reference in *Pro Cluentio* is to a Lucius Rutilius (no *cognomen*), who offered evidence in an inquiry held in 72. It is not clear if this man was a Rutilius Flaccus; nor is it clear if he was a senator in 72 as Crawford presumes; nor is it clear if he served as a judge in the trial of Cluentius in 69. However, if the Lucius Rutilius mentioned by Cicero is our moneyer, a mint magistracy in 74 is consistent with an election to a quaestorship and membership in the Senate by 72.

Rutilius' coin with its Roma head and biga reverse is of such an old style that, if hoard evidence did not date it to this time period, we would have dated it to a much earlier time on stylistic evidence. Grueber suggested that the coin type related to some event connected with the man's family, of which there was no other record. The *gens* Rutilia was neither new to politics nor unknown to the Roman people. It had provided two consuls in the last thirty years, but it is not likely that the coin refers to them, since neither was famous for military victories. Publius Rutilius Lupus had been consul in 90 and was defeated and perished that year fighting the Samnites in the Social War. Publius Rutilius Rufus, the consul of 105, spent his time in Rome taking emergency measures after his colleague led the Roman army to a terrible mauling at the hands of the Cimbri and the Teutons in Gaul. Rutilius Rufus trained the army in new fighting tactics based on gladiator techniques and turned the army over to Marius who won the victory and the glory. In 94 Rufus accompanied the proconsul Quintus Mucius Scaevola to the province of Asia as a legate. Once there he endeared himself to the people, but made dangerous enemies of the knights when his sense of justice led him to defend the province against the injuries of the tax farmers. After he returned to Rome, his enemies brought a trumped-up charge of extortion against him in 92.[2] Widely known to be innocent, he was convicted by a hostile court which, at that time, was under the control of the knights. Rutilius was sentenced to exile. He returned to Asia and was gladly received by the province he had been charged with plundering.[3] When Sulla made his reforms in 81, Rutilius Rufus' case became his best justification for returning the courts to the control of the Senate. Sulla lifted Rutilius' sentence of exile,[4] but the aging ex-consul chose not to return and was still living in Smyrna when Cicero visited him there in 78.

Since we can find nothing in the better known history of the *gens* Rutilia to make this coin a specific reference to a victory won by a family member, and since its type is so generic, it may simply be a confident expression in Rome's ability to prevail in the many wars she was waging at the time. Of the year 74, Appian wrote, 'Wars abounded. There was the war against

Sertorius in Spain, the one against Mithridates in the East, the one against pirates on the whole sea, and another around Crete against the Cretans.'[5] For a nation embroiled in so many conflicts, the simplicity of the traditional design quite eloquently proclaims that Rome has always been victorious in her wars and that Rome will always be victorious in her wars.

Although we fail to find any connection between the generic design of the coin and the family history of the moneyer, there is a family connection that may have greater relevance if Rutilius actually did hold the mint magistracy in 74. The mother of the consuls Gaius Aurelius Cotta (consul 75) and Marcus Aurelius Cotta (consul 74) was a Rutilia, the sister of Publius Rutilius Rufus, the illustrious consul of 105.[6] Gaius Cotta had even spoken on his uncle's behalf in his trial for extortion in 92. As consuls of the years 75 and 74, the Cottae were certainly in a position to promote their own relatives and it appears to me more than coincidental that Lucius Rutilius Flaccus, who is otherwise unknown, should appear as a moneyer at this very time.

Chapter 14

GNAEUS CORNELIUS LENTULUS MARCELLINUS 74/73 BCE

The moneyer who inscribed his coins CN•LEN•Q and LENTCVR⁎FL has been identified as Gnaeus Cornelius Lentulus Marcellinus who was later consul in 56, and the identification is generally accepted today. Both coins are marked with the S•C inscription designating special issues struck by decree of the Senate. The inscription Q for quaestor and the second inscription CVR⁎FL for 'curator for minting denarii,' with the symbol ⁎ used as a shorthand for denarius after the denarius was revalued at sixteen asses, confirm that this moneyer was not a mint magistrate.

Classical Numismatic Group, Inc. 66 Lot 1306

The moneyer signed his name CN•LEN on the reverse of the coin and gave his office as quaestor Q. To the left of the scepter is EX and S•C is to the right of the rudder.

Only the CN•LEN•Q coin appeared in the Roncofreddo hoard. Although Crawford estimated a production level of 5,500,000 denarii from about 200 dies for both types combined, these coins occur only erratically in later Italian hoards.[1] The coins are missing from ten of the thirteen hoards subsequent to Roncofreddo listed in Crawford's chart. Crawford concluded that this absence 'provides substantial evidence for a mint outside Italy; the issue should, I think, be connected with the war against Sertorius.'[2] The fact that the coin was issued by a quaestor, most of whom served in the provinces, does lend support to its being minted outside Italy.

In assigning the issues to Spain, Crawford followed Grueber who rejected the earlier interpretation put forward by Mommsen and accepted by Babelon. Mommsen, citing Plutarch *Lucullus* 13, felt that these coins were part of the 18,000,000 denarii voted to Lucullus in 74 for his campaign against

Mithridates.[3] Grueber did not argue the point with Mommsen that Plutarch's statement says that the Senate was about to vote 3,000 talents for a fleet, but Lucullus refused to accept the Senate's generous offer of funding, writing in a letter that he did not need such an expensive fleet. Lucullus was later praised for making his expedition self-supporting and not drawing on the public treasury.[4] Grueber felt that the coin's appearance in the Roncofreddo hoard, whose terminus he had fixed at 75, was enough to refute Mommsen's date of 74, and consequently, a different interpretation of the coin was required. On hoard evidence, Grueber assigned the coin's first appearance to 76 and associated the issue with Pompey's campaign against Sertorius in Spain.[5] Crawford, accepting the terminus date of the Roncofreddo hoard as 75, assigned a date of 76-75 and, considering the absence of this large issue from Italian hoards to be indicative of a non-Italian mint, agreed with its assignment to Spain.

Crawford, however, did not associate this S•C coinage by Marcellinus with Pompey, who first arrived in Spain in 76, but with Metellus Pius who had been waging the war there since 79. He suggested, 'The issue may have been paid for by the exactions in Gaul (Sallust, *Hist.* ii, 98M, 9) and may have been described by Sallust, *Hist.* ii, 34M *quae pecunia ad Hispaniense bellum Metello facta erat.*'[6] To better assess this suggestion, let us look at the longer fragment of Sallust's *Histories* where Crawford found his reference to the exactions in Gaul. Purporting to be a letter written by Pompey from Spain at the end of 75, it provides a most interesting glimpse of the situation in Spain. It was read before the Senate in January of 74.

> If it had been against you and the fatherland and the ancestral gods that I had undertaken so many labors and dangers the many times that, from my earliest youth, my generalship put to flight your most wicked enemies and secured your safety, you, Senators, could not have taken better action against me in my absence than that which you are now doing. Despite my youth, you have thrown me and an army, deserving of only the very best, into a most savage war, and as far as it was in your power, you have exhausted us with famine, the cruelest death of all. Was it for this that the Roman people sent sons off to war? Are these the rewards for wounds, for so often shedding blood on behalf of the Republic? Worn out with writing letters and sending legates, I have exhausted my private wealth and my hopes, since in the meantime you have given barely a year's expenses for the last three years. By the immortal gods, do you think that I stand in for the treasury or that it is possible to maintain an army without food and pay? Indeed, I admit that I set out for this war with greater enthusiasm than plan. Of course, having received from you only the

> name of commander, I did raise an army in forty days and I pushed back from the Alps into Spain an enemy already pressing at the throat of Italy. I opened up another route through the Alps more convenient than Hannibal's. I recovered Gaul, the Pyrenees, Lucetania, and the Indigetes. With raw recruits and far fewer in number, I sustained the first assault of the victor Sertorius. I spent the winter not in the towns looking to my own popularity but in camp surrounded by the most savage enemy. Why should I list the battles and the winter expeditions, the towns destroyed or captured? Actions speak louder than words. The enemy's camp captured at Sucro, the battle at the Turia River, and the enemy's general, Gaius Herennius, destroyed together with the city of Valentia and his army, are facts well known to you. In return for these things, O grateful Senators, you have given need and famine. And so the situation is the same for my army and the enemy's, for either army can come into Italy as victor. I am warning you about this and I beg you to turn your attention to this matter and do not force me to look to my needs by my own methods. Whatever part of Nearer Spain is not held by the enemy, we or Sertorius have reduced to total devastation, except for the maritime cities. Moreover, it is now an expense and a burden. The previous year Gaul furnished Metellus' army with pay and food, but now, with bad harvests, it can barely provide for itself. I have consumed not only my own means, but even my credit. You are all that is left. Unless you support us, although unwilling, and although I have forewarned you, the army will cross over from here into Italy and with it will come the whole Spanish war.[7]

Given the way Pompey had extorted from the Senate his appointment as proconsul in 77, it is understandable why the financially strapped Senate had not sent the money for which he kept begging. Finally resorting to threats, Pompey stirred them to action. His letter was especially disconcerting to the consul Lucius Lucullus who had obtained the governorship of Cilicia and expected to be placed in command of the new war against Mithridates. Pompey's return might be a serious obstacle to his appointment. Plutarch said,

> If the war in Spain came to an end, Pompey would be immediately chosen general against Mithridates. Therefore, when Pompey wrote demanding money, saying that if they did not send it, he would leave Spain and Sertorius and lead his army back to Italy, Lucullus most zealously worked to send the money lest Pompey have any excuse at all to return.[8]

Pompey got his money and stayed in Spain. Lucullus got his command against Mithridates.

Chapter 14

Now Pompey's letter said that both Roman armies had been reduced to very desperate straits, having received from Rome only one year's pay over the last three years, i.e. the years 77, 76, and 75. I have suggested that a portion of the S•C issue minted by Farsuleius provided some of the original funding for Pompey's army in 77, and no additional S•C coins have been assigned to the years 76 and 75. To pay his troops Pompey had used his own money and borrowed from friends. Pompey's letter states that Metellus received support from Gaul in 76, but Gaul could not continue to support the Spanish army in 75 due to bad harvests. The year 75 appears to have been the most difficult. The consul Cotta's speech in 75, which we saw earlier in Volteius' chapter, complained that the government was suffering from such a lack of revenues that it could not answer the pleas for money from its commanders in Spain, let alone meet ordinary expenses. This situation was not remedied until later in the second half of the year when the Senate found additional revenues from Cyrene and Bithynia. But if we are to accept the usual dating of Marcellinus' coins to the years 76 and 75 with some 5,500,000 denarii minted in Spain, how could Pompey's letter have had any validity with the Senate in early 74? How can a mintage of 5,500,000 coins extending over the two years 76 and 75 square with the ancient evidence which asserts that the year 75 was particularly lean for both armies? This defies logic and such a position is only possible to maintain if the Roncofreddo hoard does indeed have a terminus date of 75. The hoard itself has no intrinsic date, but Marcellinus' coin does have a date of a sort in the Q inscription, showing that it was issued the year of his quaestorship.

At this point we must turn to the evidence for the *cursus* of Gnaeus Lentulus Marcellinus. There is no historic information to tell us when Marcellinus held the quaestorship. The date of 74 in Broughton, given with a question mark, was based on Grueber, although I cannot understand how. Grueber dated the coins between the years 76-72, but put the terminus of the Roncofreddo hoard at 75. Only the coin marked Q is found in that hoard. Broughton in his later additions and corrections noted Crawford's revised dating of the two issues to 76-75.

The first reference we have to any office held by Marcellinus is tribune of the plebs. Cicero said that the year after he had been tribune of the plebs, he was chosen to serve as a legate.[9] Marcellinus did serve as Pompey's legate in the pirate war of 67. Hence Broughton has assigned the year of his tribunate to 68. Appian said that Africa, Sardinia, Corsica, and the neighboring islands had been assigned to Lentulus Marcellinus and Publius Atilius.[10] A Greek inscription on a dedication set up in the temple of Apollo at Cyrene in Africa confirms this sphere of activity:

Gnaeus Cornelius Lentulus Marcellinus 74/73 BCE

Gnaeus Cornelius Lentulus
son of Publius Marcellinus
legate with praetorian power
patron and savior.[11]

Marcellinus did not hold the praetorship until 60 and it is assumed that he came to that office so late after a quaestorship in 76 because he stayed with Pompey from 67 until Pompey's return in 62.

If he was quaestor in 76, Marcellinus was eligible to run for the praetorship in 68, which he apparently did not do. That he ran and lost is possible, but no recent election defeat was indicated in Cicero's speech cited earlier. Instead, he held the tribunate in 68. The fact that he was on one of the first boards of tribunes to serve after the office had been restored to its pre-Sullan position of power indicates that he had an appreciation of the popularity he could win with that office. It hints at his ambition to attain higher office. But to hold the tribunate in a year when he was eligible to run for praetor, then not run for the praetorship of the next year, but postpone his bid even further by accepting Pompey's commission in 67 is puzzling and indicates a certain misplacement in the normal *cursus*. Is this misplacement due to Marcellinus himself or to the dating of his quaestorship to 76 based on the Roncofreddo hoard? Sumner, who worked with Broughton's original date (*ca*. 74), suggested that Marcellinus held the tribunate in 68 in place of the more expensive aedileship and probably held it closer to the time he was eligible to run for aedile.[12] This means that the date of 74 for his quaestorship is more in line with that probability. If he was quaestor in 74, he would not have been eligible to run for the praetorship until 66. The position of legate offered in 67 was a great opportunity to further his career, not delay it by missing another election. The pirate war ended more quickly than anyone expected and a grateful Senate and people gave Pompey command of the war against Mithridates in 66. Marcellinus may have decided to stay on as a commander in a war that promised far greater rewards and glory than anything else he had been associated with up to that time. We do not hear of Marcellinus again until 61 when he joined with two other Lentuli in prosecuting Clodius for his sacrilege in the Bona Dea affair.

In assessing all the evidence on Marcellinus' *cursus* and taking into consideration the financial problems for the years 76 and 75 illuminated by Cotta's speech and Pompey's letter, it is better to date Marcellinus' quaestorship to 74 and to abandon the arbitrary terminus of 75 for the Roncofreddo hoard. Hersh and Walker in their more recent reassessment of Crawford's dating were apparently willing to do just that when they moved

Lucretius and Rustius into 74, but they still left Marcellinus in the years 76-75.[13]

The coin inscribed CN•LEN•Q then should be dated to the year 74. This coinage represents the money allocated to the Spanish war in response to Pompey's letter. This leaves us to next deal with the coins Marcellinus inscribed LENTCVR⁎FL. This is a unique title not found elsewhere on coinage, probably reflecting the unique position in which Lentulus found himself in the next year. He was still there in Spain minting money for the army, but no longer quaestor, so Q did not apply to his position. Nor was he a mint magistrate so he could not use IIIVIR. The authorization for the continuing production of money is apparently represented by the S•C inscription, but whether CVR⁎FL abbreviates an official title granted in the Senate decree or was invented by Lentulus to simply describe what his duty was when he was no longer quaestor cannot be determined, but it seems most likely that he minted the CVR⁎FL coins in 73. Crawford offered no separate estimate of dies used for the Q and the CVR⁎FL coins. The Mesagne hoard of 5940 coins buried in 58 suggests a possible ratio. It contained 105 coins inscribed Q and only thirty-three inscribed CVR⁎FL.

Classical Numismatic Group, Inc. 82 Lot 916

This coin bears the inscription CVR⁎FL indicating that Marcellinus issued the coins as a curator for striking denarii.

Although he changed the inscription on the coins issued in the two different years, Marcellinus used the same design both years. On the obverse, he depicted a bearded male head clearly identified as the Genius of the Roman people by the inscription G•P•R above his head. To a Roman, a genius most simply was the personality formed at one's birth. It was one's double, exhibiting the same traits and characteristics, and finally it was a separate protective being peculiar to one individual. These protective genii were attributed to families, states, provinces, colleges, and military units. Here we see one depiction of how the Roman people viewed their genius in the late Republic. The inscription G•P•R does not appear elsewhere on Republican coins, but similar figures on coins minted by Publius Cornelius Lentulus, son of

Marcellus, and Publius Cornelius Lentulus Spinther have been identified as the Genius of the Roman people, leading Grueber to say, 'It is evident that the Cornelia *gens* specially favored the cult of the Genius of the Roman people.'[14] This notion is repeated frequently in the literature, yet there is nothing in any ancient source to support this. It is hard to see how one family could claim a special relationship with a deity who derived his very nature and being from the collective citizen body and was considered to be the tutelary god of the whole people. This assumed special association between the Genius of the Roman People and the Cornelii also led Grueber to interpret the reverse design as personal in nature. On the coin's reverse, Marcellinus has the orb of the world occupying the center of the coin, a scepter with wreath is to the left and a rudder on the right. Grueber associated them with Marcellinus' Cornelian kinsman Sulla. He said that the globe was emblematic of the extended rule of Rome brought about by Sulla's recent victories in the East, the rudder recalled the naval victories of Lucullus, the scepter with wreath was a reference to Chaeroneia and Orchomenos. Instead of attributing these battles to Roma, Marcellinus attributed them to the Genius of the Roman People with whom Grueber assumes the Cornelii were specially connected.

To a Roman citizen, the Genius of the Roman People represented all the power and authority of the entire Roman state. Crawford, doubting any special relationship between the Cornelii and the Genius of the Roman People, said, 'The types associate the Genius populi Romani with domination *terra marique*.'[15] He also felt that since the coins were struck for the Spanish war they asserted 'the claims of the Roman state against those of the rebel state of Sertorius.' I feel that Crawford's simpler explanation is correct. The association of these three symbols of scepter with wreath, globe, and rudder appeared for the first time here, but the theme of domination on land and sea was not new. The sacrifice scene on Postumius' coin minted in 81 recalled the prophecy which assured Rome's position as *caput rerum*. In its earliest context that prophecy applied to Rome's sovereignty over its Latin neighbors. *Imperium* was contested over centuries until the Social War brought the final resolution for Italy. The Italian peoples ceased to fight Rome and became Roman citizens. Italy now became the *populus Romanus*. But the original prophecy of Rome's position as *caput rerum* had already looked beyond the borders of Italy growing into the belief that it was Rome's destiny to become the *caput orbis terrarum*. Roman ambition had grown to encompass the whole world. The expanded prophecy is found in Valerius Maximus, 'The fatherland of whoever makes the sacrifice of that heifer to the Aventine Artemis will possess the command of the whole world (*eius patria totius terrarum orbis imperium obtinet*).'[16] It was a goal still to be achieved in 74, but expounded with the same degree of faith as was the belief that it was America's manifest destiny to spread from ocean to ocean. Inevitably the rebel state in Spain must yield to the Genius of the Roman people. Fate is irresistible.

Numismatica Ars Classica Auction 51 Lot 31

The obverse has the head of the Genius of the Roman People identified by the inscription G•P•R. A scepter is behind his shoulder. On the reverse is a scepter with a wreath to the left of the orb of the world and a rudder to the right.

Lentulus Marcellinus' military and political career spanned the major events which were to confirm Rome as the *caput orbis terrarum*. He saw Spain yield, the pirates surrender control of the seas, and Mithridates' empire pass to Rome within a decade of his minting these coins. Marcellinus received his share in Rome's command of the whole world. He was praetor in 60 and became governor of Syria in 59. He spent two years there fending off attacks by Arabs.[17]

Although Marcellinus' military exploits in Syria were minimal, Cicero indicated that he was quite adept at ingratiating himself with the influential and powerful. He drew on this when he returned to Rome and campaigned for consul in 57. Finally at the age of at least 48, he capped his career with the consulship and immediately things began to go downhill. Having achieved his ultimate goal, Marcellinus seems to have become less ingratiating. He became involved in the wrangle over who was to restore Ptolemy to the throne of Egypt, vehemently opposing Publius Lentulus Spinther's appointment.[18] Pompey's hopes to restore Ptolemy fared no better. In March, Cicero was complaining to his brother that Marcellinus was treating Pompey rather harshly.[19]

This developing rift with Pompey became an unbridgeable chasm later in the year when Pompey and Crassus declared themselves candidates for the consulship of 55 after the legal time for announcing their candidacies had passed. Marcellinus declared their candidacies illegal. In a harangue before the people, he bitterly complained of Pompey's excessive power, 'Shout out your disapproval citizens, shout it out while you can for soon you will not be able to do so with impunity.'[20] The elections were disturbed by constant strife and on one occasion the situation deteriorated into a near riot. Marcellinus became alarmed by the violence of the opposition and refused to frequent the Senate House. He was eventually outmaneuvered by Pompey and Crassus who succeeded in getting the election postponed until the next year when they were appointed consuls by an *interrex*.

An assessment of his eloquent rhetorical style, exercised so ineffectively during his consulship, survives in Cicero's *Brutus*, 'Gnaeus Lentulus Marcellinus was never ineloquent and in his consulship he seemed most eloquent. Not slow in his expression, nor lacking in vocabulary, he had a melodious voice and sufficient wit.'[21]

Even though there is nothing more in the ancient sources on Marcellinus, a coin from the period of his consulship may give us some insight into what lay behind his rift with Pompey and the reason for his complaints against Pompey's excessive power. Consider the coin minted by Pompey's son-in-law Faustus Sulla about the time of Marcellinus' consulship. The orb of the world once again occupies the center of a coin. Marcellinus had flanked his orb with a wreathed scepter and a ship's rudder, symbolic of the power of the Roman people who are represented by the Genius of the Roman people on the coin's obverse, but Faustus surrounded the orb of the world with four wreaths, three commemorated the victories Pompey won on the three known continents, the fourth was the special wreath voted to Pompey in 63 in recognition of his extraordinary accomplishments. Cicero had said that Pompey's three triumphs bear witness that he held the whole orb of the world under his power.[22] Where was the Genius of the Roman People?

Numismatica Ars Classica Auction 54 Lot 239

Faustus Sulla's coin minted around the time of Marcellinus' consulship depicts the orb of the world surrounded by Pompey's wreaths. No Genius of the Roman People to be seen here.

Chapter 15

PUBLIUS SATRIENUS 73 BCE

The moneyer Publius Satrienus is unknown and his *gens* is not even mentioned in the surviving literature. For the date of his mint magistracy, we turn once again to hoard evidence. As noted earlier, Grueber, Crawford, and Hersh and Walker have all paired Rutilius and Satrienus as mint magistrates in the same year 77. Control numerals from I to CV on the obverse of his coins indicate that Publius Satrienus produced a sizeable number of denarii. But since they were missing from the Kerassia and Hev-Szamos hoards, as were Rutilius' coins, this suggests a date after Cassius and Volteius, whom I dated to 76 and 75. Both Rutilius and Satrienus appear as the latest mint magistrates in the Capreni hoard indicating that they minted about the same time, but in my arrangement, in order to have one moneyer each year, Satrienus must be put into a separate year. Since I think there is better reason to put Rutilius' moneyership into 74 when one of his relatives Marcus Aurelius Cotta held a consulship, I assign Satrienus to 73.

Numismatica Ars Classica Auction 51 Lot 30

Satrienus did not identify his obverse head and it is variously identified as Mars or Roma in catalog listings. A she-wolf is on the reverse. The moneyer's name is in the exergue.

On the obverse of his coin, Satrienus depicted the helmeted head of a god, which was identified as Mars by Grueber because it appeared to him rather masculine, but identified as Roma by Crawford. The exact identification remains uncertain today and may have been so even in ancient Rome, but the martial character of the deity is unmistakable.

On the reverse is a she-wolf. At first look, the reverse design seems to be nothing more than a complement to the obverse, since the she-wolf can be associated with both Roma and Mars. To Grueber, this was the she-wolf who suckled Romulus and Remus, a reference to the foundation of Rome. To Crawford, this 'type of ferocious wolf has no original connection with the wolf that nursed Romulus and Remus, but was perhaps adopted as a symbol of Rome after the defeat of those rebel Italians who likened Rome to a predatory wolf.' This, he says, would make Satrienus' wolf an anti-Italian reference. Crawford said that this was 'the she-wolf of the Capitol, apparently portrayed here.'[1]

The famous statue to which Crawford refers is called the Capitoline She-Wolf because it resides in the Capitoline Museum in Rome. It was on public display without the twins in the tenth century CE outside the Lateran Palace. The statue is remarkably well preserved except for the tail, which is restored, and there appears to be damage to the hind legs and paws as if scorched. That damage led to the Renaissance identification of this wolf as part of the famous statue group on the Capitoline depicting the twins Romulus and Remus suckled by the she-wolf. Cicero said that the statue was hit by lightning in 65 and torn off its base falling to the ground, a seemingly good explanation for the damage to the wolf's hind legs and tail.[2] Consequently, believing that this ancient statue was the she-wolf struck by lightning on the Capitoline, the lost twins Romulus and Remus were added beneath the teats of the wolf in the fifteenth century CE.

The hollow bronze statue of the Capitoline She-Wolf was perhaps originally a dedication and it certainly appears to have been a public monument, but we have no clear idea of its provenance. Moreover, it is also possible that this she-wolf did not belong to a wolf and twins group. Statues of wolves were not uncommon. We know that there were wolf statues in the temple of Mars Gradivus on the Appian Way where Roman armies gathered for a final salute before departing the city. Livy said that those statues sweat blood in 217, a dire sign portending Hannibal's arrival in Italy that year. Livy, however, used the masculine plural form of the noun so those wolves may not have been female or the noun may simply refer to the pack.[3]

The Capitoline She-Wolf underwent a restoration in 1997. Examination indicated no damage to the statue from a lightning strike. The lesions on the legs were a result of an imperfect solidification of the bronze in the original casting. The Capitoline She-Wolf is clearly not the statue struck by lightning in 65. But in solving one question, another controversy has arisen. The restorer, Anna Maria Carruba, discovered that it was cast in one piece. Since ancient Greek bronze statues were made in pieces and soldered together with carefully hidden seams, she argued that the Capitoline She-Wolf could not be an Etruscan bronze dating to the fifth century, but rather a medieval work dating closer to 700 CE when medieval technology made such casting possible. This suggestion has not yet been accepted by most scholars. First of all, there is too little comparative evidence from monumental Etruscan statues for us to assume that the Etruscan methods were the same as the Greeks. In fact, this statue might be the evidence to prove that such one-piece casting was done by the Etruscans. Moreover, analysis of the clay used in the casting shows that it came from Southern Etruria and that the metal came from Sardinia.[4] Secondly, stylistically, the she-wolf has long been recognized as Etruscan. The ancient sculptor knew wolves to have pointed noses and short ears, small heads, and particularly lean bodies, but Otto J. Brendel points out,

> Close inspection shows the Capitoline Wolf to be a composite beast, zoologically and stylistically....wolves also have hairy pelts, and that the artist made no attempt to show. Instead he chose to assimilate the animal he was to represent to the traditional representations of lions after the archaic fashion common in Etruria; hence the long hair locks strung along the spine, the collar of small curls that frame the face, and the curly mane around the neck. Wolves sport no manes.[5]

Classical Numismatic Group, Inc. 85 Lot 739

This anonymous didrachm (*ca.* 264-255) shows the most common way the wolf and twins were depicted on Roman coins from the earliest time onward.

The earliest Roman depictions of the wolf and twins found on coins, such as an anonymous didrachm (*ca.* 264-255 Crawford 20/1) and a bronze quadrans (*ca.* 217-15 Crawford 39/3), show the wolf with the twins beneath her teats. The wolf's head is twisted back as if to tenderly lick the nearest twin like a nurturing mother. The denarius minted (*ca.* 137) by Sextus Pompeius Fostulus tells a fuller story. The wolf is in the center of the coin turning to lick the twins beneath her teats. To the left side, identified by an inscription, stands Fostulus, the shepherd who found the twins. Behind the wolf is a tree and in the tree sit birds. The tree represents the fig tree that was at the spot where

Romulus and Remus washed up on the bank of the Tiber. The indistinguishable birds in the branches were the woodpeckers that Mars sent to watch over his sons. The wolf and woodpeckers were sacred to Mars. We know that such a statue grouping was erected at the spot where Romulus and Remus were found by Fostulus, but all trace of it is lost today. Later representations on coins from the Imperial period show the wolf with her head lowered but looking forward as seen on an aureus by Hadrian (BMC 444) or with the head down and slightly turned as seen on a denarius by the usurper Carausius in Britannia (RIC V/2, 512, 571). In contrast to the coin depictions of the she-wolf and twins, the Capitoline She-Wolf's head is turned and her gaze is fixed on you as if you had just come upon her suddenly and she snarls dangerously. No coins depict such a wolf.

Classical Numismatic Group, Inc. Triton VIII Lot 826

This coin by Sextus Pompeius depicts the shepherd Fostulus coming upon the she-wolf and twins. The wolf is in the same pose as seen on the didrachm.

However, the wolf depicted by Satrienus has much more in common stylistically with the statue of the Capitoline She-Wolf than nature's wolf or the typical depiction of the nurturing she-wolf who bends her head back to lick the infant twins as they nurse at her teats. Satrienus' die engraver has prominently reproduced the four teats on the left side of the belly without showing the four on the other side. The wolf's lean body is depicted by the modeling of the rib cage and the body hair is only rendered by the raised hair along the spine. The ears are upright. But the feature which most closely ties Satrienus' wolf to the statue of the Capitoline She-Wolf is that it too sports the un-wolflike characteristic of the mane, clearly delineated by the engraved lines contrasting with the smoothness of the rest of the body. Compare this wolf with the wolf on the coin by Papius Celsus which depicts a much different rendering of a she-wolf with only three teats and no mane. It is clear that Satrienus' rendering is in the artistic tradition of the Capitoline She-Wolf and may be intentionally recalling this very statue that survives today; but it is just as clear that he did not precisely reproduce this statue.

Classical Numismatic Group, Inc. 76 Lot 1273

Papius Celsus' she-wolf does not have the hairy mane around the neck and he only depicts three teats instead of the four that we see on Satrienus' she-wolf.

The Capitoline She-Wolf has all four feet on the ground and her head is turned three-quarter view. Satrienus' she-wolf looks forward and lifts her right forepaw; hence, in the catalogs she is described as walking. But if she is walking, she cannot be in the act of nursing, although the distended teats clearly show that she is lactating. We have to wonder if Satrienus' she-wolf is to be associated with the nurturing mother of the foundation myth or is this rather a predatory wolf as Crawford suggested.

The image of Roma as a predatory wolf had been an effective and widely disseminated propaganda device used by the Italians during their revolt. During the Social War, the rebel commander C. Papius Mutilus minted coins depicting a bull goring a wolf, which was an allegorical representation of the Italians, represented as the bull, overcoming the Romans, portrayed as the wolf.

Gorny & Mosch Giessener Müzhandlung Auction 141 Lot 224

Some of the propaganda from the Italian side in the Social War has been preserved on the reverse of this coin by Gaius Papius Mutilus. We see the Italian bull goring the Roman wolf that had been characterized as the ravager of Italian liberty.

Even after the Social War was over, the imagery of Rome as a predatory wolf continued to be used by the Samnite leader Pontius Telesinus. Before the battle at the Colline Gate in 82, he called for the capture and destruction of the city of Rome, reminding his troops that the wolves, the ravagers of Italian liberty, would never be gone unless they cut down the forest in which they lived. Such imagery had been clearly established in the minds of the people throughout the Italian peninsula.

There is, however, no reason to assume with Crawford that 'the type is perhaps anti-Italian in intention.' Since the *gens* Satriena is otherwise unknown in Rome, it is quite probable that the family was among the newly enfranchised Italians. Satrienus was following in an allegorical vein already opened by Egnatius, who earlier had depicted Roma herself with her foot on the head of a wolf, symbolizing the suppression of that predatory nature which ravaged Italian liberty. If Satrienus chose the Capitoline She-Wolf as the model for his allegorical Roma, the change in the stance becomes significant to the interpretation of the coin. The stance of Satrienus' she-wolf has much more in common with the way the dog was depicted on the early Roman hemi litra dating to around 235. The dog has its paw raised in similar fashion and appears to be walking. Likewise, Volteius' coin depicting Cybele in a chariot drawn by a pair of lions has one lion with its forepaw lifted. Such a pose is not intimidating.

Gemini Numismatic Auctions, LLC Auction VIII Lot 195

The unnatural mane around her neck sets this she-wolf apart from ordinary wolves and the inscription identifies her as Roma.

On Satrienus' coin we do not see a ferocious, predatory wolf snarling and holding her ground with all four feet firmly planted. In fact, we do not really see a wolf at all, but rather a somewhat mythical composite, like the Capitoline She-Wolf. Satrienus' inclusion of the inscription ROMA into the plane of the design over the she-wolf was unique. ROMA was most commonly placed in the exergue. Satrienus seems to be using the inscription ROMA to affirm an identification that many could well have made without the inscription. This mythical wolf comes to be identified as the new Roma, a less intimidating, more nurturing mother.

Chapter 16

LUCIUS LUCRETIUS TRIO 72 BCE

Nothing is known of the moneyer who inscribed his name L•LVCRETI TRIO on the reverse of two coin types. The only other occurrence of the name Trio in connection with the Lucretii was found in the obverse inscription TRIO of an earlier coin signed by the moneyer CN•LVCR and although nothing is known of Gnaeus either, his name on an issue dated around 136 tells us that the Lucretii Triones were an older Roman family. Lucius Lucretius Trio was not one of the newly enfranchised Italian citizens. Crawford dated Lucius Lucretius to 76, ahead of Egnatius Maximus, as the next to last of the non-S•C moneyers whose coins appear within the Roncofreddo hoard. The San Mango hoard evidence suggests that Egnatius be moved to an earlier date. This makes Lucretius the last non-S•C moneyer in the Roncofreddo hoard. Lucretius is the only mint magistrate in the Roncofreddo hoard who is missing from all the minor hoards used in determining the relative dating of the other moneyers. Crawford estimated that Lucretius used a total of 125 reverse dies and his absence from the smaller hoards suggests that Lucretius minted after the moneyers found in those hoards confirming his position as the latest mint magistrate in the Roncofreddo hoard. Hersh and Walker dated him to 74 which became their new terminus date for the Roncofreddo hoard.[1] In my arrangement, Lucretius must follow Satrienus and be assigned to 72, which becomes my revised terminus date for the Roncofreddo hoard.

A Tkalec AG Auction May 2005 Lot 180

Lucius Lucretius Trio put the head of Sol on the obverse and a crescent moon with seven stars on the reverse.

Our moneyer Lucius Lucretius Trio issued two different types. The smaller issue struck from an estimated thirty-six reverse dies has the radiate head of Sol on the obverse and the crescent moon surrounded by seven stars on the reverse. The name TRIO is inscribed above the crescent. The standard interpretation of the design is found in Grueber:

> This type is an allusion to the moneyer's name. The sun and moon which give the greater light (lux) are intended to refer to the gentile name, Lucretius, whilst the seven stars (septem Triones) which form the constellation of the Great Bear, are a "type parlant" of the cognomen "Trio."[2]

We have good reason to believe, however, that this design led the ancient Romans to make different associations. The moneyer P. Clodius Turrinus in 42 issued virtually the identical coin with a radiate Sol on the obverse and the crescent moon on the reverse, except Turrinus used only five stars. While the associations of the name Lucretius with *lux* (light) and the pun on Trio seem to work with a moneyer named Lucretius Trio, they cannot transfer to Clodius' name. The attempt by A. Vercoutre to identify the five stars on Clodius' coin as the representation of the constellation Taurus and make it a punning allusion to the *cognomen* Turrinus convinces no one.[3]

Classical Numismatic Group, Inc. 61 Lot 1576

> Publius Clodius Turrinus issued this coin in 42 which is virtually the same as Lucretius Trio's coin except that he has five stars around the crescent moon.

To find an interpretation that works for both men, we have to ask what the two moneyers Clodius and Lucretius had in common. Grueber points us in the right direction in his discussion of Clodius' design, suggesting that the type may relate to the early history of the Claudii who were of Sabine origin. During the consulship of P. Valerius Volusi and Titus Lucretius Tricipitinus in 504, the Sabine Attius Clausus broke ranks with his countrymen who wanted to continue waging war with Rome. He transferred his family and allegiance from Regillus to Rome where he was given citizenship and land on the further side of the Anio river, and became known as Appius Claudius.[4] Clodius Turrinus' depiction of the head of Sol and the crescent Moon in the starry sky recalls his family's Sabine origin, reminding us that Titus Tatius, the Sabine king who became joint ruler in Rome with Romulus, was the first to build an altar to the Sun and Moon in Rome.[5]

That the same design with its Sabine allusions appeared first on the coin of Lucretius Trio should not come as a surprise to us, since we have met with the name Lucretius as one of the consuls in the year Claudius transferred to Rome. The consul Titus Lucretius Tricipitinus was the father of Lucretia, the wife of Tarquinius Collatinus, who killed herself when raped by king Tarquin's son. Her death stirred Brutus into action and it was in Lucretia's Sabine hometown, Collatia, where the revolt began which led to the overthrow of the Tarquins and the establishment of the Republic.

Lucretius' coin, like Clodius Turrinus', was designed to recall the moneyer's Sabine roots and it is likely that the name Lucretius has more to do with the name of the mountain Lucretilus in Sabine territory than with the word *lux* (light). We have here a candidate who felt that allusion to his Sabine roots would be advantageous to him in his upcoming election bid for the quaestorship. The Sabines were the second most ancient ethnic group incorporated into the Roman state and they had a reputation for being virtuous and brave. We will see more of this emphasis on Sabine origin. Although the sun and moon indicate Sabine origin rather than a pun on the name Lucretius, it is quite probable that the use of seven stars on Trio's coin, as opposed to the five used on Clodius', does allude to Lucretius' *cognomen* Trio. The constellation we know as the Big Dipper was called the Septentriones by the Romans.

Lucretius' second type was a much larger issue that Crawford estimated at eighty-nine reverse dies. Lucretius depicted Neptune wreathed with laurel on the obverse. He is clearly identified by the trident over his shoulder. Keeping with the naval theme, on the reverse a winged child rides a dolphin. Who is this winged boy? Since Trio seemed to be alluding to his own name in the reverse design of his first type, interpretations of his second coin type have continued in the same vein. Crawford postulated a possible etymological allusion between the name of the sea goddess Leucothea and the name Lucretius, since he felt that it was not inconceivable that the reverse depicted Palaemon, the son of Leucothea, who was rescued from drowning in the sea by a passing dolphin.[6]

However, not only is the name Leucothea a long stretch to Lucretius, but Palaemon was not winged. Moreover, this coin's dolphin is bridled and guided by reins, suggesting some kind of taming rather than a chance rescue. This would also seem to rule out Taras who rides an unbridled dolphin on

Tarentum's coins. Grueber identified the child as a genius, but the genius of what he did not say. Noting the laurel in Neptune's hair, not one of his normal attributes, Grueber said that the coin referred to some naval victory. Grueber felt that this coin recalled the naval commands of a family member, Gaius Lucretius Gallus.[7]

Classical Numismatic Group, Inc. Inventory no. 810442

A laurel wreathed Neptune is on this obverse die marked XIIII while a winged Cupid rides a dolphin on the reverse. The laurel seems to suggest some kind of naval victory.

In 181, two naval commanders, Lucretius Gallus and Gaius Matienus, were placed in charge of guarding the Italian coastline. Matienus' province was from the promontory of Minerva up the west coast of Italy to Massilia; Lucretius Gallus' province was from the promontory round to Barium on the east coast of Italy. Each officer had only ten ships in his command. None of Lucretius' activities for 181 are reported, but the record of Matrienus' service makes it clear that the main purpose of the command was to police piracy along the coast.[8] When he was praetor in 171, Gallus again commanded a fleet which he sailed to Cephallenia and then turned it over to his brother.[9] Although these Lucretii commanded fleets, there does not appear to be any significant naval victory connected with their commands.

It is not impossible that a naval command of a Lucretian ancestor was on Trio's mind when he minted this type, but it is questionable how many Romans might recall anything about the minor commands of Gaius Lucretius Gallus or his brother. Apparently the moneyer Mn. Cordius Rufus saw no specific Lucretian reference when he depicted the boy on a bridled dolphin design (*ca*. 46). On Cordius' coin the identity of the winged boy is clear. All commentators identify him as Cupid because of Venus on the coin's obverse. We should also expect that most Romans recognized Lucretius' winged boy as Cupid. After all, the sea is a natural playground for a boy whose mother was born from the waves.

We have met with Cupid already on the coins of Egnatius and discussed how he represented the peace restored by the Sullan settlement. Cupid who gambols through the waves on his pet dolphin on this coin's reverse conveys a sense of peaceful and carefree enjoyment of the sea. This was something that Rome and her allies had not enjoyed for some time now, for the Mediterranean Sea was not a safe place in the 70s due to pirates. Mithridates, using the tactic of state sponsored terrorism, had first unleashed the pirate menace when he recruited their help in 88 for his war against the Romans. When Mithridates made peace with Sulla in 85, the pirates were left without homes and livelihood. Appian said that having grown to like their way of life, they chose to harvest the sea instead of the land.[10] As their success grew, they began to think of themselves as minor potentates and thought that if they should unite their forces they would be invincible. They chose the rocky coast of Cilicia as their main base and set up an entire industry of shipbuilding and arms making, constantly bringing in raw materials for the craftsmen whom they kept chained to their tasks. They also had lookout posts, forts, desert islands, and retreats throughout the Mediterranean. In 74 an unprecedented special command had been entrusted to Marcus Antonius in order to deal with the problem, but he was making little headway.

Classical Numismatic Group, Inc. 61 Lot 1413

The obverse die is marked with the number LXIIII.

Grueber's and Crawford's widely accepted dating of Lucretius to 76 puts the coin into a period when there were no recent naval victories to commemorate and has forced us to look somewhat further into the past than necessary. The imagery of a laurel wreathed Neptune clearly indicates that Lucretius was alluding to a naval victory. If Lucretius minted in 72 as I propose, it is most likely that this imagery would call to mind the recent naval victories won by Lucullus over Mithridates in 73. Lucullus' naval victories and his success at Cyzicus forced Mithridates to withdraw and as Mithridates made for his kingdom of Pontus, Neptune himself further aided the Roman effort by sending a storm which destroyed a great portion of Mithridates' fleet. Appian said that the storm cost Mithridates 10,000 men and about sixty ships.[11]

Lucius Lucretius Trio 72 BCE

With Mithridates defeated and licking his wounds in Pontus, the Romans finally had reason to hope that the seas, long harassed by the pirates he sponsored, would soon become safe to sail again. Cupid's peaceful enjoyment of the sea on his pet dolphin suggests that the Mediterranean Sea was once again a Roman lake. Lucretius' optimism, however, was premature; the pirate problem would get worse.

Chapter 17

LUCIUS RUSTIUS 72 BCE

Since the moneyer Lucius Rustius is unknown except for his coin, there is no prosopographical evidence to help in dating. The presence of the coin in the Roncofreddo hoard, whose terminus I have dated to 72, gives us the latest date for his minting, but all other hoard evidence is lacking for the years between 78 and 72. Rustius was not found in any of the smaller hoards used in dating the moneyers to this point, so it is consistent with the hoard evidence to look for a date close to the terminus of the Roncofreddo hoard. Both Crawford and Grueber approximated the date of 76, one year before their terminus of Roncofreddo. But the coin is an S•C issue and the financial picture painted by Cotta's speech and Pompey's letter showed a Rome hard pressed for cash, unable to send adequate funds to support the war in Spain and failing to meet other important needs in the years 76 and late into 75. An absence of special issues of coinage for the years 76 and 75 accords well with the picture found in the surviving literary evidence. Hersh and Walker re-dated Rustius to 74, which became their terminus for the Roncofreddo hoard.[1]

When we move the date down to the years between 74 and 72, a small feature of Rustius' coin becomes more significant. The coin is inscribed with a mark of value ⳩ for denarius. This mark had last been used as a mark of value on coins that Crawford called 'restored issues' (Crawford 369, 370, and 371). Since they appear in no hoards before San Miniato, Crawford dated those 'restored issues' to 82-80. They have the identical reverses of the earlier coins nos. 263-5 dated to 127; the obverses, however, are all of Apollo instead of Roma. Crawford felt that the coins with the Apollo obverses were restored by Sulla in memory of the men whose names appeared on them. These issues are problematic to say the least, but their mark of value clearly imitates the previous coinage of 127. Except for the 'restored issues,' the mark of value had not been used since about 107.

Grueber said the appearance of Rustius' ⳩ was 'purely accidental.' Crawford called it 'merely an archaism.' But Gnaeus Lentulus Marcellinus had just used this symbol on his S•C coinage in 73 in his title CVR⳩FL, 'curator for minting denarii.' Marcellinus' ⳩ was not used as a mark of value, but as part of his office title, as an abbreviation for the word denarii. Rustius' use of the symbol ⳩ becomes more intelligible if he was the moneyer who took over from

Lentulus Marcellinus. Since his issue is marked S•C, which suggests to me that he was not a mint magistrate, Rustius may have been Pompey's quaestor who replaced Marcellinus in 72. Picking up the 𐆖 from the title CVR𐆖FL, he stamped 𐆖 on the coin as a mark of value.

A.Tkalec AG Auction May 2005 Lot 179

> The obverse head is not identified by inscription. The mark of value 𐆖 for denarius is below the chin. A finely rendered ram is on the reverse and the moneyer's name L•RVSTI is in the exergue.

On the obverse of his coin, Rustius depicted a god in a crested helmet just as Satrienus did; Rustius also placed a single animal on the reverse just as Satrienus did. Rustius' animal is a finely rendered ram. No inscription identifies the god on the obverse, but the ram on the reverse led Crawford to identify the helmeted head as Minerva, saying, 'The constellation Aries was the astrological "house of Minerva" and a ram was doubtless chosen as reverse type to complement the head of Minerva on the obverse.'[2] But interpretation is never doubtless and Grueber believed that the obverse head was Mars. He noted that the ram was the emblem of the month of March, which related the reverse to the Mars obverse.[3] There is no way to distinguish between these two interpretations and neither offers anything special. We might have remained content with this simple speculation had not Grueber directed our attention to an Augustan moneyer named Quintus Rustius who depicted two ram heads on his coinage. This puts us on a track that may better illuminate our Republican coin.

The Augustan coin with the inscription Q•RVSTIVS FORTVNAE ANTIAT depicts co-joined heads representing the two aspects of the goddess Fortuna of Antium: Fortuna Victrix and Fortuna Felix. The temple of Fortuna, where oracles were given through the interpretation of lots, was Antium's most famous attraction and Horace addressed Fortuna as the goddess who rules over the pleasant town of Antium.[4] Beneath the co-joined heads is a bar with ram's head finials at each end. The appearance of rams on two coins by moneyers named Rustius minting so many years apart led Grueber to suggest that the ram was a family crest. The way the ram is used on our Republican coin does look like a family crest, but the way the ram heads appear on the Augustan coin looks more like they are connected with the worship of the goddess Fortuna.

Classical Numismatic Group, Inc. Triton XI Lot 711

The Augustan moneyer Quintus Rustius depicted the draped co-joined busts of Fortuna Victrix, who is in front wearing a round helmet, and a diademed Fortuna Felix who is behind. Beneath the heads is a bar terminating at each end in ram's head finials.

Quintus Rustius' reference to the Fortunae of Antium led Wiseman to suggest that the Rustii came from that town. This is a reasonable assumption and we do find the name of a Rustius on an inscription from Antium.[5] But are we to associate the ram with the Rustii as the Republican coin by Lucius suggests or is the ram to be associated with the goddess Fortuna of Antium as the Augustan coin suggests? These two choices are not mutually exclusive and both may be correct, for the thing that the Fortunae and the Rustii had in common was their hometown Antium.

Antium was a harbor-less coastal city of Latium situated on masses of rock some thirty-eight miles (61 km) south of Rome. In early times, it was a Volscian stronghold and the inhabitants took to ships and made their living by piracy, but those days were long gone. Antium had been sacked by Marius in the civil war only a short time before Rustius minted this coin and was in the process of rebuilding. It was not yet the fashionable resort town popular with the nobility in Augustan times. Strabo said that all of Latium was fertile and produced everything, except for the marshy and sickly area between Antium and Lanuvium as far as the Pomptine marsh. He said that the rocky hills were not tilled either, but that area was not wholly useless for it afforded rich pasture to flocks and herds.[6] Grazing flocks on these hills had provided livelihood for the inhabitants from the most ancient times. The coastal hills south of Antium were said to be home to the mythical Laestrygonians of Homer's *Odyssey*, a fierce cannibalistic race of giants famous for their flocks of sheep and herds of cattle. The whole area around Antium was replete with traditions derived from Homer's *Odyssey*. The town of Antium itself boasted of its foundation by

Antias, a son of Ulysses and Circe.[7] About thirty miles (48.2 km) south of Antium was a mountain called Circaeum, which had a little city and a temple to Circe and an altar to Minerva. One of the prize exhibits that the town displayed was a bowl they claimed belonged to Ulysses who visited this part of Italy shortly after he left the Cyclops in Sicily.[8] In fact, even today this coastal region is called *La Riviera d'Ulisse.*

For a people living in sheep country and proud of their ancient origin from Ulysses, the large fleecy ram which Rustius depicted may well have called to mind Ulysses' famous adventure with the Cyclops. Unaware of the crude nature of this race of one-eyed giants who had no regard for human or divine law, Ulysses and twelve companions had ventured into the cave of Polyphemus and awaited his return from pasturing his flocks. They expected the Cyclops to offer them gifts and have them to dinner as was customary with guest friends. However, upon discovering his unwanted guests, Polyphemus snatched up two men, smashed their brains out against a rock, and had them for dinner. In sheer terror, the rest would have fled for their lives, but the Cyclops had placed a huge boulder at the entrance of the cave in order to enclose his flock. In the morning, two more men became breakfast before the Cyclops drove his sheep to pasture. The boulder again trapped the hapless men. But Ulysses, guided by the counsel of Minerva, had time to plan his escape. When the Cyclops returned, Ulysses ventured forward to offer the wine he had brought as a gift to his host. Its superior flavor was a taste unknown to the uncivilized Cyclops and as he grew heavier with the wine he offered Ulysses the special privilege of being eaten last. But once the wine took its full effect, Ulysses with the help of his companions lifted up a tree trunk specially sharpened and hardened in the fire. He could not use it to kill the Cyclops or he and his men would be forever trapped in the cave by the huge boulder, which they could not move. So he drove the pole into the single eye of the Cyclops. Immediately sobered by the pain Polyphemus roared and thrashed about for his attackers whom he could no longer see. Now at the disadvantage, he nursed his wound until morning when his bleating sheep demanded his attention. He had to remove the boulder so the sheep could leave. Standing at the entrance he ran his hands over the backs of all the sheep as they left, but the wily Ulysses had tied three sheep together and bound his comrades to their underbellies where Polyphemus did not think to search. Ulysses reserved for himself one exceptionally large ram, the prize of the flock; and so the survivors made good their escape.[9] The ram well symbolized Ulysses' fortunate escape from the Cyclops and so may have factored in the worship of the Fortunae of Antium.

That the Cyclops story was popular in this area of Italy is affirmed by the Villa of Tiberius discovered in 1957 at Sperlonga which is about fifty miles

(80.46 km) to the south of Antium. Ulysses sailed right past Sperlonga on his way to Circe's home at Circaeum which is visible from Sperlonga. The main attraction of the villa is a cave near the beach where a square basin had been constructed with a rectangular island which served as a dining room with special seating for a view into the inner cave. Four different scenes from Ulysses' life were recreated in sculpture. The central and largest group was the scene of Ulysses and three companions blinding the drunken, reclining Cyclops twice their size.

Numismatica Ars Classica Auction 46 Lot 893

The obverse head may be Minerva who had an altar at Circaeum.

Given all the associations with Ulysses in this area of Italy, it is more likely that the head on the obverse of Rustius' coin is Minerva, who had an altar at Circaeum and was Ulysses' counselor and protector. Considering the economic importance of sheep to Rustius' area of Italy, the mythical associations to be made with the ram that saved Ulysses, as well as the foundation myth of Antium by Antias, a son of Circe and Ulysses, it is not surprising that Rustius chose a ram for his reverse type. It is even likely that he traced his family line to Ulysses, just as the Mamilii did.

Chapter 18

GAIUS POSTUMIUS 71 BCE

Even though the large issue by the moneyer Gaius Postumius was not found in the Roncofreddo hoard, Grueber dated his coin to the year 77. Crawford noted that there were nine other hoards whose only addition to the list of coins found in the Roncofreddo hoard was Gaius Postumius' coin.[1] This was decisive evidence that Postumius belonged after the terminus of Roncofreddo, which for Crawford meant that Postumius dated to 74. This relative dating to the year after Roncofreddo's terminus should be maintained. Since I have dated the terminus of the Roncofreddo hoard to 72 with the issue of Lucretius Trio, I date Gaius Postumius to 71.

Grueber wrote that this moneyer was unknown, but subsequent scholarship has shed a glimmer of light that brings Gaius Postumius out of the depths of the unknown darkness. It seems that for centuries Gaius Postumius had been lurking unnoticed in the text of Cicero's *Pro Murena* under the misspelling Gaius Postumus. In the elections of 63, Lucius Licinius Murena had won the consulship of 62 and was subsequently being prosecuted for election bribery by the defeated candidate Servius Sulpicius Rufus and his son. In the speech which Cicero delivered in defense of Murena, he made references to a certain Gaius Postumus, otherwise unknown, as one of Murena's prosecutors. G. V. Sumner proposed the emendation to Gaius Postumius. The best grounds for restoring the missing [i] of Postum[i]us is that Servius Sulpicius was married to a Postumia and it is reasonable to assume that he was supported in his suit by his wife's relatives.[2]

Something of Gaius Postumius' character and oratorical style may be found in a passage of Cicero's *Brutus* if another emendation by Sumner is to be accepted. The passage reads, 'Not even T. Postumius is to be despised in speaking. On behalf of the Republic he was no less vehement an orator than soldier. He was unbridled and extremely bitter, but he was well versed in constitutional law and institutions.'[3] Although all the ancient texts give T. as the *praenomen*, its emendation seems obligatory, since no T. Postumius is mentioned elsewhere in the whole history of the Republic. Munzer had earlier emended it to L, which is far more common for the Postumii Albini, but Sumner felt that C was better.[4] These two textual corrections by Sumner in the *Pro Murena* and the *Brutus* are indeed reasonable, but it is the inscription

C•POSTVMI in the exergue on this coin that really tells us that a Gaius Postumius even existed at this time.

If our moneyer was the same man who prosecuted Murena in 63, we gain an additional piece of prosopographical information useful for dating this coin. A passage in Cicero's speech makes it clear that Postum[i]us abandoned his campaign for praetor that year and joined Sulpicius in the prosecution of Murena.[5] Presumably, he did not expect to win office now that his relative had lost the consulship and had his influence diluted by defeat. Postum[i]us' candidacy in 63 for the praetorship indicates a minimum age of 39, giving the year 102 as his latest date of birth. A moneyership about the age of thirty-one in the year 71 fits within my working criteria for the age at which a mint magistrate held office.

Classical Numismatic Group, Inc. Inventory no. 732959

Diana on this obverse has her hair twisted into sections which are drawn up into a knot at the top of her head. A hunting dog is on the reverse with a hunting spear beneath him. The moneyer's name C•POSTVMI is in the exergue.

It escapes no one's notice today that the draped bust of Diana with bow and quiver over her shoulder on the obverse of Gaius Postumius' coin recalls the types of earlier moneyers from the Postumii Albini. On the reverse is a hunting hound with both front paws off the ground in a running gait and a hunting spear is below. Sumner wrote of Gaius Postumius that 'the typology of his coins associates him with previous moneyers from the Postumii Albini.' Since the ancient evidence indicates the Postumia who was married to Servius Sulpicius was from the Albini branch of the family, Sumner suggested that Gaius Postumius was her brother or some other close relative.[6]

However, before we affirm Gaius Postumius' close blood relationship with the Albini, we must reconsider the name C•POSTVMI inscribed in the exergue. The previous Postumii who minted were less interested in inscribing their *nomen* on the coin, never spelling it out further than POST. They were more interested in their *cognomen*, sometimes using only it for identification.

This Gaius Postumius inscribed his *nomen* POSTVMI on the coin while his *cognomen* below the C•POSTVMI is only a ligature, an A with a line over the top. This same ligature is found beside the head of Titus Tatius on the coins of Vettius and Titurius. On these coins, the TA clearly stands for Tatius; but no similar point of reference on Postumius' coin allows us to determine whether Postumius' ligature is to be read TA or AT. If we fail to note that line atop the A, we might think that the A was the first letter of Albinus, but the line over the A makes it clear that his *cognomen* was not Albinus, which means that we really have no reason to believe that he was from that famous branch of the Postumii Albini. Furthermore, his *praenomen* Gaius was not used by the Albini, who used Aulus, Spurius, and Lucius. By using Diana as a type, as did the Postumii Albini, our moneyer is inviting us to make an assumption that is not necessarily true, linking his less well known branch of the *gens* Postumia with the more famous Albini. Possibly he hoped to gain an election advantage from the famous name. He inscribed his less well-known *cognomen* in an ambiguous ligature and we barely pay attention to the difference in the name. So subtly effective is the imagery that it seduces us even today into connecting him with the Albini, as evidenced by Sumner's quote above, and many a Roman may have come to the same conclusion at first glance.

Diana, of course, was not just connected with the Postumii. We have seen in earlier chapters how Diana factored in the *caput orbis terrarum* theme and in the propaganda of the Sertorian war. That war had been successfully brought to an end early in 72 and Rome's attention had now shifted to Asia where Mithridates offered a greater challenge to Rome's dominant position. The literature makes it clear that Diana continued to be useful propaganda in the Mithridatic war. An event strangely reminiscent of the sacrifice of the heifer on the Aventine survives in Plutarch's account of Lucullus crossing the Euphrates in 69. Lucullus was leading his reluctant army on an invasion of Armenia where Mithridates had taken refuge with Tigranes his son-in-law. At the point of his crossing, there were heifers pasturing in the fields. The cows were branded with the symbol of a torch to mark them as sacred to Persian Diana. Reserved solely for her sacrifices, they were left free to roam at large and were very difficult to catch. As soon as the Romans crossed over the river, one of these heifers, of its own accord, came to a rock sacred to Diana, stood upon it, lowered its head, and offered itself to Lucullus as a sacrifice.[7]

Diana's appearance on Gaius Postumius' coin in 71, besides having family significance, is part of a steady stream of propaganda that used Diana to promote Rome's claim that it was her destiny to become the *caput orbis terrarum*. The imagery has changed slightly. The hunting hound and a spear on the reverse side of Gaius Postumius' coin are symbols designed to emphasize

Diana's huntress aspect and are not symbols of armed conflict. This same hunting imagery is to be found on the coin by Lucius Axius which also seems to date to the year 71. The hunting theme may actually have been inspired by the way in which Lucullus was conducting the war against Mithridates. At the very start of the war in 74, Archelaus, one of Mithridates' generals who had defected to the Roman side, advised Lucullus that, if he invaded Pontus while the king was still absent, he would control everything immediately. Lucullus replied that he would not show himself more cowardly than a hunter, marching into an empty lair having by-passed the beast.[8] Lucullus went instead to engage Mithridates at Cyzicus on the Propontus and when Mithridates was defeated and forced to flee, the chase was on.

Classical Numismatic Group, Inc. Inventory no. 197341

On this obverse die, Diana's hair is done in straight strands and drawn up into the knot at the top of her head.

Chapter 19

LUCIUS AXIUS NASO 71 BCE

The coins issued by the moneyer who inscribed his *cognomen* NASO on the obverse and L•AXSIVS•L•F in the exergue rarely appear in the hoards of this time period. Even among the 5,940 pieces of the Mesagne hoard, only one coin by this moneyer was found. The Villa Potenza hoard is the only one that is useful in establishing Axius' date of minting. Its latest mint magistrates were Gaius Postumius minting in 71 followed by Cossutius whom I date to 70. Axius' S•C coin was not found in the Frascarolo hoard whose latest mint magistrate was C. Postumius, so it would appear that Axius' relative dating is close to Gaius Postumius and Cossutius and he should be dated either to 71 or 70. Since his type of Diana emphasized the hunting imagery similar to Postumius' design on the regular issue, I think that the year 71 seems the best date for Axius' coin. Also, the obverse head that is usually identified as Mars is appropriate to a military issue authorized by Senate decree. Two distinct types of helmets are worn by the god: a helmet with only plumes appears on coins with control numbers from I to X. Valerius Maximus noted that it was not uncommon for Mars to wear plumes on his helmet and the moneyers Titus Veturius, Gaius Poblicius Malleolus, and Quintus Minucius Thermus have similar representations of Mars.[1] On coins with control numbers XI to XX, the helmet has plumes and a crest. The crested helmet of the second series is similar to the crested helmet on Rustius' coin and I have dated Rustius to the year before Axius. However, the added plumes on the helmet identify this god as Mars, whereas Rustius' god may be Minerva.

Classical Numismatic Group, Inc. Triton X Lot 522

This coin marked by the control number VII has Mars wearing a helmet with two plumes. On the reverse, Diana drives a biga of stags with three hunting dogs running alongside and behind.

Classical Numismatic Group, Inc.82 Lot 918

On this second type marked XVIII, Mars wears a helmet with crest and plumes.

The inscription recording the name Lucius Axius Naso, son of Lucius, on this coin is one of our earliest notices of this rare family name which he spelled Axsius. The name of a banker Lucius Axius also appeared on a near-contemporary *tessera nummularia* (ILLRP 1019) and Crawford was convinced that our moneyer was the same man as the banker.[2] Otherwise we know nothing of this moneyer.

In the surviving literature, Quintus Axius, son of Marcus, is the only member of the *gens* Axia attested to have reached the Senate. He was a friend and fellow tribesman of the historian Varro. Quintus Axius survives in literature as one of the speakers in Varro's *De Re Rustica*.[3] We know from Varro that he came from the town of Reate. Cicero stayed at his villa there when he arbitrated a dispute between Reate and Interamna in 54.[4] This S•C coin by Lucius Axius Naso suggests that we have another member of the *gens* whose name can be added to the Senate's roster.

Because the *nomen* Axius is so rare, it is generally assumed that our moneyer also came from Reate and was related to Quintus. The filiations of the two men make it clear that they were not brothers or father and son; but cousins, or uncle and nephew, are possible relationships. Grueber's suggestion that our moneyer was the Naso proscribed by the triumvirs in 43 is quite speculative since Appian only used the *cognomen* Naso which was common to too many men.[5]

Longperier interpreted the coin's reverse design depicting Diana driving a biga of stags to be a punning allusion to the family name Axia, citing Pliny's mention of a strange animal found in India called *axis*, which had the hide of a fawn, but with more spots and whiter in color.[6] This suggestion was frequently repeated in catalogs. Pliny, however, specifically said that the *axis* was sacred to Liber not Diana.[7] Moreover, it is difficult to see how or why an Italian family would derive its name from an obscure and virtually unknown

Indian animal. Crawford is surely right in saying the *axis* is 'of no conceivable relevance to the reverse type.'[8]

However, the name Axius is not unknown in Greek mythology and offers a better reason why a Roman family might take the name Axius and spell it using the letters xs to transliterate the Greek letter ksi. Two heroes who fought for Troy, Pyraichmes and Asteropaeus, came from the banks of the Axius River in Paionia, whose stream Homer called 'the loveliest on earth.' Although a very minor character, Pyraichmes found fame perishing at the hands of Patroclus fighting over the body of Sarpedon.[9] Asteropaeus earned greater fame by perishing at the hands of Achilles. Before their single combat, Asteropaeus boasted of his lineage. He was the son of Pelegon and Periboia, and his father was the son of the river Axius. The combat began with the ambidextrous Asteropaeus throwing two spears at Achilles at the same time. One spear hit the shield but did not break through; the other grazed Achilles' right forearm and drew blood giving Asteropaeus the distinction of being the only warrior on the Trojan side in the *Iliad* to draw blood from Achilles. Achilles' answering spear cast also missed its mark and stuck fast in the ground. Drawing his sword, Achilles rushed upon Asteropaeus as he frantically tried to draw Achilles' spear from the ground. Too swiftly Achilles buried his sword in Asteropaeus' belly and so he perished on the eleventh day after his arrival at Troy.[10] Our moneyer's family may well be associating their line with this hero descended from Axius.

At first glance, Axius' design exhibits nothing that one can claim as unique to the *gens* Axia or, for that matter, to the *municipium* Reate which was famous for its mules not stags. In fact, Axius' design seems heavily influenced by earlier issues. The reverse design of Diana driving a biga of stags had been used twice before. The earliest appearance was an anonymous issue dated to about 143. Although the deity in the biga holds a torch in her right hand rather than a bow, she is clearly identified as Diana by the quiver over her shoulder and the crescent moon below the stags. The moneyer Gaius Allius Bala used the biga of stags again (*ca.* 92). Bala's deity can also be identified as Diana by the quiver over her shoulder and she too holds a torch in her right hand. Her left hand holds not only the reins but also what appears to be a scepter or possibly a spear. Bala's coins were numerous and were in wide circulation when Axius minted, so the design was not novel to the eye. Although Axius' deity does not have the quiver over her shoulder, she does carry the spear and drive the biga of stags. The imagery clearly establishes her as Diana. These three similar appearances of Diana in a biga of stags by moneyers from three different families suggest that the type was more likely generic than a specific reference to the *gens* Axia.

Numismatica Ars Classica Auction 61 Lot 942

This anonymous issue dated to about 143 depicts Diana in a biga of stags carrying a torch. The bow and quiver over her shoulder and the crescent moon under the stags make the identification certain.

Numismatica Ars Classica Auction 46 Lot 356

This coin by Gaius Allius Bala depicts Diana in a biga of stags. Again the bow and quiver over her shoulder make the identification certain. She holds a torch and what has been identified as a scepter, but may be a spear.

However, if the Axia *gens* did associate themselves with a Homeric hero from the region of the Axius River, Axius' Diana might also have a connection to that region. As we have noted, Axius' Diana carries a spear, but the bow and quiver which usually identify her are not there. One of the more important gods of the Paionians was Bendis, whom the Greeks most often associated with Artemis. By the fifth century, Bendis' cult was well established in Athens.[11] By the fourth century her image could be found in Italy as seen on an Apulian krater (*ca*. 370) in the Boston Museum of Fine Arts. She is dressed in Thracian clothing, a body suit with long sleeves covered by a long dress down to the top of her hunting boots tied with a belt around the waist, and an animal skin cap on her head. She carries a spear with no bow or quiver to be seen.[12] A skyphos attributed to the Phiale Painter shows her dressed in similar fashion with two spears, no bow or quiver to be seen.[13] The poet Cratinus used the epithet '*dilonchon*' of her. The grammarian Hesychius seemed unsure of the meaning of '*dilonchon*' and offered three possibilities in his lexicon, one of which was that she bore two spears. We might recall that the Paionian Asteropaeus was ambidextrous and hurled two spears at once at Achilles.

Axius' Diana appears somewhat similar to the Paionian version of Diana; she carries a spear, not a bow and quiver, she has a cap on her head and a dress tightly cinched at the waist, but her arms appear to be bare and boots cannot be seen. Axius did expand on the hunting scene by adding three hunting hounds, two behind the chariot and one below. He seems to be picking up the theme used by Gaius Postumius who coupled Diana's head on the obverse with the hunting hound and the spear on the reverse. The hunting theme of Axius' reverse, however, does not have any relationship with the obverse design as does Postumius' coin. Axius' obverse has a martial look and the helmeted head is usually identified as Mars.

Lucius Axius' coinage is an S•C issue and we must ask what need may have occasioned the decree of the Senate authorizing this special issue. Axius' issue was the smallest mintage of the S•C coins for the period following Sulla's reforms. It is not likely that this money was minted for the Mithridatic war for Lucullus claimed not to have made any demands on the treasury.[14] Nor is it likely that it funded Crassus' army fighting against Spartacus since Crassus raised his own army and we know the name of his quaestor for 71, so Axius cannot be assigned to his army. I have assigned the S•C issues of the previous years to quaestors in Pompey's army. The necessity of paying Pompey's troops did not end with the completion of the war; they were still under arms. The Sertorian war had ended in 72 and Pompey was engaged in settling affairs in Spain when the Senate sent him a summons to hasten his return home in order to help Crassus put down the slave revolt of Spartacus. Crassus quickly regretted this decision to ask for Pompey's help and doubled his efforts to bring the revolt to an end before Pompey arrived to share in the glory. Crassus succeeded in bringing Spartacus to a decisive battle in which Spartacus was killed and his army put to flight. Some fugitives from the battle fled right into the path of Pompey who was returning in early 71. Pompey immediately fell upon them, killing the whole remnant reported as 5,000 in number; and then Pompey anticipated Crassus' own dispatch to the Senate, announcing that he, Pompey, had finished off the war wholly and entirely.

With the end of the slave revolt, there was no longer need to keep troops under arms in Italy and the Senate sent orders for Pompey and Crassus to discharge their soldiers. Pompey temporized. The relief and joy that Rome felt over the successful completion of the Sertorian war and the end to the slave revolt was tempered by the fear that Pompey might now refuse to dismiss his army and use it instead to establish himself in absolute power just as Sulla had done. Minds were put somewhat at rest when Pompey promised to dismiss his troops immediately after his triumph.[15] But time dragged on as Pompey found excuses for delaying the celebration of his triumph. His refusal to dismiss his troops contrasted sharply with the actions of Quintus Caecilius Metellus Pius who dismissed his army as soon as he crossed the Alps into Italy. Crassus also refused to dismiss the troops that he had commanded against Spartacus on the grounds that Pompey still retained his army.[16] These two armies camped under arms in the vicinity of Rome increased tensions.

It soon became obvious what Pompey hoped to achieve by this tactic. Backed up by his army, Pompey requested of the Senate that he be allowed to run for the consulship of 70 despite being only thirty-five years old and never having held any of the required offices of the *cursus honorum*. Pompey was exceedingly popular because of his victorious campaigns and his long service did merit special concessions, but the retention of his army was certainly a tacit threat. The Senate preferred not to test Pompey's resolve and passed a decree granting the exemption.

Keeping troops under arms required money and supplies. Where did it come from? It is difficult to see how the Senate having asked Pompey to bring the army back to Italy to aid in the slave war would refuse to authorize the funding to pay them. In the previous chapters, I suggested that the coins issued by Gnaeus Lentulus Marcellinus as quaestor and curator for minting denarii were for the expenses of Pompey's army for the years 74 and 73 and that Lucius Rustius' issue covered the year 72. Axius, perhaps as Pompey's quaestor, minted this money in 71 after the war had ended in Spain and the soldiers were summoned home for the slave revolt, hence the smaller mintage.

Chapter 20

TITUS VETTIUS SABINUS 71 BCE

The coin by the moneyer Titus Vettius Sabinus does not appear in hoards until the Kavalla and Mesagne hoards whose latest coins are those of the curule aediles Scaurus and Hypsaeus dated to 58. No one, however, assigns the coin to this late a date. It is usually dated in the 70s on stylistic grounds. Grueber noting the coin's similarity in fabric and style to the joint issue of Calenus and Cordius and the issue of Manius Aquillius dated all three issues to 72. Crawford was equally impressed by the similarity, but his dating moved the joint issue of Calenus and Cordius to 70 and he wrote, 'the other two issues, on grounds of style and fabric, go closely with it; for what my opinion is worth, it is that the issue of Mn. Aquillius belongs in 71, the issue of T.Vettius Sabinus (with that of Kalenus and Cordus) in 70.'[1]

Dating on stylistic grounds is always subjective, but our moneyer Titus Vettius Sabinus may not be completely unknown and the scanty prosopographical evidence that survives may well support dating this coin to the 70s. Crawford wrote that the moneyer had 'probably already been Quaestor when he became moneyer and went on to be Pr. 59.'[2] The quaestorship to which Crawford refers was held in Sicily under the governorship of Gaius Verres who was propraetor there for three years from 73 to 71. Broughton says that Vettius' quaestorship is better attested for 71 than 73 since he was excluded from a *consilium* which tried a case against Sicilian captains following the capture of pirates by the quaestor L. Caesetius in eastern Sicily in 72.[3]

Absolute certainty with the identification of our moneyer Titus Vettius Sabinus as Verres' quaestor Titus Vettius is clouded by the moneyer's *cognomen* SABINVS which appears on the obverse of the coin. The *cognomen* of Verres' quaestor was not recorded, but we know that he was the *frater* of a certain Publius Vettius Chilo who was Verres' brother-in-law. Verres was married to Publius Vettius Chilo's sister.[4] If we assume that the quaestor Titus Vettius' *cognomen* was also Chilo, being a brother of Publius Vettius Chilo, then his identification as our moneyer is not likely, although it is not impossible that they were brothers with different *cognomina.* It is also possible that *frater* does not mean brother here but cousin, a usage not uncommon to Cicero and we note that Cicero does not refer to Titus as also being a brother-in-law of Verres as would be the case if Titus and Publius were brothers.

There is one other point we should note about the *cognomen* SABINVS. Sabinus might only have been an affectation, a name assumed by our moneyer when he entered upon his political career. In a letter written in 45, Cicero jokingly asked whether a candidate who went by the *cognomen* Sabinus was really a Sabine or by chance had 'he too suddenly seized upon this name, using the license of candidates.'[5]

Numismatica Ars Classica Auction 46 Lot 384

Titus Vettius depicted the head of Titus Tatius identified by the ligature for TA under the chin on the obverse. The inscription SABINVS behind his head confirms that it is Titus Tatius and also gives the moneyer's *cognomen*.

We have noted how well such references to a non-Roman heritage played with the newly enfranchised Italians and Vettius may have simply decided to advertise his Sabine roots with an assumed, more politically significant *cognomen*. He further emphasized his Sabine connections by depicting on the obverse of his coin the bearded portrait head of the legendary Sabine king, Titus Tatius who is clearly identified by the ligature for TA.

Classical Numismatic Group, Inc. Triton XII Lot 476

This earlier coin by Lucius Titurius Sabinus gives us the same portrait bust of Titus Tatius that was probably a reproduction of the head from the familiar statue of the king. The ligature for TA beside the face and the inscription SABINI behind makes the identification of the head as Tatius clear. Vettius' obverse almost appears a copy of Titurius' obverse.

Tatius was king of the Sabines when the Romans under Romulus snatched the Sabine women to be their wives. This famous act of Roman treachery, a representation of which had appeared only a few years earlier on the coins of Lucius Titurius Sabinus, drove the Sabines to take arms against Rome. The conflict was only resolved by the intervention of the Sabine women pleading for a political settlement that joined the two communities under a joint kingship held by Romulus and Titus Tatius. Titus Vettius Sabinus' representation of Titus Tatius closely resembles that on the earlier coin by Lucius Titurius Sabinus. He is rendered in the idealized Greek style of kingly portraits with his eyes looking slightly heavenward. His portrait displays none of the rugged character lines chiseled on the faces of Republican magistrates. This portrait may have been derived from a statue, for we know that there was a statue grouping of all the kings in Rome.[6]

Vettius' emphasis on a Sabine heritage has colored the modern interpretations of his reverse design. A Roman magistrate wearing a toga and carrying a magistrate's staff in his left hand rides in a chariot drawn by a pair of stately horses with raised front hooves indicating a slow, processional walking pace. The inscription IVDEX which Vettius used to identify this particular Roman causes great confusion. The term *iudex*, usually translated as judge, applied most commonly to each of the members of a panel of jurors who sat in judgment at trials. There was no regular office of *iudex*, but only the temporary function of arbiter in a dispute or investigation and once the verdict was rendered the service of *iudex* was terminated just as in the case of modern jurors. At various times in Roman history any member of the senatorial or equestrian orders could serve as a *iudex*. Who is this particular *iudex*? Looking for a link with the moneyer's family traditions, the early commentators identified the figure as the Sabine king Titus Tatius or possibly the Sabine king Numa as chief judge of the state; they suggested that the ear of grain to the right of the figure referred to Numa's distribution of land. Others saw the figure as the Spurius Vettius the *interrex* who, following the death of Romulus, finally called for the election which resulted in Numa's appointment as king. But an *interrex* was not a *iudex*, and if our moneyer was so anxious to make a family reference to famous Sabine ancestors, why did he identify by name the easily recognizable head of Titus Tatius on the obverse and only identify the reverse figure by a title? Crawford rejected the Titus Tatius, Numa, and Spurius Vettius identifications for the reverse figure saying, 'It is simplest to identify the type as portraying a magistrate engaged in judicial activity, perhaps over corn distribution; it is doubtless intended to convey a family or political allusion now lost.'[7] Perhaps the allusion is not lost; perhaps we are just looking in the wrong place. This is an S•C coin and in applying my theory on S•C coinage, I would expect that Vettius was not a mint magistrate but a quaestor or higher magistrate authorized to mint coinage for a special purpose. If our moneyer is the same Titus Vettius who served as Verres' quaestor in Sicily, the earliest year he could have minted as quaestor was 73 and the latest was 71. If he minted while serving in Sicily, the reverse design becomes somewhat more intelligible. Sicily was the main supplier of grain to Rome and paid an annual tithe of almost 3,000,000 modii of wheat in taxes. The ear of grain on Vettius' coin may be a reference both to where he served his quaestorship and the reason the Senate authorized the special minting of this coin.

We have a precedent for quaestors minting money by decree of the Senate in order to purchase grain. The first time the EX•S•C inscription appeared on a denarius was the issue by the quaestors Lucius Calpurnius Piso Caesoninus and Quintus Servilius Caepio dated to 100. The reverse shows the two quaestors seated on their quaestor chairs with ears of grain flanking them. An inscription AD•FRV•EMV, *ad frumentum emundum*, declares that these coins were issued by decree of the Senate for the purpose of buying grain.

Classical Numismatic Group, Inc. 122 Lot 282

The reverse of the coin declares that the quaestors Lucius Calpurnius Piso Caesoninus and Quintus Servilius Caepio issued these denarii by decree of the Senate for the purpose of buying grain.

One of the duties of the Roman governor in Sicily was to oversee the sale of the tax tithes. The Romans did not have a tax collecting agency, but sold the right to collect the taxes to tax farming companies. The contract went to the highest bidder who paid the bid price to the Roman treasury, usually in installments. The tax farmers made their profit by collecting more than what they bid for the contract. If the tax farmers failed to collect the price bid they would lose money, not the Roman treasury. This system seems strange to us and inherently dangerous for the poor souls who must pay the taxes. But the tithe contracts were not a license for the tax farmers to collect as much as they could possibly extort from the farmers. A tithe is a fixed rate of ten percent and that is all that the tax farmers had the right to collect from the grain farmers. Bidding tax contracts was a lot like speculating on the modern commodities market and just as big a business. The contractor bet on what the harvest was going to be and what price it would bring. Bids were not submitted on blind guesswork. Records existed on how many farmers were in each tax district, how many acres were planted, and the average yields from the land. In order to keep things fair for both the tax collector and the grain farmers, laws were in place prescribing penalties should the tax collector demand more than the required ten percent; and there were penalties should the grain farmer try to conceal part of his harvest by not bringing it to the threshing floor. If a dispute should arise, either party could request the praetor to appoint a panel of judges called *recupatores* or the plaintiff could ask for a single *iudex* to decide the issue.[8]

Classical Numismatic Group, Inc. Inventory no. 157813

On the reverse a togate figure carrying a magistrate's staff drives a chariot to the left. An ear of grain is behind him on the right. Above the horses is the inscription IVDEX. The moneyer's name T•VETTIVS is in the exergue. Classical Numismatic Group, Inc. felt that this was possibly the finest example known.

Now if the ear of grain behind the *iudex* sets the scene of the coin in Sicily where Vettius served his quaestorhip, it also makes intelligible that figure whom Vettius has identified as a *iudex*. He is one of the arbiters who are sent to the different districts by the praetor to resolve the various disputes arising over the collection of the tithe of grain. The scene does not relate to the distribution of grain but rather the acquisition.

By 74 the demands of war and the activities of the pirates had made grain scarce and expensive in Rome. The acquisition of additional resources of grain became necessary to alleviate the situation. In 73 the consuls passed the *lex Terentia et Cassia*, a major grain bill, providing for a distribution of five *modii* per month[9] at the price of six and one-third asses.[10] The *lex Terentia et Cassia* provided for additional purchases of grain in Sicily. What we know of its workings comes from Cicero's speech against Verres, the man whom the Senate made responsible for carrying out the law's provisions for grain acquisition in Sicily.

By decree of the Senate and from the *lex Terentia et Cassia*, it was Verres' duty to purchase grain in Sicily. There were two types of purchases: one a tithe amount, the other, requisitioned over and above the tithe, was to be equally divided throughout the districts. The tithe amount was to be the same as was the tax tithe; the amount of the requisitioned grain was to be 800,000 modii of wheat. The price for the tithe grain was set at three sesterces per modius; for the requisitioned wheat, the price was set at three and one-half sesterces. Therefore, 2,800,000 sesterces were decreed for Verres to pay to the farmers each year for the requisitioned grain and almost 9,000,000 sesterces for the second tithe. So in each of his three years he was paid almost 12,000,000 sesterces for the purchase of Sicilian grain.[11]

Unfortunately, this ambitious program was placed in the hands of a man who was to so ruthlessly plunder the province that his name and reputation has lived on for two thousand years as the epitome of Roman greed. Part of the funding came from the treasury and part directly from the tax farmers. The bulk of the funding for the purchases was to come from an assignment of the revenues collected by the companies collecting the pasture taxes and import duties in Sicily.[12] Instead of sending the money to the Roman treasury when the installments were due, they were to pay it to Verres for the purchase of the grain. Pompey's special command against the pirates in 67 would be financed in the same way.[13] Verres found a very interesting opportunity here. Since this money technically belonged to the Roman treasury and had been assigned to him for the purchase of grain, why not charge interest on it while it remained in the hands of the tax farmers? He set the rate at two percent per month, but, of course, the proceeds never went into the Roman treasury. His own brother-in-law Publius Vettius Chilo was one of the directors of a tax collecting company who complained bitterly about this scheme.[14] He demanded to see the official records and if they did not show that the money collected as interest was paid into the treasury, he said he would demand it be paid back to the companies. This was just one of the reasons why the program of the *lex Terentia et Cassia* did not work out as planned. Cicero laid out the other charges in his indictment of Verres' crimes.

> This great amount of money given to you from an impoverished and exhausted treasury, given for grain, the staff of life and health, given in order that the Sicilian farmers, on whom the Republic has placed such great burdens, should be compensated, this money I claim was so squandered by you that I could prove, if I so chose, that all this money was diverted to your own coffers... Regarding this public money, there were three types of theft: first, when the money was deposited among the companies whence it was assigned, he charged the companies two percent interest per month; secondly, he paid

> nothing at all to very many cities for their grain; and finally, if he did pay any city, he subtracted as much as he liked, to none did he pay what was owed.[15]

Cicero's prosecution of Verres laid bare such brazen criminal activities of the governor and his staff that Verres ran into exile rather than face his trial in 70. Cicero had to settle for publishing his speeches rather than delivering them in court. From these speeches we have no evidence that the quaestor Titus Vettius shared in Verres' schemes. If he was a praetor in 59 as suggested by Cicero's text of *Pro Flacco* 85, his career was apparently slowed but not ruined by his association with Verres. But it is difficult to believe that the Senate would have entrusted a position of financial responsibility to him in the years immediately following his service in Sicily. Since Vettius issued the coin by decree of the Senate, it is best to date this coin to 71 before Vettius would have been tainted by the public scandal that attended Verres' prosecution. This small mintage (estimated by Crawford at less than twenty-two reverse dies) then was struck to pay for grain purchases authorized by the *lex Terentia et Cassia.*

If these coins were counted into the hands of the farmers to pay for the grain, the reverse design was intended to depict the fair and evenhanded way in which the Romans handled the grain tithe and how the parties had recourse to a *iudex* to settle any dispute. In other words, 'If you do not like it, you can always submit the matter to the arbitration of the *iudex*.' But Verres subverted the whole established system by having his own henchmen buy up the contracts at outrageous prices and exact as much as they could extort. Should anyone complain, Verres selected the arbiters from the members of his staff sharing in the plunder. Cicero's speeches reveal the true situation under Verres.

> Truly, there was that famous little clause in your edict, which proclaimed that you yourself would provide a board of arbiters for any dispute that arose between a farmer and the tax collector, if either party so wishes. First of all, what dispute could there possibly be, when he who ought to request the grain, simply takes it and moreover takes not as much as is owed, but as much as he likes, and yet the man who was robbed has no chance of recovering his property in court? And then in drafting this edict, this corrupt fellow wants to be a clever fox, writing, 'If either party so wishes, I will provide the board of arbiters.' How cleverly he thinks he commits his theft. He gives to both parties the power to appeal, but it makes no difference whether he wrote, 'if either party wishes' or 'if the tax collector wishes,' for the farmer will never want that board of your arbiters.[16]

Chapter 21

GNAEUS POMPEIUS MAGNUS 71 BCE

The day before he assumed the consulship, Pompey finally celebrated his long postponed triumph. No description of the triumphal procession survives in the ancient literature, but one golden moment from it remains and has passed into our hands today in the form of an extremely rare aureus bearing the obverse inscription MAGNVS. The triumphal chariot on the reverse makes it clear that it was issued to celebrate one of Pompey's triumphs, but the aureus has not always been recognized as belonging to Pompey's Spanish triumph. There is absolutely no hoard evidence to help in the dating. The coin itself provides the only clues as to its date and its imagery has led many commentators astray.

On the obverse, Pompey depicted the head of Africa wearing an elephant's skin. Behind the head is the inscription MAGNVS. Beside the head are a *lituus* and *capis*. The whole is encircled with a wreath. The elephant skin, an obvious reference to Africa, led commentators to assign the coins to Pompey's first triumph that he celebrated in 81 for his victory over Iarbas in Africa.[1] This, however, created a problem in interpreting the reverse design.

On the reverse, Pompey depicted the triumphal four-horse chariot in procession. On the near horse is a young rider and this feature confirms our assumption that we are dealing with a triumph, for it was customary to allow underage sons to ride on the trace-horse of the triumphal chariot.[2] We assume that Pompey is the figure in the chariot. He holds a palm branch in his right hand and is about to be crowned with a wreath by a flying Victory. The problem in identifying this triumph with the African triumph of 81 is twofold. First the title PRO•COS is inscribed in the exergue and Pompey conducted his African campaign with the title of propraetor.[3] He did not hold the title of proconsul until his command in Spain, which means that we must date the coin to some time after 77. Secondly, the boy on the horse could not have been Pompey's son in 81 since he had no children when he celebrated his African triumph. Gnaeus was born some time between 80 and 76.

G. F. Hill tried to resolve the problem by arguing that the coin referred to the African triumph, but was minted later when Pompey was proconsul. He claimed that gold coinage was never minted in Rome, which meant that this coin had to be issued in a province. He suggested that Pompey issued it to commemorate his African triumph some time between 76 and 72. However, Hill's argument that the aureus had to be issued in the provinces has no substantiation and the evidence we have seen about Pompey's problems with money during the Spanish war argues against a gratuitous commemorative issue while in Spain. Moreover, Hill's solution still left the problem over the identity of the mounted boy. Hill answered that problem saying that the boy does not have to be Gnaeus; he could be another relative.[4] Yet the natural assumption any Roman would make about the boy on the horse was that he was the son of the *triumphator*.

©Trustees of the British Museum

This extremely rare example of Pompey's aureus comes from the British Museum. The head of Africa wearing an elephant skin is on the obverse. A *triumphator* in a four horse chariot is on the reverse. A young rider is on the trace-horse.

Things begin to fall into their proper place if we accept what is most obvious. Since the coin is gold and of very small mintage, it is most likely a commemorative or donative issue minted on the occasion of a triumph, not a field issue by a general on campaign. The title PRO•COS indicates under what office Pompey held *imperium* when he triumphed. This eliminates the African triumph but still leaves two possibilities: the Spanish triumph of 71 and the Mithridatic triumph of 61 to which Grueber assigned the issue. The head of Africa does not fit the theme of Pompey's triumph in 61 in which Pompey emphasized that having won his third triumph in Asia he had conquered all three continents, Africa, Europe, and Asia and, hence, led the whole world captive.[5] The African head only alludes to one triumph.

Crawford dated the coin to the Spanish triumph of 71 saying that it provided the better context for the obverse type.[6] He noted that the reference to Africa was surprising, 'but is intelligible if one remembers that the swift and decisive victory in Africa was a more striking achievement than the victory in Spain,' and that it was 'less recent and less charged with bitterness.'[7]

There is no doubt that the obverse design was intended to recall the African war and Pompey's African triumph, so let us take a look at what memories survived in the histories. Plutarch said that it only took Pompey forty days to annihilate the enemy's army and gain control of Libya.[8] His soldiers not only saluted him as *imperator*, but addressed him for the first time by the name Magnus, the Great. On his return to Rome after his African victory, Pompey was warmly greeted by Sulla who loudly addressed him as Magnus, thus confirming the soldiers' title. Sulla told all those present to salute Pompey in the same way. Plutarch said that Pompey was the last man to actually use the title Magnus, doing so only after a long time. It was while fighting Sertorius in Spain that he began to sign dispatches and letters as Pompeius Magnus.[9] Pompey, by placing the name MAGNVS on the obverse of this coin near the head of Africa, reminded his fellow citizens of the source of the *cognomen* he was now using.

The reward Pompey expected in 81 from his service in Africa was greater than just a Great *cognomen*. When he defeated Iarbas, Pompey captured some of the king's elephants and had them shipped to Rome in anticipation of celebrating a triumph. Although such an honor was legally granted only to a consul or praetor, Pompey, who was not yet even a senator, demanded a triumph for his African victory. Sulla at first refused, but undaunted, Pompey persisted and finally Sulla yielded in disgust. After he received permission for his triumph, some of his soldiers who had not gotten rewards to match their expectations threatened to disrupt the celebration. Pompey said he would forgo the triumph rather than curry to the soldiers. Hearing that, Publius Servilius Isauricus, who had opposed Pompey's request in the Senate, proclaimed that Pompey really was Great and did deserve a triumph. Pompey intended to make his triumphal entry into Rome riding in a chariot drawn by four of the captured African elephants, but the city gate was too narrow so he had to use the traditional four-horse chariot.[10] The head of Africa in an elephant's skin on the obverse of this gold coin reminded the Romans of the elephants which Pompey had captured and displayed in the triumph of 81 and in a way allowed him to celebrate it a second time.

There is an even more subtle reason why Pompey chose to represent Africa in an elephant's skin on a coin celebrating his Spanish triumph. Pompey was a proud man and rightly so, but he was self promoting and jealous of other men's accomplishments even to the point of robbing them of due recognition. In early 71, when Pompey slaughtered the fugitives escaping from the battle in which Crassus had killed Spartacus, he anticipated Crassus' own dispatch to the Senate, writing to them that Crassus had certainly defeated the gladiators in a pitched battle, but that he, Pompey, had finished the war off entirely and completely. Plutarch said that Pompey was so popular in Rome that everyone liked repeating this remark and that, as far as Spain was concerned, no one even in jest maintained that the entire credit was due to anyone but Pompey.[11] Perhaps this explains why only Pompey issued a commemorative triumphal aureus even though Metellus also celebrated a triumph for the Sertorian war.

On this aureus Pompey wanted the people to see that his exploits surpassed Metellus' to the point that he had even accomplished something that Metellus could only lay claim to as part of family tradition. The elephant had been emblematic of the Caecilii Metelli ever since Lucius Caecilius Metellus had captured over 100 elephants from Hasdrubal in a battle at Panormus in Sicily in 251.[12] Five different coin types with depictions of elephants were minted by various Metelli to commemorate the event. These coins were already in circulation when Pompey minted this coin. Ten years beforehand, Metellus Pius himself had issued a coin depicting a walking elephant. This was all ancient history for Quintus Metellus Pius, but Pompey had himself captured Jarbas' elephants about the same time Metellus minted his elephant coin. Metellus relied on ancient family history; Pompey was making family history. And lest Metellus have any other advantage over him, Pompey seems to have taken note of a second coin Metellus issued. This coin depicted a *lituus* and *capis* within a wreath, symbols of the augurate.

Classical Numismatic Group, Inc. Triton VIII Lot 868

This coin was minted by Quintus Caecilius Metellus Pius (*ca.* 82/81). The elephant was frequently used on coins minted by the Metelli recalling the 100 elephants that Lucius Metellus captured from Hasdrubal in 251.

Pompey managed to incorporate these three same elements on this aureus. The head of Africa is flanked by a *lituus* and *capis* and the whole design is enclosed within a wreath. These insignia of the augurate are the earliest evidence for Pompey's holding that priesthood. Their pairing with the African elephant does not prove that he held the priesthood by the time he celebrated his African triumph in 81, but only indicate that he was augur by the time he minted in 71. When it came to celebrating his own accomplishments, Pompey had seen to it that Metellus Pius could in no way surpass him.

Classical Numismatic Group, Inc. Nomos 5 Lot 219

Metellus Pius had encircled his *lituus* and *capis* with a wreath on this coin that was minted to pay Sullan soldiers during the civil war.

It is probable that Pompey's aureus represents largess distributed to the soldiers on the day of Pompey's triumph in 71. This gold was a fitting bonus. At the beginning of the next year Pompey became consul thanks to his loyal troops who had remained under arms to support his claim to that office.

Numismatica Ars Classica Auction 63 Lot 220

This coin appeared for auction in May 2012. In the catalog description the seller noted that this coin is only the fourth known specimen and the only one in private hands. He also says, 'This example links the two previously known varieties of this rare issue; the other three known specimens are in the BM, Bologna (which shares obverse dies with this specimen), and an example published by Riccio. This coin is reported to have been found in Spain.'

Chapter 22

LUCIUS COSSUTIUS SABULA 70 BCE

In my arrangement which assigns only one non-S•C coin to each year between 81 and 64, the relative dating of Cossutius' coin becomes rather precisely fixed by hoard evidence. It was absent from the Roncofreddo hoard whose terminus I set at 72. The Frascarolo hoard of 1,000 coins adds only the very large issue of Postumius to those found in Roncofreddo, making Postumius' date 71. The Cosa hoard of 2,004 coins adds only Cossutius to the coins found in the Frascarolo hoard. This hoard evidence suggests that Cossutius should follow Postumius making his date 70. Cossutius' mintage estimated at thirty-one reverse dies was considerably smaller than that of the mint magistrates of the preceding years and this reduction in coinage is consistent with testimony in the historic sources that there was a shortage of money in the year 70.[1] Mintages remained small for the next two years as well.

Lucius Cossutius Sabula is unknown and there is very little known of the *gens* Cossutia. A certain Cossutius, called a Roman citizen by Vitruvius, was the architect who designed the great sanctuary of the temple of Olympian Zeus in Athens when Antiochus undertook its completion in the 160s.[2] Apparently, the Cossutii held Roman citizenship long before the Social War. In the 80s, a certain Cossutia had been betrothed to Julius Caesar, but the engagement was broken in favor of Cornelia, the daughter of the consul Cinna. Cossutia's family was described by Suetonius as 'an equestrian family, but quite rich.'[3] It would seem that prior to the Sullan constitution none of the Cossutii had reached senatorial status, but Cossutia's betrothal to Caesar makes it clear that the family could travel in an illustrious circle. Although the family failed to make a marriage connection, a later coin by the moneyer C. Cossutius Maridianus minted in 44 with Caesar's head and the inscription Caesar Parens Patriae shows that the family maintained its connections with Caesar. In 44, Cossutius Maridianus could only dream what might have been had Cossutia become Caesar's wife.

The theme of Lucius Cossutius Sabula's coin is a wholly Greek myth recalling the adventures of Bellerophon and the winged horse Pegasus. On the obverse, Cossutius depicted the head of Medusa, the mother of Pegasus. Medusa and her two sisters lived beyond the Ocean in the farthest reaches of the world toward Night and the land of the Hesperides. The three sisters were Gorgons, terrible frightening creatures. Early Greek vase paintings depicted them having heads entwined with coils of snakes, their mouths filled with large teeth and protruding boar's tusks. A tongue usually protruded from the toothy grins. Frequently their faces were blackened with beard stubble. It is no wonder that the sight of Medusa's face turned men to stone. Moreover, the Gorgons' hands were bronze and from their backs sprouted wings that were of gold.[4] Medusa alone of the sisters was mortal. She was slain by Perseus while she slept. He cut off her head and took it with him, using it as a weapon to turn men to stone in his later adventures. Eventually Medusa's head was to end up on the aegis of Minerva and the terrifying aspect of the Medusa was popular on the shields of Greek soldiers who hoped that the Medusa would strike numbing fear into the enemy who must look on her face.

Classical Numismatic Group, Inc. 66 Lot 1307

The head of a lovely Medusa with her snaky hair is on the obverse. The wing over her temple alludes to the birth of Pegasus who is depicted on the reverse.

In the course of time, the artistic rendering of Medusa underwent dramatic changes becoming less grotesque until, during the course of the fifth century, she became a graceful winged creature. The tusks are gone, thin delicate lips give no hint of that once gaping toothy grin, her cheeks are smooth. She is now rendered as a beautiful girl, just having a perpetual bad hair day, for the snakes still remain about her head. This is the Medusa the Romans came to know in their literature. Ovid said that Medusa, a beautiful girl with lovely hair, was pursued by many lovers. Unfortunately, she attracted the attention of Neptune who raped her in Minerva's temple. The abashed virgin goddess punished the girl for her carelessness by turning her hair to snakes.[5] Cossutius has rendered his Medusa as this beautiful girl with the snakes arranged as thick curls of hair, a little wild over her forehead, but tied with a fillet to keep them neatly arranged in the back. The wing depicted over her temple is not usually found on Medusa's head. In some early paintings her feet are winged, but usually the wings sprout from her back. While the wing may recall that Medusa was a winged creature, it more likely recalls that after Perseus cut off her head, the winged horse Pegasus sprang from her bloody neck. The wing sprouting from Medusa's head on Cossutius' coin represents Pegasus about to be born.

Leaving behind the distant land of his mother, Pegasus flew off to Greece to roam the Corinthian plain. Such a wondrous creature could not escape the notice of the Corinthians. Bellerophon, the grandson of Sisyphus, the cleverest of all Corinthians, was possessed by a passion to capture and tame the horse, but a winged horse was not as easy to catch as the normal variety and he was completely frustrated in his efforts. He sought the advice of the seer Koiranides, who told him to sleep near the altar of Minerva. In a dream the goddess came to him with a golden bridle. She told him to take this magic for the horse and to sacrifice a bull to Neptune. When he awoke a golden bridle lay beside him. Bellerophon made the sacrifice to Neptune and successfully bridled the elusive Pegasus as he drank from the Pirene spring .[6]

But that success was soon followed by an unfortunate incident that compelled Bellerophon to leave Corinth in exile. The murder of a brother is hinted at, but not sufficiently illuminated in the sources. Driven from Corinth, Bellerophon took refuge with King Proitos in Tiryns. Anteia, the king's wife, fell in love with him and wanted to sleep with him. When he would not succumb to her charms, she denounced him to her husband for attempting to seduce her. Beside himself with anger, Proitos plotted Bellerophon's murder. He asked Bellerophon to take a letter to Iobates, king of Lycia, Anteia's father. Unaware of its content, Bellerophon carried the message ordering his own death. But the Lycian king shrank from bloodying his own hands with the murder and sent Bellerophon on a mission that promised certain death. He was to slay the chimaera, an unapproachable beast having the front of a lion and a tail of a snake with a goat head in the middle which breathed fire. Following the commands of the gods, Bellerophon succeeded in killing the chimaera. Next he was sent against the Solymoi. He defeated them, and when he met the Amazons in battle, he overcame them as well. The Lycian king tried one last time by laying an ambush; but when none of those handpicked men returned, the king knew Bellerophon to be the offspring of a god (Hesiod said he was the son of Poseidon) and offered him the hand of his daughter and half of his kingdom.[7]

Paintings of Bellerophon and Pegasus attacking the chimaera were on Corinthian vases before the mid-seventh century. They became quite popular on Attic vases of the later fifth and early fourth centuries. An even greater interest is found on the pottery of South Italy in the fourth century. Most vase paintings show Bellerophon mounted on Pegasus flying above the chimaera, but some early vases show him flying above the Solymoi or the Amazons. His arm is raised, ready to throw his spear downward on his victims below. This is the pose that our moneyer has used for Bellerophon on the reverse of his coin, but he has not depicted the victim, leaving us to fill in the blank.

Another important part of the Bellerophon/Pegasus myth is that at some point in their travels they came to Mount Helicon, the haunt of the Muses, and with the stamp of his foot Pegasus brought forth the most famous stream of water in all of Greece which came to be known as the Hippocrene or 'horse spring,' the favorite of the Muses.[8]

Since the story of Bellerophon and Pegasus is a Greek myth having no direct association with Rome, Grueber noted, 'The types of Medusa and Bellerophon in connection with the *gens* Cossutia have not been satisfactorily explained.'[9] Grueber speculated that an ancestor may have held a position in Greece and that the type related to an event connected with his family. Crawford noted that there were Cossutii operating as businessmen in the Greek East and he suggested that they may have been attracted to the motif while there.[10] But a Roman did not have to go to Greece to be influenced by the story of Bellerophon, and Pegasus had already appeared on very early Roman bronze coins. If we are to be guided by the interpretation of the earlier coins by Mamilius Limetanus and Strabo, it is, indeed, most likely that the moneyer is heralding his family's descent from Bellerophon. Perhaps a hint of that is found in the moneyer's name.

Gemini Auction II Lot 232

The moneyer's *cognomen* SABVLA on the obverse may be a way of recalling the famous springs that Pegasus brought forth with the blow of his hoof.

Bellerophon's part in the creation of the Hippocrene was illustrated by a later sculpted fountain which Pausanius saw standing in the rebuilt city of Corinth in the second century CE. The artist used a clever device to recall how the legendary spring was created. Bellerophon was mounted on the winged Pegasus who had water flowing from his hoof.[11] The sculpture makes a very visual connection between Bellerophon and the creation of the Hippocrene. The Cossutii, in claiming descent from Bellerophon, may be making the same association with a clever use of their *cognomen*. The name SABVLA inscribed next to the head of Medusa is not common. The Latin word *sabulum* means 'sand' or 'gravel.' In a passage of Pliny dealing with methods of finding water, various types of soil are discussed. Pliny wrote, '*sabulum* sends forth thin and muddy trickles of water; gravel gives intermittent, but good tasting water; *sabulum masculum* or carbunculus sand produces steady and constant and healthful springs.'[12]

Chapter 23

PUBLIUS CORNELIUS LENTULUS SPINTHER 70 BCE

The moneyer who signed his name P•LENT•P•F L•N, Publius Lentulus, son of Publius, grandson of Lucius, issued his coin by decree of the Senate while serving as quaestor as indicated by Q•S•C on the obverse. He has been identified as Publius Cornelius Lentulus Spinther, the consul of 57. Absolute certainty in this identification was clouded by Degrassi who claimed to observe traces of the letter C after P.F in the consul Spinther's name as found on fragment 39 of the *Fasti Capitolini Consulares*.[1] This means that Spinther's name on the *Fasti* must be restored as CN.N. He should then be traced back to Gnaeus Lentulus, the consul of 146, through a Publius not otherwise known. With a grandfather named Gnaeus, Spinther could not be the same man as our moneyer whose grandfather was named Lucius. However, what looked like the trace of a C to Degrassi looked more like the tip of the hasta of L to Sumner. Moreover, Sumner felt that Cicero's words in the *Brutus* referring to P. Lentulus Spinther and L. Lentulus Crus as *duo Lentuli* meant that they were closely related, possibly brothers or cousins. He reconstructed their possible line of descent in the stemma below.[2]

Lucius Lent., L. f., L. n.
consul 199

|

Publius Lent., L.f., L.n.
consul suffect 162

|

Lucius Lent. ——— Publius Lent., P.f.
consul 130

|

Lucius Lent. ——— Publius Lent.
praetor by 83 legate 90

|

Publius Lent., P.f., L.n. Spinther? ——— Lucius Lent. Crus, P.f.
quaestor 72? consul 49

Degrassi's reading of C in the *Fasti*, already disputed by others, was not decisive enough to deter Crawford from identifying our moneyer as Publius Cornelius Lentulus Spinther, consul of 57, and this remains the dominant opinion today. The hoard evidence, scanty though it is, certainly dates this coin to the proper time period when Spinther would have held the quaestorship. The coin did not appear in Italian hoards until Cosa and Palestrina whose latest mint magistrate was Cossutius. Grueber dated both Cossutius and Lentulus to 74. Broughton accepted this date for Lentulus in his *Magistrates of the Roman Republic*, but also cited Sydenham who dated Lentulus to 72. Crawford followed Grueber in dating Lentulus to 74. Hersh and Walker more recently dated Cossutius to 72 and moved Lentulus to 71. My dating system has moved Cossutius down to 70, which gives that year as a terminus to the Cosa and Palestrina hoards; and we are now approaching a date more in line with what we would expect from the evidence of Lentulus Spinther's *cursus.*

Spinther was curule aedile in 63, praetor in 60, and consul in 57. All these offices, if held *in suo anno,* point to a birth date no later than 100. But we know from Cicero that he did not hold them in his first year of eligibility,[3] which pushes his latest year of birth back at least one year to 101. He was then at least thirty-one years old in 70. In light of Spinther's later *cursus*, Crawford's dating of his quaestorship to 74 seems rather early. If he was thirty-one in 74, he was forty-two when he held the aedileship in 63. I find it difficult to understand why a man of great personal wealth with the illustrious family name of the Cornelii Lentuli would hold the unnecessary office of aedile two years after he was eligible for the praetorship. We would expect him to have run for the praetorship not the aedileship. The same problem exists if he was quaestor in 72. Based on the evidence of the hoards and Lentulus Spinther's *cursus*, the year 70 appears to be the best date for his quaestorship.

Numismatica Ars Classica Auction 51 Lot 32

The obverse head is usually identified in catalogs as Hercules, yet none of his usual iconography is present which makes the identification uncertain.

On the obverse, Spinther depicted a bearded head usually identified as Hercules. This is questionable because none of the iconography which identifies Hercules is present. The style is similar to the head of Hercules on the earlier coin by Publius Lentulus Marcellinus (*ca.* 100), yet the lion skin and club over his shoulder, which clearly identifies the god as Hercules on Marcellinus' coin, is missing from Spinther's depiction. The hair is rendered in the same tufty fashion, but the beard is much heavier on Spinther's coin.

Numismatica Ars Classica Auction 61 Lot 1182

Publius Cornelius Lentulus Marcellinus (*ca.* 100) depicted Hercules with the same hair, but the beard is much heavier on Spinther's coin.

Spinther's representation seems to have more in common with the male head on Oscan denarii issued in Spain. Grueber noted that Eckhel even mistook the inscription Q•S•C for OSCA.[4] The most similar head on Roman coinage is found on the coin minted by Gaius Domitius Calvinus who was appointed governor of Spain by Octavian in 39. His male obverse head has the same tufty hair and heavy beard. Although he wears a necklace and has none of the iconography of Hercules, he is usually identified as Hercules. Again, without the club and lion skin this identification is questionable. But a Spanish reference is clear from the inscription OSCA beside the head.

Classical Numismatic Group, Inc. Inventory no. 886109

C. Domitius Calvinus' coin minted while governor in Spain has nearly the same male head as seen on Lentulus Spinther's coin and the inscription OSCA makes the Spanish association clear.

On the reverse of Spinther's coin, a bearded male figure sits on a curule chair facing forward. His head is veiled and he is naked to the waist. He holds a large cornucopia in his right hand and a scepter in his left. His right foot rests on the orb of the world and under his left foot is an object that cannot be identified. Victory flying in from the figure's left is about to place a wreath on his head. Harold Mattingly saw in this type a reference to the Sertorian war in Spain, in particular 'the triumphal banquet of Metellus, when he was crowned at the feast by a Victory.'[5] Plutarch told how on one occasion Metellus was so puffed up by a victory he had won over Sertorius that at a celebration banquet, as choirs of boys and women sang victory hymns in his honor, he had mechanical Victories lowered down from the ceiling holding golden crowns and trophies in their hands.[6]

Spinther's type does seem proper to the celebration of a victory, but the scene on this coin does not fit that dinner occasion; the curule chair is not a dining couch, the scepter is not proper for a victory dinner, nor was it the custom for Romans of this period to wear beards. The beard and scepter were attributes of the Genius of the Roman People depicted on Gnaeus Cornelius Lentulus Marcellinus' coins, which I have dated to 74-73. On analogy with Marcellinus' coin discussed earlier, Spinther's figure on the reverse is more reasonably identified as the Genius of the Roman People. It is possible, then, that the head on the obverse is the same Genius of the Roman People.

In the depiction of the Genius of the Roman People on Marcellinus' and Spinther's coins, Crawford saw the assertion of 'the claims of the Roman state against those of the rebel state of Sertorius.'[7] The Spanish references do seem clear. However, both coins by these Lentuli also clearly go beyond any narrow claim of *imperium* limited to Spain. Spinther's imagery repeats the *caput orbis terrarum* theme already seen on Marcellinus' coins of 74-73.

It is particularly important to note that the orb of the world under the right foot of the Genius of the Roman People is symbolic of world domination; the scepter in his left hand and the curule chair on which he sits are both insignia of *imperium*. The goddess Victory is awarding him the crown of victory, and in his right hand the cornucopia symbolizes the fruits of peace which Roman *imperium* bestows.

If we re-date this coin to 70, it could not have been minted for the military campaign in Spain which ended in 72. From the size of the issue, estimated by Crawford at only seven reverse dies, we can assume that it was not used to pay a large army. Although too small for a military issue, the imagery does indeed suggest military victory. Moreover, the bearded head on the coin's obverse is similar to the head on Oscan coinage of Spain, while the Genius of the Roman People had already appeared on money specially minted to pay Pompey's troops. The coin type is strongly flavored with the essence of victory in Spain. This is why most commentators have continued to look to the

Sertorian war for interpretation of this design and date it to the war years. But re-dating to 70 does not eliminate the connection with the Sertorian war. It actually seems to herald the successful completion of that war. The victory in Spain was another step toward the fulfillment of the *caput orbis terrarum* prophecy.

Numismatica Ars Classica Auction 54 Lot 220

> On the reverse, the Genius of the Roman people crowned by a flying Victory sits on a curule chair holding a cornucopia in his right hand and rests his right foot on the orb of the world.

It was also in this year of Pompey's consulship that the Senate took up the last piece of business relating to that war: the issue of land for the discharged veterans from Pompey's and Metellus' armies. Pompey owed this favor to his troops. Not only had they won his victory over Sertorius, they had remained under arms in Italy until he won the consulship of 70 and finally celebrated his triumph. As consul, he was in a position to repay their loyalty by securing passage of the *lex Plautia*. This bill to procure farmland for the soldiers required special funding. These coins may represent the initial money minted for the program. Spinther may have been an urban quaestor entrusted with the minting and the record keeping. The cornucopia he placed in the right hand of the Genius of the Roman People may have alluded to the fruits the soldiers expected to reap from their new farms. Unfortunately, there was too little money in the treasury to carry out the distribution of the promised land, and it had to be postponed.[8]

We know nothing of the career of Spinther for most of the decade following his quaestorship in 70 until he made his name well known among the populace in 63 by impressing them with the extravagant games he held during his aedileship. The goodwill he won then brought him to the urban praetorship in 60. In 59 he held the governorship in Nearer Spain, and was still there when his good friend Cicero was driven into exile by Clodius in 58.[9] Spinther returned to Rome later in 58 to campaign for the consulship and made it known that he would work for the return of Cicero. He brought up the subject his very first day as consul on 1 January 57.[10] During the next months he held public meetings pleading Cicero's case and even induced Pompey to speak on his behalf.[11] Foremost in the efforts to restore Cicero, Lentulus earned not only Cicero's undying gratitude, but also public favor. During his presentation of the *Ludi Apollinares*, the people openly expressed their joy for the vote to return Cicero from exile.[12]

The fate of another exile was also to occupy Spinther's attention during his consulship and beyond. Ptolemy Auletes had been confirmed as king of Egypt by the Roman Senate in 59 after promising Caesar a bribe of 6,000 talents. In 57 he was driven from the throne by his disgruntled subjects on whom fell the burden of Ptolemy's new debt. Ptolemy fled to his friends in Rome and asked the Senate to restore him to his throne. Spinther managed to secure this potentially lucrative appointment since he had already been assigned the governorship of Cilicia which had a standing army capable of effecting Ptolemy's restoration. But the tribune of the plebs Gaius Cato forestalled his mission with the revelation of a Sibylline oracle which foretold trouble if the king of Egypt should be restored to his throne with the use of an army. Although the revelation of the oracle was patently motivated by political rivalry, the religious scruples still had to be dealt with and the project was put up for reconsideration.[13] Cicero, eager to repay the source of his salvation, worked tirelessly to have Spinther's commission approved. He overcame Gaius Cato's next proposal to recall Spinther from his proconsulship; however, he was ultimately outmaneuvered by Ptolemy who widely distributed bribes in an effort to have the commission transferred to Pompey. But Pompey would not openly lay claim to the commission stripped from Spinther, thus allowing jealousy and infighting to continually delay any resolution. The year 56 passed with nothing done. Ptolemy's restoration was only resolved when Gabinius, governor of Syria, undertook the task on his own authority early in 55. Spinther remained in Cilicia until he was replaced by Appius Claudius in 53. He distinguished himself in battle with marauding tribes and was hailed *imperator* by his troops.[14] He returned to Rome to celebrate a triumph but its celebration was delayed for unknown reasons until the end of 51.[15] At the outbreak of the civil war in 49, Spinther joined the senatorial forces led by Pompey. He recruited ten cohorts of new troops and held the town of Asculum in Picenum. When Caesar made for the town with two veteran legions, Spinther abandoned it and was deserted by most of his recruits.[16]

With his few remaining troops, Spinther made for Domitius Ahenobarbus who had twenty cohorts at Corfinium. Convinced he could stop Caesar's rapidly advancing forces there, Domitius continued to hold the town despite Pompey's orders to withdraw. Hoping that Pompey would change his mind, he called on him to come to his support and end the war there. Too quickly Caesar invested the city and relief was impossible. Pompey went south to Brundisium to evacuate his forces from Italy, leaving those at Corfinium to fend for themselves. Domitius made plans for his personal escape, but they were discovered and the soldiers were on the point of turning him over to Caesar when Spinther called down from the walls for a conference with Caesar. The record of that meeting survives in Caesar's words.

> He pleaded with Caesar for his own safety and begged him to spare him. He reminded him of their old friendship and listed the benefits Caesar had conferred on him, which were very great. Through Caesar's influence he had entered into the college of pontiffs, with Caesar's influence he had held the province of Spain after his praetorship, and he had been supported by Caesar in his campaign for the consulship.[17]

As a result of the conference, mercy was granted to all at Corfinium and Spinther retired to his estates at Puteoli.[18] He sent a letter to Cicero expressing his gratitude to Caesar over the treatment at Corfinium.[19] Yet he was uncertain over what he was to do now. He told Cicero that he felt he had done his duty by Pompey and how he dreaded another fiasco like Corfinium. Influenced by Caesar's kindness, but influenced even more by future prospects, he again threw his lot in with Pompey and joined him in Greece.[20] Looking to their future prospects on the eve of the fateful battle at Pharsalus, Domitius Ahenobarbus, Metellus Scipio, and Lentulus Spinther spent their time quarrelling over who would become Pontifex Maximus once Caesar was defeated. Stunned instead by Caesar's victory, Spinther took ship with Pompey in flight from Greece. Separating from Pompey, Spinther made for Rhodes where he was refused any kind of help. His subsequent fate is unknown, but he probably perished shortly thereafter for his son remained particularly bitter about the Rhodians' refusal to receive his father in his time of need.[21] Caesar's treatment of Spinther in his *Civil War* would have posterity recall how Spinther had misused his friendship. But for Cicero, Spinther was always to be remembered in a different light. In his oratorical work *Brutus* Cicero wrote:

> Publius, that avenger of my injury, the author of my salvation, obtained whatever skill of oratory he had from training; the tools of nature were lacking. But the brilliance and scope of his mind were so great that he did not hesitate to acquire for himself all those honors which belong to illustrious men and he held them with every dignity.[22]

Chapter 24

LUCIUS PLAETORIUS 70 BCE

The S•C coin issued by the quaestor Lucius Plaetorius was not found in the Frascarolo, Rignano, or Cabeca hoards whose latest mint magistrate was C. Postumius. It did appear in the Pontecorvo, Cosa, and Palestrina hoards which contained the coins of Cossutius. To Crawford and Grueber, this indicated a date of 74, to Hersh and Walker, a date of 71. Since the hoard evidence associated him most closely with Cossutius, whom I have dated to 70, this same year seems to me to be the best date for Lucius Plaetorius as well. His election to the quaestorship some time before 66 is confirmed by Cicero's reference to him as a senator present in the court during the trial of Cluentius in 66.[1] No other mention of Lucius Plaetorius survives.

Classical Numismatic Group, Inc. Inventory No. 873071

Juno Moneta is on the obverse. The mint was in her temple. The quaestor Lucius Plaetorius placed his name on the reverse near a naked runner carrying a palm branch in his right hand and what has been identified as a *caestus* in his left hand. This is a rare issue and it is hard to find pristine coins.

The obverse of Lucius' coin depicts the draped bust of Juno Moneta wearing a diadem. She is clearly identified by the inscription MONETA behind her head. Juno came by the title Moneta in 390 when the Gauls invaded and sacked Rome. The city below had been given up to plunder, but a strong garrison held the Capitoline. The Gauls, unsuccessful both in their direct assaults and in their siege effort, decided to try a secret nighttime assault. They approached so silently that not even the dogs heard them. However, Juno's sacred geese, which had been spared from the cooking pots, raised the alarm with their cackling and flapping wings alerting the sleeping Romans. The garrison repulsed the attack and Juno gained the title Moneta meaning 'Warner.'[2] A temple was vowed to her in 345 by the dictator Lucius Furius Camillus for the victory over the Aurunci and the temple was dedicated the next year.[3] The Roman mint was eventually located in her temple and from that new association comes our English word 'money.'

The Q•S•C inscribed on the reverse shows that Plaetorius issued this coin during his quaestorship. Juno Moneta on the obverse suggests that he held his office in Rome, not a province, making him a quaestor urbanus for the year 70. The reverse design depicts a naked athlete running. In his right hand, he carries a palm branch extending over his shoulder. The object in his left hand is more difficult to determine. The item is usually described as a *caestus*, a leather thong worn by boxers on their fists. Grueber assumed that Lucius was making a punning allusion to the *cognomen* Cestianus borne by a branch of the *gens* Plaetoria.[4] Crawford accepted the identification of the *caestus* and its punning allusion. He thought that Lucius was a Cestianus, perhaps a cousin of Marcus, the curule aedile who minted in 68, and that both men were grandsons of the senator Lucius Plaetorius, son of Lucius, recorded in the decree of the Senate regarding the Pergamine territory in 129. Crawford also suggested that our moneyer was the father of the Lucius Plaetorius Cestianus who issued the famous EID MAR coin for Brutus in 42.[5] The stemma below gives the suggested lines of descent.

L. Plaetorius, L. f. Papirian tribe
senator in 129

L. Plaetorius	M. Plaetorius aedile of Tusculum
L. Plaetorius (Cestianus) quaestor 70	M. Plaetorius Cestianus curule aedile 69
L. Plaetorius Cestianus moneyer of EID MAR coin	

All of this seems reasonable. But if the point of the coin was to make a punning allusion to the *cognomen* Cestianus, Lucius has been particularly obtuse. The *cognomen* means 'the Cestian' showing that at some point a member of the *gens* Cestia was adopted by a Plaetorius. Without the name Cestianus inscribed on the coin, how did Lucius Plaetorius expect his countrymen to make this additional association? Did Lucius really expect his fellow citizens to recognize the item in the runner's hand to be a *caestus*? If so, why is it in the hands of an athlete who is running, not boxing, or even in a boxing stance? The problem is not solved by Crawford calling him a 'victorious boxer running.' This naked athlete gives no hint of being a boxer. Imhoof-Blumer saw the item dangling from the runner's hand as a fillet[6] and many a Roman may have seen it the same way. If Lucius really wanted to stress the *cognomen* Cestianus, he could have spelled it out as did the other two Plaetorii Cestiani.

If the above stemma is correct, the adoption which produced the *cognomen* Cestianus has to go back at least to the grandfather, in order for the *cognomen* to be common to both the quaestor Lucius and the curule aedile Marcus. The other possibility is that Lucius Plaetorius was not a Cestianus. Marcus may be the adopted son, and the name Cestianus started with him and proceded down his line, making the Lucius Plaetorius Cestianus, who minted the famous EID MAR coin, his son. This produces the following stemma.

L. Plaetorius, L. f.
senator in 129

L. Plaetorius ——————— M. Plaetorius

L. Plaetorius quaestor 70	M. Plaetorius Cestianus curule aedile 68
	L. Plaetorius Cestianus moneyer of EID MAR coin

If the emphasis of the design is not the moneyer's name, what then is the message of Lucius' coin? Grueber suggested that the design may be intended to 'record some great athletic feat achieved by an ancestor of the moneyer.'[7] Pride in athletic prowess was a Greek characteristic, as was the tradition of competition in the nude. This was not something of which a Roman senator was likely to boast, nor would it win him any respect in the eyes of Roman citizens. Grueber's second suggestion that the coin may have been issued on the occasion of some public games is a better possibility, but it has remained largely unexplored and overshadowed by the supposed punning allusion to the *caestus*.

The symbols which Lucius used for control marks (the oil amphora, discus, hoop, stigil, torch, and wreath) also relate to athletics implying a wider range of athletic competition than just running. The palm branch over the naked runner's shoulder signifying victory clearly relates to games. However, the presentations of the major agonistic festivals in Rome were entrusted to the aediles and the praetors, and it is difficult to see why Lucius Plaetorius as a quaestor would be minting. That the Senate would authorize the quaestor urbanus to mint money for games, rather than the aedile or the praetor who presented them, is puzzling and not likely.

Numismatica Ars Classica Auction 46 Lot 896

On the reverse between the legs of the runner, Plaetorius used the symbols of the discus, hoop, stigil, torch, wreath, and an oil amphora as on this coin. All are associated with games that suggest that this special issue is also to be associated with games.

However, if the coin is correctly dated to the year 70, we do have an occasion on which public games were presented outside the normal religious calendar. These were the votive games that Pompey gave during his consulship. The only reference to them in all the ancient literature comes from Cicero's first Verrine oration. Cicero said the games were scheduled to start the third week of August and to last for fifteen days.[8] This generous time period allowed for an extensive series of games as was befitting Pompey's recent victory in Spain. The Senate may have authorized additional public funds for the fulfillment of the vows made on behalf of the state and Pompey as consul in 70 saw to their disbursement through the quaestor Lucius Plaetorius. Instead of an extremely obtuse allusion to a missing *cognomen*, we may have here a far more tangible testament to the votive games of Pompey than the barest mention left us by Cicero.

Classical Numismatic Group, Inc. 172 Lot 150

A discus is the symbol on this reverse die.

Chapter 25

QUINTUS FUFIUS CALENUS 69 BCE

The denarius bearing the name KALENI on the obverse and the name CORDI on the reverse was the first coin to be jointly issued by two moneyers since Sulla's reforms in 81. Hoard evidence offers little help in dating this issue. Forty-eight coins were found in the Mesagne hoard, which suggests only that they were minted before the hoard's terminus of 58. The coin's appearance in the Hev-Szamos hoard should be considered to be a later insertion.

This issue was struck on serrated planchets. The practice had not been used for six years after Egnatius' issue of 77 until it appeared again on Vettius' S•C issue of 71. The other moneyers of 71 and 70 did not follow suit, but after Cossutius the hoards contain serrated issues by three mint magistrates: Crepereius, Aquillius, and Hosidius. The serrated flans of KALENI/CORDI suggest that their issue be associated with the other three serrated issues of this period, but a more precise date can be obtained from prosopographical evidence. Since Calenus is known, I will discuss him and his obverse design first and then deal with his colleague CORDI in the next chapter.

Numismatica Ars Classica Auction 51 Lot 33

Calenus shared this issue with his colleague who signed his name CORDI on the reverse. Calenus put his name KALENI on the obverse under the co-joined heads of Honos and Virtus.

The name KALENI on the obverse is a *cognomen* which means simply 'a man from Cales.' The spelling of KALENI with the letter K transliterates the Latin C to the Greek kappa reflecting the Greek influence in the area of Campania where Cales was located. Our moneyer gave neither his family name nor his *praenomen*, but he is usually identified as Quintus Fufius Calenus, whose praetorship in 59 shows that he had to be starting his political career about ten years beforehand. Crawford dated Calenus to 70; Grueber had dated his coin to 72. Hersh and Walker dated him to 68. A praetorship in 59 shows that Calenus had to be at least 30 years old in 69, and this is an age at which I would expect him to hold the mint magistracy, so I date his coin to 69 as the first of the serrating mint magistrates after Cossutius.

Calenus depicted the co-joined heads of two deities. The god in the forefront is crowned with laurel and wears his hair in ringlets, a style frequently seen on Apollo. However, the inscription HO identifies him as Honos. The more martial god depicted behind him wears a crested helmet and is identified as Virtus by the inscription VIRT. Most interpretations of the coin are made by relating the obverse design to the reverse whose theme of reconciliation between Rome and Italy makes the stronger and more obvious political statement. Grueber said that the obverse shows that the reconciliation of Rome and Italy was under the patronage of the gods Honos and Virtus.[1]

To make this interpretation one must assume that the two moneyers KALENI and CORDI shared a common theme. This is not necessarily so, as the shared issue by Aemilius Lepidus and Scribonius Libo in 63 and the issue by Scaurus and Hypsaeus in 58 show. Since these moneyers chose to inscribe their names on separate sides of the coin as did the moneyers of 63 and 58, I will consider each moneyer's design as a separate statement.

Individually, the gods Honos and Virtus are personifications of abstracts and can be used allegorically. However, the fact that Honos and Virtus are paired here is perhaps more a concrete reference to the temple of these gods than abstract ideas, for Gaius Marius had dedicated a temple to this pair of gods to commemorate his victory over the Cimbri and the Teutons in 101.[2] All other monuments in honor of Marius had been overthrown and destroyed by Sulla. Due to its consecrated nature, the temple to Honos and Virtus was probably the only Marian monument to escape the Sullan purge. Certainly the temple was the most conspicuous Marian survivor; and, as such, the depiction of the co-joined heads of Honos and Virtus could have been recognized by the Roman people as an allusion to Marius whose image could not lawfully be displayed.

Calenus' reference to Marius' temple may have been influenced by recent events. Early in the year 69, Caesar gave a public funeral oration in praise of his aunt Julia, who had been the wife of Gaius Marius. In her funeral procession he had the audacity to display the family portrait bust of Marius, an image which had not been seen since the time he had been declared a public enemy by Sulla. Plutarch said, 'although some cried out against Caesar, the people responded by receiving him with applause and marveled how after so long a time he was bringing back to the city, as if from Hades, the honors of Marius.'[3]

Numismatica Ars Classica Auction 25 Lot 296

> The gods Honos and Virtus are depicted on Calenus' obverse. Gaius Marius had dedicated a temple to them in 101.

Caesar's funeral speech for his aunt Julia in 69 revealed the latent sentiments of the people and Calenus' design played to that feeling. The co-joined heads of Honos and Virtus revealed his Marian sympathies and gave notice of the type of politics he would pursue. Four years later latent public sentiment was to burst forth into open declarations when Caesar, during the public displays of his aedileship in 65, again set up images of Marius and golden figures of Victory carrying trophies, together with inscriptions commemorating Marius' victories over the Cimbri. Plutarch said,

> Offering encouragement to one another, the Marians were amazed by the size of the crowd which suddenly appeared and filled the Capitol with its applause. Tears of joy filled the eyes of many looking on the face of Marius and in their encomiums they extolled the greatness of Caesar, how he above all men was one worthy of Marian kinship.[4]

It should come as no surprise, then, that Calenus' subsequent career was closely tied to Caesar and the group of politicians termed *populares* by Cicero.[5] Calenus' first noted political impact came during his tribunate of the plebs in 61. Rome had just been treated to the scandal of Clodius being caught in women's clothing in Julius Caesar's house during the celebration of the rites of Bona Dea, whose worship was restricted to women only. There was debate regarding the manner in which the trial for sacrilege was to be handled. The first bill proposed that the jurors be chosen by the praetor urbanus rather than through the usual selection by lot. Calenus opposed that measure on the grounds that it gave prerogatives to the Senate and constituted an encroachment of senatorial power on the *lex Aurelia* of 70, which specified that juries were to be chosen from the knights, the Senate, and the *tribuni aerarii*. Calenus offered an alternate bill on jury selection that was carried instead.[6]

The next notice of his career involved another piece of judicial legislation passed in his praetorship in 59. Although the *lex Aurelia* had divided the composition of the juries among three orders, the verdict was given only by the total number voting to condemn or to acquit. This allowed each order to take credit for any good decision and attribute any outrageous one to another order. Calenus carried a bill that required that the orders should cast their votes separately. Each individual vote remained secret, but it was now possible to recognize the disposition of each order.[7]

Calenus' year as praetor coincided with Caesar's consulship and mutual support between Caesar and Calenus is evident from Cicero's statement to Atticus that those opposed to the triumvirate hissed and heckled Calenus wherever he went.[8] Caesar had probably been influential in Calenus' election to the praetorship. His immediate activities following his praetorship are not known, but in 51 we find him serving as one of Caesar's legates in Gaul.[9]

He was back in Italy before Caesar crossed the Rubicon in 49 and he may have been in attendance at the meetings of the Senate that led to the declaration of Caesar as a public enemy. With the outbreak of the civil war, Calenus decided to support Caesar and rushed to meet up with him at Brundisium in early March. On the way, Calenus stopped to visit Cicero at Formiae, where he expressed his total disgust with 'the crimes of Pompey and the folly and stupidity of the Senate.'[10] Calenus loyally supported Caesar for the duration of the civil war. He served in Spain and escorted the defeated Pompeian troops out of the province in 49.[11] When Caesar went to Dyrrhachium, Calenus shared with Mark Antony the responsibility of bringing the remaining troops across to Epirus.[12]

After landing his troops, Calenus was sent to secure Achaea, where he was still occupied in winning over cities to Caesar's cause when Caesar defeated Pompey at Pharsalus. Caesar summoned one of the legions from Calenus and hastened to pursue Pompey to Egypt, leaving Calenus still in command in Achaea. Many of the defeated Pompeians surrendered to Calenus who showed himself to be most moderate in his behavior toward his defeated foes, both Greek and Roman.[13] Cicero, however, hesitated to make his supplication to Calenus, whom he termed as one of his most bitter personal enemies.[14] This sentiment may have been nurtured from the time of Clodius' trial for sacrilege in 61, for Cicero blamed Calenus' jury selection law as partially responsible for Clodius' unbelievable acquittal.

After Caesar's return to Rome in September 47, the dictator rewarded Calenus for his faithful service by appointing him to a consulship for the remainder of the year.[15] When Caesar was assassinated in 44, Calenus was inclined to side with Mark Antony. He tried to dissuade the Senate from what seemed to him the same folly and stupidity that had forced Caesar into rebellion in 49. Cicero was the main voice of opposition to Antony and Book 46 of Dio Cassius' history opens with a very long speech by Calenus answering many of Cicero's charges against Antony that Calenus believed specious. Calenus' long indictment of Cicero's character is an ancient counterweight to Cicero's illustrious modern reputation. In the Senate, the consul Vibius Pansa, who was married to Calenus' daughter, frequently called on Calenus to be the first to express his opinions. Calenus' calls for moderation only prompted Cicero to direct much of his fiery rhetoric of the *Philippics* against Calenus.

When the triumvirs Octavian, Antony, and Lepidus made their compact and agreed on the elimination of their enemies, the *Philippics* sealed Cicero's death warrant. Antony demanded Cicero's head and he was hunted down and killed in 43. Although Calenus did not mourn Cicero's death, he apparently did not participate in the slaughter of the proscriptions. In one of his villas he even hid Varro, the old soldier and scholar, who had commanded some of those defeated Pompeian troops Calenus escorted out of Spain in 49.

When Octavian and Antony fought the battle of Phillipi, Calenus remained in Italy in command of two legions belonging to Antony. On Antony's orders, these legions were turned over to Octavian when he returned to Italy and Calenus took command of Antony's troops in Gaul, where he stayed until his sudden death in 40.[16]

The Marian references of Calenus' coin are dulled by the passage of time, but this coin with the name KALENI inscribed beside images of Honos and Virtus serves as a fitting memorial to a man of amazing constancy in a time of fluctuating loyalties, a man who guided his life keeping those images of Honor and Virtue ever before his eyes.

Chapter 26

CORDIUS 69 BCE

The moneyer who signed his name CORDI on the reverse side of the joint issue with Calenus is unknown. The name CORDI itself presents an immediate problem in how to read the Latin form. Does it stand for the *cognomen* Cordus or the *nomen* Cordius? Grueber and Crawford assumed that it was the *cognomen* Cordus in the genitive case paralleling the *cognomen* KALENI on the obverse. In late Republican times, the *cognomen* Cordus could be associated with the Caesii, Cremutii, Julii, and Servii, but both Grueber and Crawford, looking back into the earliest years of the Republic, identified the moneyer as a Mucius Scaevola who traced his line back to Gaius Mucius Cordus.

When the Tarquins were expelled from Rome in 509, they sought the help of Lars Porsena, the Etruscan king of Clusium. In his attempt to restore the exiled Tarquins, Porsena laid siege to Rome and hoped to starve it into submission. The young aristocrat Gaius Mucius, incensed by this humiliation, won permission from the Senate to make his way into Porsena's camp to assassinate him. When he arrived, it happened to be payday for the army and the king was seated on a raised platform with his secretary nearby. Both the king and his secretary were dressed alike and Mucius was unsure which of the two the king was. He did not dare ask lest he expose himself, so he decided to attack the man whom the soldiers kept addressing. He rushed forward and stabbed him, but was quickly surrounded and seized by the guards. He had guessed wrong. Dragged before the king, he was unmoved by fear. To the king's questions he replied that he was a Roman who had come to kill his enemy Porsena and having failed he had as much courage to die as he had to kill. Porsena was enraged and demanded that he reveal who else was involved in the plot or else be burned alive. With the cry, 'Look, that you may know how cheap the body is to those who see great glory,' he thrust his right arm into the flames kindled for a sacrifice and held it there unflinching. Astounded, Porsena leapt up to his feet and had Mucius dragged away from the fire. Admiring his courage, he granted him his life and freedom. Mucius, as if to thank him, told Porsena that three hundred such young men were ready to draw lots for the honor of assassinating him. He was but the first. Porsena realized the resolve of the Romans and shortly after Mucius was released he sent envoys to negotiate peace terms. In honor of his heroic act, Gaius Mucius was afterwards known as Scaevola, the Left-Handed Man.[1]

Crawford said that this story as told by Livy was 'redolent with the themes of *honos* and *virtus* and it is reasonable to suppose that a later Mucius would wish to claim descent from the legendary hero and would advertise his achievement and the esteem which followed.'[2] Convinced that the moneyer was a Mucius, Crawford identified him as Publius Mucius Scaevola who was attested as pontifex in 69.

Classical Numismatic Group, Inc. Inventory no. 886103 ex Leu 75 Lot 1430

The moneyer's name CORDI in the exergue has frequently been interpreted as a *cognomen* associated with the Mucia *gens* and the coin is referenced as Mucia 1 in *Roman Silver Coins*. The moneyer's reverse design shows Italia on the left and Roma on the right clasping hands. Roma has her foot on the orb of the world.

I see two problems in identifying our moneyer as a Mucius Scaevola. First, Gaius Mucius earned the *cognomen* Scaevola for his act of bravery and that name epitomized his virtue, not the *cognomen* Cordus. In fact, Livy never even mentioned that Mucius' original *cognomen* was Cordus. Nor can the *cognomen* Cordus again be found for any later Mucii who proudly bore the name Scaevola. Scaevola, not the obscure *cognomen* Cordus, evoked the images of Gaius Mucius' heroic act.

Secondly, there is nothing in the reverse design that alludes to Mucius' attempt to assassinate Porsena. The moneyer CORDI depicted the personifications of Italia on the left identified by the ligature ITAL and Roma on the right identified by the inscription RO. They stand clasping each other's right hand. Italia wears a long chiton and holds a cornucopia cradled in her left arm. Roma, on the right, is diademed and wears a slightly shorter chiton. She holds what appears to be a spear in her left hand, which is so identified by Grueber, but Crawford calls it a *fasces*. This picture recalls the two fatherlands Cicero said each townsman of the Italian *municipia* shared, one of nature, one of citizenship. In this design one readily sees the reconciliation between Italy and Rome following the Social War. The caduceus behind Italia and the cornucopia in her arm symbolize both peace and prosperity; the clasped hands show reconciliation and cooperation. Beneath Roma's right foot is the orb of the world, as seen earlier under the foot of the Genius of the Roman People on Lentulus Spinther's coin. Our moneyer's design celebrates Italia's shared role in exercising Roman *imperium* over the orb of the whole world.

This new state of affairs brought far more satisfaction to the Italians than to the old Roman citizens, many of whom considered the townsmen from the *municipia* foreigners. Cicero advised his friend Lucius Manlius Torquatus that such contempt was misguided, and perhaps, fatal to one's hopes of winning office.

> Chosen from the whole of Italy they will soon contend with you for every office and honor. Beware of calling any of them 'foreigners' lest you are buried by the votes of foreigners. If they bring energy and industry, believe me, they will drive that boastful talk from you and make you wake up, nor will they allow themselves to be surpassed by you in office, unless beaten by excellence.[3]

The figures for the census taken 70/69 revealed the huge number of new citizens who had been added to the rolls. To the almost 400,000 Roman citizens before the Social War, some 500,000 new Italian citizens had been added. With the representation of Italia, this moneyer acknowledged the importance of the Italian voters for election to Roman magistracies. Our moneyer appears to associate himself with those Italians who will not be surpassed unless beaten by excellence.

If the two sides of this coin function separately, we no longer need assume that CORDI is a *cognomen* in the genitive like KALENI. This brings us to the other possibility that the name is the *nomen* Cordius. CORDI would be the normal way a Cordius would abbreviate his name on a coin whether he intended it to be in the nominative or the genitive. Manius Cordius, triumvir of the mint in 46 inscribed his name MN•CORDI (Crawford 463/1b).

The Cordia *gens* is virtually unknown in Roman history. Our first certain notice of the name in Rome was when the moneyer Manius Cordius Rufus placed it on coins in 46. Manius Cordius' obverse depicting the co-joined heads of the Dioscuri suggests that the family came from Tusculum where there was a special cult to the Dioscuri. This assumption is further supported by the survival of a local inscription from Tusculum recording a Manius Cordius Rufus, son of Manius, who had held the offices of praetor, proconsul, and *aedilis lustrando Monti Sacro.*[4] It seems better to me to identify the CORDI of this coin as Manius Cordius Rufus from Tusculum, the father of the Caesarian moneyer. Since he probably shared a similar *popularis* political philosophy with his fellow moneyer Calenus, we are not surprised to find the family name Cordius connected with offices under Caesar's dictatorship.

This moneyer who only signed his name CORDI may have been the first of the *gens* Cordia to enter into the stream of Roman politics, an opportunity made easier by the enfranchisement of so many new Italian voters. His coin design testifies to the importance that new men placed on the Italian voters from the *municipia*.

Chapter 27

QUINTUS POMPONIUS RUFUS 69 BCE

The moneyer who signed his name Q•POMPONI on the reverse and RVFVS on the obverse is unknown. To further complicate matters, his coin does not appear in any of the hoards of the period, including the Mesagne hoard. Crawford dated Pomponius to the year 73 because of the similarity of his obverse to that of Publius Lentulus Spinther, whom he dated to 74, and the similarity of his system of control marks to that of Crepereius, whom he dated to 72.[1] This relative arrangement of Lentulus, Pomponius, and Crepereius had already been determined by Count de Salis, whose work Grueber followed to arrive at his date of 74. When Hersh and Walker lowered Crepereius' date to 69, they kept Pomponius in the same relative position but moved him to 70.

Classical Numismatic Group, Inc. Nomos 1 Lot 133

> Quintus Pomponius Rufus' coin is one of the rarest of Republican issues. Jupiter is on the obverse and his eagle standing on a scepter is on the reverse. The number VII on this reverse die is below the eagle's foot and a scorpion is on the right by his wing.

Pomponius' control marks on the reverse are helpful in determining a relative date for his coin. The moneyers immediately following the Sullan reforms in 81 were more inclined to use control marks than the later moneyers. Fourteen of the twenty-four moneyers up to and including Crepereius used control marks. Of the ten not using control marks, seven of them minted between 72 and 69 which indicates that the practice was passing. After Crepereius only four other Republican moneyers used control marks on their issues: Marcus Plaetorius who immediately followed Crepereius; Roscius Fabatus, in imitation of his fellow townsman Papius; Cassius, who used the letters of his own name; and Piso Frugi, who copied his father's earlier issue. For his control marks, Pomponius used Roman numerals from I to VIII and associated each with a different symbol: I with bee, no example of II has been found, III with prawn, IIII with bird, V with fish, VI with snake, VII with scorpion, VIII with frog. The control numbers tell us that Pomponius' issue was small, since no more than one set of dies was used for each pair of control marks. The pattern of pairing numbers with animals parallels that of Crepereius who paired Roman letters with marine animals. It seems that one system inspired the other, suggesting that we associate Crepereius and Pomponius in a fairly close time period.

The S•C inscription of the coin indicates that this money was minted for a special purpose. Is there anything in the design that can hint at its purpose? The laureate head of Jupiter occupies the obverse. The reverse depicts an eagle perched on a scepter with his right foot raised holding a wreath. A supposed relationship between the design and the moneyer was found by Grueber in the claim of the *gens* Pomponia to be descended from Pompo, a son of Numa. Grueber wrote that 'the type of Jupiter and his eagle may refer to the tradition that to Numa were revealed the conjurations for compelling Jupiter himself to make known his will by lightning and the flight of birds.'[2] The claims of the *gens* Pomponia to descent from Numa were well known in antiquity and already proclaimed on a coin (*ca.* 97) by Lucius Pomponius Molo who depicted Numa standing before an altar. However, the head of Jupiter and his eagle on Pomponius Rufus' coin do not immediately call to mind Numa who is nowhere on the coin. Crawford felt that the eagle was present on Rufus' coin only as an attribute of Jupiter, the chief god of the Roman state.

If the same relative dating which has Pomponius minting the year before Crepereius is maintained, Pomponius Rufus' coin must be dated to 69 in my arrangement. This was a year very special to Jupiter and his eagle, for their Capitoline temple which had burned to the ground in 83 had finally reached a point where it could be rededicated. Later coins minted by the moneyer Petillius Capitolinus in 43 affirm the special relationship between the god, his eagle, and the temple. Petillius depicted the head of Jupiter and his eagle on a thunderbolt on the obverses of separate coins that had common reverses depicting the temple of Jupiter Capitolinus. The Capitoline temple that was home to Jupiter and his eagle is missing from Rufus' coin design, but the temple would have been easily incorporated into the picture in the minds of the Romans who celebrated the spectacular rededication of the temple in 69.[3]

The original temple of Jupiter Capitolinus dedicated in 509 burned on 6 July 83. Quintus Lutatius Catulus won the privilege of reconstructing the temple upon the death of Sulla in 78. We saw in Volteius' chapter that he preserved the original size of the temple, but as befitted Rome's new imperial status, he undertook extensive embellishment. The golden gleam of the gilded bronze roof tiles could be seen at a great distance, adding majesty.[4] Enough of the temple structure was completed to be dedicated and opened for worship in 69, but the detail work went on for years. During his praetorship in 62, Caesar claimed that this work was still only half done and he tried to have Catulus' name removed from the dedicatory inscription, charging him with embezzlement and demanding an accounting of the expenses.[5] But Catulus weathered this attack and his name remained engraved in the dedication until the temple was again destroyed by fire in 69 CE.

Classical Numismatic Group, Inc. 81 Lot 952

Classical Numismatic Group, Inc. Triton XII Lot 515

These two coins by Petillius Capitolinus in 43 show the close connection that Romans made between Jupiter, the eagle, and Jupiter's temple.

Caesar's quarrel with Catulus makes it clear that the funds for reconstruction were state moneys administered by Catulus. It is not likely that special coinage was issued for the sundry construction costs of the temple, but the dedication of the temple was something special, a one time event requiring a special allocation of money for public entertainment. We do know that there were dramatic performances given in the theaters in Rome and Pliny tells us that Catulus was the first in Rome to go to the added extravagance of having canvas awnings spread to provide shade for the spectators.[6] We do not have the details on the dedication ceremonies, but Tacitus' description of the ceremonies held for the rededication of the site in 70 CE for the temple that replaced Catulus' preserves some important aspects of the rites. The rubble was cleared from the site and the whole area to be dedicated was marked off by a line of fillets and wreaths. A procession of soldiers with propitious names carried auspicious boughs into the area. The Vestal Virgins followed. They thoroughly sprinkled the site with water drawn from springs and streams. Then the praetor, guided in the ritual by the pontifex, sacrificed a pig, sheep, and bull and offered the entrails on an altar of turf. Then he put his hands on the fillets tied around the foundation stone at which sign the other officials and priests, senators, and knights strained on the ropes and pulled the stone into place.[7]

The prominence of the fillets and the wreaths used in the rededication of the temple's site in 70 CE suggests that the wreath held in the claw of Jupiter's eagle is something other than a victory wreath, perhaps a dedicatory wreath. And what about the scepter? Every other representation of the eagle on Republican coinage depicts him standing with both feet planted firmly on a thunderbolt as on Petillius' coin. Here the imagery has been changed; he stands on a scepter, grasping it with only one foot while extending a wreath in the other. Why does the eagle stand on a scepter? We should recall that originally when construction started on the foundation of Jupiter's temple, a human head was discovered with features intact and that it was interpreted as a portent that Rome would become the *caput rerum*.[8] Tacitus said the temple was the 'seat of Jupiter, founded by our ancestors under propitious auspices as a pledge of our *imperium*.'[9] With the rededication of the temple, not only was Jupiter once again enthroned in his temple, but the promise that Rome was to be the head of world was reaffirmed. The re-dating of the coin opens up the possibility that it was minted to cover the costs of the dedication of the temple in 69. The S•C designation, the small mintage, and the theme of Jupiter and his eagle are consistent with such an expenditure.

A. Tkalec AG Auction 2005 Lot 184

This variant has the number IIII on the scepter and a bird to the right of the eagle.

Chapter 28

PUBLIUS SULPICIUS GALBA 69 BCE

Publius Sulpicius Galba, whose name is inscribed on his coin as P•GALB, minted an S•C issue as curule aedile and is one of the few moneyers from this period for whom we have any historical information. This is fortunate since all hoard evidence is lacking before his coin appears in the Mesagne hoard. In a letter to Atticus in July 65, Cicero wrote that Publius Galba was the only candidate actively campaigning so early for the consulship of 63, but his haste had so far only brought him rejection.[1] Galba failed to win the election, but his candidacy in 65 for the consulship of 63 attests to an unrecorded praetorship which he must have held by 66. This gives us a birth date by 106. His S•C coin inscribed AED CVR or AE CVR is the only evidence of the aedileship which he would have been eligible to hold in 69. This date then becomes the year of his coinage. Cicero characterized Galba as *sobrius et sanctus*. *Sobrius* translates as reasonable, even-minded, and circumspect and was a trait Cicero had to respect in the man whom Verres had rejected from the panel of judges in his trial for extortion in 70. Galba had a reputation for severity and Verres felt he would not be able to win over Galba even with a bribe.[2] The second adjective *sanctus* is better illustrated by the images on his coin.

Classical Numismatic Group, Inc. 79 Lot 928

Vesta on the obverse coupled with the priestly implements on the reverse advertises the priesthood of pontiff which Galba held at the time he minted as curule aedile. This reverse die has a ligature for AED to the left of the knife and CVR to the right of the axe.

The head of Vesta or a Vestal Virgin occupies the obverse. The reverse has three sacrificial implements: a knife and an axe used in the blood sacrifice of the victim flank a single handle vessel variously called a *simpulum* or *culullus*, a vessel used for pouring out liquids. Grueber said that these implements related to the 'priestly functions as curule aedile.'[3] The aedileship, however, was not a priesthood. A denarius minted by Gaius Antonius (Crawford 484) shows two of the same implements that we see on Galba's coin. Antonius' inscription PONTIFEX beneath the implements shows that Galba's symbols are an allusion to the pontificate. A passage from Livy illuminates the functions of a pontifex as established by Numa at the time he chose Numa Marcius the first pontifex.

> He entrusted to him all the sacred rites, having written down and spelled out what victims to use, on what days and in what sanctuaries the sacrifices were to be performed, and even from what source the money was to be sought for those expenses. All the other rites both public and private he made subject to the decree of the pontifex so that the plebs would have someone to whom they could go for consultation, lest there be confusion over any divine law either through neglect of our own ancestral rites or the adoption of foreign rites. And the pontifex not only teaches on the ceremonies of the gods in heaven, but also on the proper funerary rites and placating the spirits of the dead; and he teaches what prodigies sent either by lightning or in some other form should be recognized and propitiated.[4]

Freeman and Sear Mail Bid Sale 14 Lot 366

> Many reverse dies have only AE for the office of aedile. This coin came from the Mesagne hoard.

The head of Vesta on the obverse shows the close connection the pontificate had with Vesta and the Vestal Virgins. The pontiffs had oversight of the ceremonies of Vesta. The Vestal Virgins attended most of the pontifical ceremonies and also attended the pontifical banquets. Trials of delinquent Vestal Virgins were referred to the pontifical college for judgment on their lives.[5] The priesthood was originally restricted to the patricians. After Numa, the number was soon increased to four. In 300, it was opened to plebeians and four more members were added.[6] Sulla increased the number of the college to sixteen, including the pontifex maximus. Membership was by a combination of cooption and election. When a vacancy occurred, the members of the college nominated two candidates who were then voted on by seventeen tribes selected by lot.

A piece of trivia found in Macrobius' *Saturnalia* offers a glimpse into the privileged position of the members of the college.

> Accept it as a fact that the most important dignitaries lacked no luxury. I refer to a pontifical dinner of the distant past which is described in these words in the fourth catalog of the pontifex maximus Metellus. On the ninth day before the Kalends of September, the day when Lentulus was inaugurated as the flamen of Mars, the house was decorated, and the ivory couches were arranged in the dining hall. The pontiffs Q. Catulus, M. Aemilius Lepidus, D. Silanus, C. Caesar, the chief priest, P. Scaevola Sextus, Q. Cornelius, P. Volumnius, P. Albinovanus, and L. Julius Caesar, the augur who inaugurated Lentulus, reclined on two couches. On the third couch were the Vestal Virgins Popilia, Perpennia, Licinia, and Arruntia, and Lentulus' wife Publicia, and his mother-in-law Sempronia. This was the dinner: the hors d'oeuvres were sea-urchins, raw oysters as many as they wanted, shellfish, mussels, thrush on asparagus, fattened hens, a dish of oysters and scallops, black mussels, white mussels, then a second round of mussels, shellfish, sea nettles, fig-peckers, goat loin, boar loin, fattened hens wrapped in pastry, more fig-peckers, and two types of purple fish. For the main courses, boar heads, a dish of fishes, a dish of sow udders, ducks, rabbits, boiled teal, roasted fattened hens, cakes and bread of Picenum.[7]

Generation after generation of Sulpicii Galbae can be found in the college of the pontiffs. Publius followed in the footsteps of family tradition and it was this priesthood he chose to advertise to his fellow citizens thereby cultivating his image as *sanctus*, a pious and holy man. Galba's membership in the college is attested for the year 57 when Cicero returned from exile and requested of the Senate that his house on the Palatine be restored to him. Clodius, who had it leveled and in its place consecrated a shrine to Libertas, opposed Cicero's request on the grounds that the site was now sacred. The matter was referred to the college of pontiffs which unanimously absolved the property from sanctity. Galba was mentioned as one of the members of the college and this is the last notice we have of the man.[8] The implements of the pontifex on this coin offer evidence that Publius Sulpicius Galba was already a pontifex when he minted as curule aedile in 69.

Publius Sulpicius Galba 69 BCE

This was the first time under the Sullan constitution that an aedile minted. With an estimated fifty-three reverse dies, Galba's S•C issue is a good bit larger than any of the previous four S•C issues. Are we able to determine what program required special money to be issued and administered by a curule aedile? One clue comes from the earlier coin minted by the plebeian aediles Marcus Fannius and Lucius Critonius discussed earlier. The ears of grain beside their chairs clearly indicate that they were involved in grain acquisition. Can a similar purpose be reasonably postulated for Galba's issue even though there is no hint of it in his design? The *lex Terentia et Cassia* of 73 attempted to alleviate severe grain shortages which plagued Rome. Extra grain was to be purchased from Sicily and paid for by an assignment of the revenues from the tax farming companies and the state treasury. Verres' misappropriation of the funds allocated to buy additional grain from Sicily had done serious damage to the Senate's efforts to alleviate the problem. Vettius' S•C coinage suggests that Sicilian revenues had fallen short in the last year of Verres' praetorship and extra money had to be minted. Grain had become even more scarce and expensive since the Sicilian farmers had withdrawn land from grain production rather than have the fruits of their labor stolen by the governor. When Metellus took over the province in 70, he had a major public relations problem trying to convince the farmers to return to their farms and plant grain.[9] The need that had generated the *lex Terentia et Cassia* had not gone away, but only grown worse. If Galba's coin is dated to 69, it falls within the span of time following Verres' prosecution in 70 (hence, no reference to such purchases in Cicero's *Verrine Orations*) and the appointment of Pompey to the Pirate War in 67. Grain still had to be purchased and the program may have been placed under the control of the curule aediles of 69.

Chapter 29

QUINTUS CREPEREIUS ROCUS 68 BCE

Quintus Crepereius Rocus is another moneyer who only made his mark in history by leaving his name on coinage. Crepereius' coin was in the Ossero hoard with Cossutius and it was in the Tolfa hoard with Cossutius, Lucius Plaetorius, and Lentulus Spinther, all of whom I have assigned to 70. This suggests that his mint magistracy should be assigned to 69 following Cossutius, but I feel that the prosopographical evidence for Fufius Calenus, whose coin seldom appears in hoards, indicates that his coin belongs in the year 69. Therefore, I have assigned Crepereius to 68. Crepereius' coin like the joint issue of Calenus and Cordius has a serrated flan.

Numismatica Ars Classica Auction 46 Lot 383

A lovely unidentified sea goddess graces the obverse of Quintus Crepereius' coin. The control marks are a D and a fish. Neptune on the reverse rides on the tails of two hippocamps holding the reins in his left hand. Q•CREPEREI ROCVS is inscribed beneath.

The artistic rendering of the design on the coin of the moneyer Quintus Crepereius who inscribed his name Q•CREPEREI ROCVS on some dies and Q•CREPER•M•F ROCVS on others is somewhat more lovely than what the Romans had come to expect. Instead of ending the portrait bust of the goddess at the neck, the moneyer has included her shoulders and the upper portion of her back. Her face is in profile looking over her right shoulder, but the perspective is from behind her back. Her back is twisted slightly so that her chin and her right shoulder are in a vertical straight line. Her gown dips across her back and flows up over her shoulder in a wave effect. A braid of hair sweeps down from the right side of her head and flows across her bare back separating at the end into wavy strands that blend with her loose hair. The artistry appears more Greek than Roman.

The coin's reverse, at first glance, has the appearance of a typical two-horse chariot design. The horses' heads and forefeet are depicted in the usual way of horses pulling a chariot, but the rear portion of the horses is drawn out into the tails of fish. These were the special sea horses of Neptune, the fanciful Greek creatures called hippocamps. There is no chariot; Neptune rides the tails of the hippocamps. Neptune's appearance on the reverse has led to the identification of the goddess on the obverse as Neptune's wife, Amphitrite, who was one of the fifty daughters of Nereus. Without the benefit of an inscription, this identification cannot be certain, but the special system of control marks that Crepereius devised to keep track of production reinforces the impression that the goddess is indeed a marine deity. Ten different marine animals were used on the obverse dies. Each animal is paired with a given letter, which appears on both the obverse and reverse: A/Dolphin; B/Turtle; C/Crab; D/Fish; E/Octopus F/Squid; G/Flat fish; H/Sponge; I/Sea anemone; K/Heron.

Numismatica Ars Classica Auction 54 Lot 222

This die variant has a sponge and an H for the control marks.

Crawford noted that the name Crepereius appeared among those of businessmen operating in the Greek East and suggested that the marine types and control symbols 'are tolerably appropriate for a man with such a background.'[1] However, there is certainly more working here than a statement of his business connections. Grueber suggested that the marine deities referred to some naval victory in which an ancestor took part.[2] There is no reason for us nor was there for Crepereius' fellow Romans to believe that any Crepereius had a significant role in any naval victory. The only surviving mention of the family name in literature names a Marcus Crepereius, an elected military tribune for 69, who was a juror in Verres' trial for extortion in 70. On some dies, our moneyer declared himself son of Marcus, which has led to speculation that Verres' juror was our moneyer's father or an older brother. The twenty-four elective offices of military tribune were open to men who had served a minimum of five years in the army and the office was usually held prior to the time a man ran for the quaestorship, so it is most likely that Marcus was the moneyer's older brother. Cicero said that Marcus Crepereius was from 'a family of knights distinguished by the strictest discipline.'[3] The fact that his family was still called *equestris* suggests that none of its members had reached a position high enough to be in command of a fleet. The tribune Marcus and our moneyer Quintus are the earliest known Crepereii in Rome.

Crepereius is most likely claiming divine ancestors just as other moneyers had done before him. Crepereius is offering the Roman voters his pedigree. He is descended from powerful marine deities. Since the goddess on the obverse is unnamed, he allows us to draw our own conclusions about who she is and we readily identify her today as Amphitrite because of Neptune on the reverse, but she could be any one of dozens of sea nymphs. An article on the *gens* Crepereia by Barbara Levick and Shelagh Jameson provides us some additional information on the family.

> The Crepereii came from the centre of the peninsula, ultimately from Sabine territory. The name occurs at Capena, a town in southern Etruria which lies very near the borders of Sabine country, and at Nomentum, a Sabine town proper. In confirmation of the Sabine origin of the Crepereii we have Varro's statement that the word *creper* itself meaning 'obscure' is Sabine, and at Bononia or Mutina we find a Crepereia with the *cognomen* Sabina.[4]

Quintus Crepereius' *cognomen* Rocus is rare and, although it belonged to Romilius the consul in 455, it was not a word of common Latin usage. In a context of sea imagery, it may be onomatopoeic for the sound of the crashing waves and may well be derived from the Greek word 'rhokthos' which means 'the roaring of the sea.' But perhaps a clearer indication that the Crepereii looked to marine deities for their origin can be seen in an inscription found at Vienna which recorded a certain businessman named Lucius Crepereius Marinus[5] whose *cognomen* translates 'of or belonging to the sea.'

Numismatica Ars Classica Auction 44 Lot 345

On this die, the moneyer spelled his name Q•CREPER•M•F ROCVS.

Chapter 30

MARCUS PLAETORIUS CESTIANUS 68/67 BCE

The moneyer Marcus Plaetorius Cestianus issued seven different coin types. All are S•C issues and two are marked AED•CVR indicating that he was curule aedile when he issued them. None of the issues appear until the Kavalla, San Gregorio, and Mesagne hoards and of the seven only the two types inscribed AED•CVR are found in these hoards. Using two passages from Cicero's speech *Pro Cluentio*, which was delivered in 66, we can fairly closely date the year in which Cestianus held the curule aedileship. Cicero remarked that Cestianus and Flaminius were serving as judges in the second and third sections of the murder courts that year.[1] Earlier in the speech Cicero said that he had recently argued a case on behalf of Decimus Matrinius before these two men when they were curule aediles. This sets 67 as the latest year for their aedileship. Cicero's client had been degraded to a lower order by the censors of 70.[2] This date then becomes the upper limit. But in 70, Cestianus brought a suit in the extortion court against Marcus Fonteius who had served as governor of Gaul. Cestianus would not prosecute such an action while serving as an aedile, so the year 70 is eliminated. We have already assigned Sulpicius Galba to 69 and since we know that Cestianus' colleague was Flaminius, not Galba, we are left with the years 68 and 67 as the only choices. Unfortunately, nothing more is known of Cestianus' colleague Flaminius to be useful in dating their aedileship. Grueber, following de Salis, assigned his aedileship and all his coins to 68.[3] Broughton felt that the year 67 was more likely for Cestianus' aedileship citing the example of Julius Caesar who served as a judge in the murder courts the year right after his aedileship. Crawford accepted Broughton's date of 67.[4]

Broughton's suggestion took no notice of the association to be made with the other AED•CVR coin issued by Galba within the same close time frame. Galba and Plaetorius Cestianus were the only two curule aediles to mint between 81 and 58 and I have suggested that after Verres made such a fiasco of the *lex Terentia et Cassia* that the Senate entrusted the program to the curule aediles and the S•C coinage issued by Galba in 69 was used to pay for grain. The grain shortage only continued to grow worse in 68 and the Senate could not abandon the program. It is reasonable to see in Cestianus' AED•CVR issue a continuation of the grain program into 68 and, therefore, I date Cestianus' aedileship to 68. These two S•C issues by the curule aediles Galba and Cestianus then fall into the years between the crisis created by Verres' mishandling of the *lex Terentia et Cassia* and Pompey's appointment to deal with the grain problem in 67.

Since we have a better time frame for the dating of Cestianus' two AED•CVR coins, we will deal with them first. On the obverse of one of his coins is the turret-crowned head of Cybele. Long locks of hair fall down her neck. A forepart of a lion is behind her shoulder on some dies, recalling the lions that draw her chariot as seen on Volteius' coin. On other variants there is a cornucopia for fertility. Beneath her chin is the orb of the world indicating that she is the Great Mother. One of the duties of the curule aediles was the presentation of her games, the *Ludi Megalenses*. The coin is simply emblematic of the office of curule aedile. Along the left edge of the coin is the moneyer's *cognomen* CESTIANVS. On the reverse is the curule chair surrounded by the inscription M•PLAETORIVS AED•CVR EX•S•C. This coin is basically a repetition of the type that the curule aedile Furius Crassipes used in the late 80s. Commentators have speculated that Furius' issue was used to purchase grain.

Gemini Numismatic Auctions, LLC Auction VIII Lot 203

Cestianus used a turret-crowned Cybele on his curule aedile coin, adding the orb of the world beneath her chin. The forepart of a lion is over her shoulder. The control mark on the reverse is a serpent.

Classical Numismatic Group, Inc. Inventory no. 786861.

This variant has a poppy over her shoulder and a rare butterfly for the control symbol on the reverse. The curule chair is intended as a symbol of his office of curule aedile.

Classical Numismatic Group, Inc. Triton IX Lot 1280

This coin minted by Publius Furius Crassipes in the late 80s was in circulation when Cestianus minted his similar type as curule aedile.

The deity on Plaetorius' second AED•CVR type is much more enigmatic and intriguing. The goddess wears a crested helmet like Minerva, her hair falls in long ringlets like Apollo's, she is winged like Victory, and carries a bow and quiver like Diana. The wreath of laurel, grain, poppy, and lotus on the helmet recalls the Egyptian goddess Isis. Babelon, followed by Grueber, identified the goddess as Vacuna. Horace mentioned Vacuna in *Epistles* 1.10.49 and from the scholiast Porphyrion we learn that Vacuna was a Sabine deity of uncertain form and nature; some thought she was Bellona, some Minerva, others Diana; Varro identified Vacuna with Victory.

Classical Numismatic Group, Inc. Triton IX Lot 1298

The enigmatic deity on the obverse of Cestianus' second AED•CVR coin is usually described in catalogs as a helmeted and draped bust with attributes of Isis, Minerva, Apollo, Diana, and Victory.

Crawford said that the traditional identification of Cestianus' figure as Vacuna was impossible and felt that Alfoldi's suggestion that it was Isis was perhaps correct and that the eagle on the reverse represented a Ptolemaic eagle. The problem with the identification is finding a goddess that the whole range of attributes will fit. In discussing this goddess on Plaetorius' coin in Appendix Fifteen of his book on the Nile mosaic at Palestrina, P. G. P. Meyboom points out, 'The only goddess who may have a cornucopia as well as armour and wings is Fortuna.'[5] This is the best suggestion for the enigmatic goddess.

The Plaetorii were apparently from the town of Tusculum. An inscription from Tusculum recorded the service of a Marcus Plaetorius, son of Lucius, as a local aedile who was entrusted with the care of the temple of Fortuna.[6] Moreover, a senator Lucius Plaetorius was recorded as a member of the Papirian tribe and Tusculum was in the Papirian tribe.

A.Tkalec AG Auction May 2005 Lot 188

On the reverse a young boy holds a tablet inscribed SORS which refers to the temple of Fortuna at Praeneste. The Plaetorii Cestiani were closely associated with the town that was most famous for its temple of Fortuna.

However, our moneyer's *cognomen* Cestianus indicates that either he or an earlier family member was adopted into the *gens* Plaetoria from the *gens* Cestia. This adoption has been discussed earlier in the chapter on Lucius Plaetorius and it seems probable that Marcus Plaetorius Cestianus himself was the man who was adopted. Inscriptions from Praeneste have been found with the family name Cestius,[7] and Cestianus' reverse design on one of the non-AED•CVR coins is useful to consider here for the light it sheds on his family line. The young boy on the reverse holding a tablet marked SORS can readily be identified with the temple of Fortuna at Praeneste. A passage from Cicero's *De Divinatione* illuminates the significance of this design.

> What is casting lots (*sors*)? It is much like playing mora, casting knuckle bones or throwing dice, games which depend on chance and luck, not reason and plan. The whole thing was devised in deceit, either for profit or to promote superstition and error. And so, just as we did in the case of soothsaying, let us investigate the traditional origin of the most famous lots. The annals of Praeneste declare that Numerius Suffustius, an honorable and noble man, became thoroughly terrified by repeated dreams which had finally turned threatening, ordering him to cut open a flint rock lying in a certain place. He set about the task in spite of the ridicule of his fellow townsmen. When the rock had been broken open, lots inscribed in ancient letters on pieces of oak leapt forth. The spot is piously enclosed today. It is located near the statue of the infant Jupiter who,

> nursing together with Juno, sits in the lap of Fortuna reaching for her breast, a statue most piously revered by mothers.
>
> At the same time and in the same place where the temple of Fortuna now stands, they say that honey flowed from an olive tree and the soothsayers said that those lots would be held in the highest repute. At their bidding a chest was made from that olive tree and the lots were placed in it. Today the lots are drawn from the chest at the direction of Fortuna. How then can one have confidence in these lots which at Fortuna's direction are mixed around and drawn out by the hand of a boy? How were those lots deposited in that place? Who cut the oak, worked it, and inscribed it? People respond, 'There is nothing which god cannot do.' Would that god were able to make the Stoics wise so that they not believe everything with superstitious anxiety and distress! But now, indeed, common usage has rejected this type of divination. Still, the beauty and antiquity of the shrine at Praeneste even now retains the name of Sors, that is, among the common folk. For what magistrate or what reputable man consults lots? Indeed, in all other places lots have lost their appeal, which, according to Clitomachus, prompted Carneades' remark that he had never seen Fortuna more fortunate than at Praeneste.[8]

It would seem then that Cestianus' SORS type refers to the temple of Fortuna at Praeneste and is an allusion to his hometown, just as Papius' and Procilius' depiction of Juno Sospita was an allusion to their hometown Lanuvium. Since Plaetorius Cestianus may be associated with Tusculum by adoption and with Praeneste by birth, and since neither of these towns were Sabine towns, there is no particular reason to assume that Cestianus would depict the obscure Sabine goddess Vacuna on his coins. At Tusculum we have evidence of a Plaetorius connected with the temple of Fortuna and since the Cestii's town Praeneste was most famous for its temple of Fortuna, the goddess most likely to be of influence in Plaetorius Cestianus' life was Fortuna.

Can the strange goddess on Plaetorius' AED•CVR coin really be Fortuna? No description of the specific iconography of Praeneste's Fortuna exists, only her epithet Primigenia survives. An inscription was found at Praeneste reading *Orcevia Numeri / nationu gratia / Fortuna Diovo fileia / Primogenia / donom dedi,* which has been translated, 'Orcevia Numeria in gratitude for the birth of my child makes this gift to Fortuna, the First Born Daughter of Jupiter.'[9] But the meaning of Primigenia is uncertain. The basic meaning is 'first of its kind' or 'original.' But Cicero interpreted Primigenia to mean, 'our companion from birth,' '*a gignendo comes.*'[10] It is understandable why the meaning 'First Born Daughter of Jupiter' would not come to Cicero's mind if there was a statue of Fortuna suckling the infants Jupiter and Juno. The statue would suggest that her birth preceded Jupiter's, making her one of the first born or original gods. Clearly, things are confused.

The one thing that the inscription and the statue do show is that the people of Praeneste worshiped Fortuna chiefly as a fertility goddess. So if Cestianus' goddess is actually Fortuna, how do we explain her various attributes? The attribute most commonly depicted with Fortuna is the cornucopia.[11] This symbol of fertility appears under the chin of the goddess on Cestianus' coin. What about the wreath of laurel, grain, poppy, and lotus identified with Egyptian Isis? These are clearly fertility symbols not improper to any fertility goddess and they may have been intentionally imported into the worship of Fortuna at Praeneste. A beautiful mosaic survives from the temple at Praeneste depicting a Nile scene suggesting that the Isis connection to Fortuna was already made by the 80s. A later inscription which preserves the title *Isityches* for Isis shows that Isis could be assimilated with the Greek goddess Tyche (Fortuna).[12] What about the wing? Since Fortuna was also associated with Tyche who has wings to indicate her fleeting nature, the wings seen on Cestianus' goddess need not be equated with Victory. But how do we account for the military aspect of the crested helmet? A more martial aspect of the goddess was familiar to the people of Rome. Following a defeat at the hands of Hannibal, which cost him 1,200 men, Publius Sempronius Tuditanus, the consul of 204, vowed a temple to Fortuna Primigenia if he should be victorious in his next battle. His prayers were answered with a total rout of Hannibal's forces.[13] The Roman temple of Fortuna Primigenia, finally dedicated in 194, was located on the Quirinal.[14] The Roman Fortuna Primigenia had a martial origin so a crested helmet on her cult statue in her Quirinal temple would not have been out of place.

Classical Numismatic Group, Inc. 76 Lot 1227

The combination of all the attributes of crested helmet encircled with a wreath of laurel, grain, poppy, and lotus, the bow and quiver over her shoulder, the wing, and a cornucopia below her chin can be associated with Fortuna. The obverse head then is more likely the goddess Fortuna Primigenia as she was seen in her temple on the Quirinal.

I think that Cestianus' AED•CVR coin has preserved for us the iconography of the goddess Fortuna Primigenia most probably as she was worshipped in her temple in Rome. The identification of the goddess as Fortuna makes it easier to interpret the eagle holding the thunderbolt on the coin's reverse as simply emblematic of Jupiter, who was either the father of Fortuna Primigenia or was suckled by Fortuna Primigenia.

Now we must address another question. Do Cestianus' five types not inscribed AED•CVR belong to the year of his curule aedileship? Grueber dated all seven coin types to the same year but noted that the quality of workmanship was not consistent. He wrote, 'if we are to attribute all the coins struck by M. Plaetorius to one year, it is evident that the dies must have been executed in separate *officinae*, at which different sets of workmen were employed.'[15] Crawford separated the types, dating the five types without the AED•CVR to a moneyership in 69. This dating was widely accepted until the discovery of the Mesagne hoard. Although both types of the AED•CVR coins appeared among those 5940 Measgne coins, none of the other five types were found in the hoard. Yet, Crawford recorded 116 control marks used on the five different types and recent catalog listings have listed new control marks indicating that these types were issued in rather large numbers. Hersh and Walker felt that their absence from the Mesagne hoard was a compelling reason to move these coins to a date after 58. Since the coins were found in the Sustinenza and Frauendorf hoards, a date around 57 seemed best to them, suggesting that perhaps Cestianus was minting as a propraetor. Their new date of 57 has been adopted in most catalog listings. We know that Cestianus did hold a propraetorship, but much earlier than 57. Broughton assigned Cestianus' praetorship to 64 and his propraetorship in Macedonia to 63-62 based on a Greek inscription which referred to Plaetorius as *strategos.* Lucius Manlius Torquatus, the propraetor of Macedonia, returned to Rome in 63 and we know that Antonius arrived in 62. Since the other years were filled, Broughton felt that Cestianus must have been propraetor in Macedonia in 63/62, the only time open for him.

We know nothing more of Cestianus' career until 56 when he was in Rome actively supporting Lentulus Spinther's efforts to win the commission to return Ptolemy to the throne of Egypt. In 55 Cestianus traveled to Cilicia to join Lentulus, presumably as a member of his staff or as a legate.[16] In my study of the moneyers who minted between 63 and 49, I felt that for Plaetorius to mint so late in the 50s after he had already held the praetorship and a propraetorship was anomalous. I opted not to treat Plaetorius as a moneyer of the 50s. Clearly he was not a mint magistrate and clearly the money was authorized by the Senate for some specific purpose. Hersh and Walker offered no reason why he would have held a propraetorship in 57 or what occasioned the special need for him to mint these denarii.

Despite their absence from the Mesagne hoard, I still think that the five non-AED•CVR coins belong in the 60s and the coins themselves offer hints for this earlier dating. The 116 control marks noted by Crawford, which allow us to estimate the size of the mintage, appear out of place on coinage minted in the 50s. As discussed in the chapter on Pomponius Rufus, after the mid 60s control marks virtually disappear from Republican coinage. If Cestianus is to be dated to the 50s, his use of control marks is another anomaly. One might argue that Cestianus simply followed the practice he had used when curule aedile, but of the two coins minted during his aedileship, one has control marks, one has none. The use of control marks was common in the 70s and early 60s, but seldom used after 66. Roscius Fabatus who minted in 62 and imitated Lucius Papius' earlier issue was the last to use an extensive system of control marks. It is better to look for a date for Cestianus' other five types in the 60s closer to the time he minted as curule aedile, but not the year of his curule aedileship.

The year 67 offers a most interesting context for the five non-AED•CVR coins. The grain crisis had only intensified due to the unchecked depredations of the pirates. They had bested the Roman commanders sent against them and they continued to sail the Mediterranean disrupting all shipping. Plutarch said that their numbers had grown until they had over 1,000 ships, many with gilded sails, purple awnings, and silvered oars. They did not confine their plundering to ships at sea, but also attacked coastal cities capturing some 400. With no regard for the gods, they plundered sanctuaries and violated sacred sites. Abducting wealthy Romans and holding them for ransom was a particularly profitable enterprise.[17] The story of Caesar's capture by pirates is well known, but hardly unique. On one occasion, pirates boldly marched up a Roman road and fell upon two praetors dressed in their purple-bordered togas and attended by their retinue of slaves and lictors. The pirates captured them and carried them off. Eventually their power extended over the entire Mediterranean with the result that shipping and commerce came to a standstill. The Romans, long since dependent on imported grain, found themselves in a stranglehold which had to be broken.

In 67 the tribune of the plebs Aulus Gabinius drafted a law proposing that Pompey be given supreme command over the entire Mediterranean Sea and the mainland to a distance of fifty miles (80.46 km) inland. Gabinius reminded the Romans of the good service Pompey had done them.

> Remember how many and what sort of reverses we suffered in the

> war against Sertorius because we lacked a general. We could find no one either from the younger men or the older men suited to the purpose, except this man Pompey, and then, at a time when he had not yet even reached the proper age nor was even a senator, we sent him out in place of both consuls. We should wish that we had many such good men, and if one had but to pray for this, we would pray. But virtue is not a matter for prayer and it does not come to someone automatically. One must have a natural inclination toward virtue, learn what is advantageous, and put into practice what is fitting, but most of all he must enjoy good Fortune, all of which I suppose to be the rarest combination in the same man. When you find such a man, it is necessary that all of you with one accord make use of him and support him, even if he is unwilling.[18]

Pompey's proposed command would cover virtually the whole of the Roman world. The most influential senators opposed such extensive power in the hands of one man and tried to dissuade the people from voting the bill into law. But the Senate's earlier attempts to deal with the problem had been disappointing and ineffectual. The people eventually passed legislation giving Pompey almost twice as many forces as in Gabinius' original proposal. Pompey was assigned two quaestors and allowed to select twenty-four legates in addition. He was allowed to recruit as many troops as he thought necessary and to take not only from the treasury, but from the provinces and from the tax farmers as much money as he needed. That he did receive money from sources outside Rome is known, for Lucullus recorded handing over to Pompey money that he had won in the Mithridatic War. Five hundred ships were manned and 120,000 infantry and 5,000 cavalry were raised. Appian said that the money amounted to 6000 Attic talents, i.e. 24,000,000 denarii. He divided his command into thirteen regions and placed squadrons of ships, infantry, and cavalry under the command of thirteen legates who were given praetorian powers. This allowed each commander to have full control over his own area and not be drawn afield by endlessly chasing pirates throughout the Mediterranean. Pompey reserved for himself sixty ships and toured the whole area coordinating operations. It had been assumed that the war would be very difficult, so Pompey's commission was voted for a period of three years.[19] However, so efficiently did he manage the war that within three months it was over. Pliny said that Pompey captured 846 ships.[20] About 10,000 pirates were killed and another 20,000 taken as prisoners. These men were treated mercifully and resettled with their families in thinly populated towns away from the sea.

Plutarch said that immediately upon Pompey's appointment as commander in the pirate war the price of all foodstuffs dropped and soon the marketplace was overflowing.[21] The anxiety caused by the grain crisis may have ended with Pompey's appointment, but the massive forces that were assembled required massive logistical support. Supplies and equipment had to be purchased and pay provided. For this Pompey needed people experienced in procurement. If Cestianus was already engaged in minting money presumably for the acquisition of grain as curule aedile, he may have been enlisted by Pompey as a legate and retained in this capacity to mint money for the acquisition of grain, supplies, and payment of troops. It is not likely that all the money needed was readily available in coin and we should expect increased levels of production. However, neither of the issues that I have assigned to the mint magistrates for 68 and 67 is exceptionally large; and Cestianus' special S•C issues can reasonably be seen as part of the 24,000,000 denarii voted to Pompey by the Senate's decree. Pompey's command covered the whole of the Mediterranean and a traveling mint makes sense to meet expenses in different locations. That brings us back to Grueber's statement, 'it is evident that the dies must have been executed in separate *officinae*, at which different sets of workmen were employed.' And it may help explain their absence from the Mesagne hoard. Given the extraordinary nature of Pompey's new command, it is likely that the Senate authorized additional coinage and Cestianus' five non-AED•CVR types are the only S•C coins issued in large numbers since the war with Sertorius that can possibly be dated to the early 60s.

Numismatica Ars Classica Auction 59 Lot 779

> The obverse head is frequently identified as Fortuna and its association with the SORS reverse makes that identification probable. She closely resembles the Fortuna Populi Romani seen on Sicinius' coin.

Let us now consider the coin designs of the five non-AED•CVR types. Since the reverse scene of the SORS coin depicted the giving of lots at Fortuna's temple in Praeneste, the goddess on the obverse is frequently identified in catalogs as Fortuna, usually with a question mark, but she is not specifically identified as Fortuna Primigenia of Praeneste. I do think that her identification as Fortuna is quite correct, but she does not resemble the figure on the AED•CVR coin whom I have identified as Fortuna Primigenia depicted in a martial aspect appropriate to her temple in Rome. The head on the SORS coin, however, is what one might expect to see on the statue of Fortuna Primigenia at Praeneste nursing Jupiter and Juno. In this aspect she is very similar to the Fortuna Populi Romani identified by the inscription FORT before the face and P•R behind the head on Sicinius' coin minted in 49 that is pictured below.

Numismatica Ars Classica Auction 44 Lot 377

Sicinius identified his female head with the inscription FORT before the head and P•R behind the head for Fortuna Populi Romani.

The goddess on the SORS coin may well be a depiction of Fortuna Populi Romani, but Grueber felt that Fortuna Populi Romani was the goddess on the coin below with the anguiped reverse, the snake-footed figure in a temple tympanum, although he did add a question mark.[22] This goddess' hair is drawn to the back of her head and held in place by a hair net. She wears a circular earring and a winged diadem. Although the wing is missing on the diadem of Fortuna Populi Romani on Sicinius' coin and on Cestianus' similar coin, we have already seen that the wing can be associated with Fortuna.

Gemini Numismatic Auctions, LLC Auction II Lot 248

The Gemini catalog described this coin as 'an extraordinary example of this very rare but poorly executed type.' The obverse figure is usually referred to simply as a female bust in catalog listings. The temple tympanum on the reverse also remains unidentified.

Now if this head with the winged diadem is also Fortuna, is this temple with the anguipedic figure in the tympanum on the reverse a temple of Fortuna, and where was that temple? We can no longer precisely determine what temple was depicted on this reverse. Cestianus certainly expected his contemporaries to recognize the temple from the sculpture of the tympanum. But if we cannot place the temple, can we connect its theme with Fortuna? The monster with snakes for feet is one of the Giants whom Hesiod said were born from the blood that dripped on Mother Earth from the severed genitals of Ouranos. Pausanius said that it was absurd to claim that the Giants had snakes for feet,[23] but they are frequently so depicted in Greek art and even Latin authors describe them with serpent feet. After Zeus defeated the Titans and established himself as the chief god, Mother Earth stirred the Giants to conquer heaven and free the Titans from their chains. So huge were the Giants that they lifted whole mountains as their weapons. In Greek myth, they sprang from the soil of Phlegra in Macedonia. But the Romans had their own version in which they sprang from the Cumaean plain of Italy, also known as the Phlegraean Plain, an area of volcanic activity in which Mount Vesuvius was located. They could only be overcome by a god and a hero working together. Hercules assisted Jupiter in defeating these monsters and after enclosing them again inside the earth, Hercules brought the area under cultivation.[24] The volcanic soil was rich and fertile, but the ongoing volcanic activity of the area testified to the subdued presence of the Giants below the surface. Grueber identified the item cradled in the Giant's left arm as a club, but Crawford's suggestion that it is a cornucopia is better in light of the agricultural activity of the area where the Giants were defeated and buried. Why might an anguipedic Giant decorate the tympanum of a temple of Fortuna? The theme of abundance indicated by Fortuna's attribute, the cornucopia, offers one connection. But the elusive title Primigenia might offer another. The title Primigenia and the statue of Fortuna nursing Jupiter and Juno that Cicero saw at Praeneste show that Fortuna was born in the earlier generation of gods. The primordial Giant in the tympanum is a reminder of that ancient status.

Turning now to the other coins in the series, we see that two other obverses have busts of a third goddess who is similar to the goddess with the winged diadem. These coins depict a goddess whose hair is pulled to the back and confined in a hair net. Her hair is ornamented with poppy heads. Her ear has a circular earring and above the ear there appears to be a horn instead of a wing. This may simply be hair pulled together and held in place by the hair net, but the shape is unmistakably a horn. Is this meant to suggest the cornucopia? The identification of this goddess too is uncertain. Her usual identification as Ceres or Proserpina depends on the reverse symbols of jug and torch, recalling the torches Ceres used to find Proserpina. Crawford cited the caduceus on the other reverse as an additional association with the underworld. He said that the goddess is clearly Proserpina.[25] He felt the reference was to a cult with which the moneyer was connected. Yet the main reason that the identification is uncertain is that Proserpina is usually depicted with grain in her hair. Here grain is conspicuously absent. The torch on the reverse becomes the most compelling connection to Ceres/Proserpina, but by the mid-fourth century the assimilation of Tyche (Fortuna) with Demeter (Ceres) was already evident in a statue that Pausanius saw in Thebes made by Xenophon the Athenian and Callistonicus the Theban. The statue depicted Tyche holding the infant Ploutos, a son of Demeter, which Pausanius said was a clever idea to show that Tyche was his mother or nurse.[26] The statue Pausanius saw is lost, but a similar statue of a turret-crowned Tyche holding a cornucopia in one arm and the infant Ploutos in the other is in the Archaeological Museum of Istanbul. The assimilation of Tyche with Demeter means that the jug and torch on the reverse are not limited to the cult of Ceres or Proserpina. In context with Cestianus' other types, this goddess may be another manifestation of Fortuna. There is an additional small feature that supports this. Proserpina usually wears a drop or triple drop earring, but the earring on Cestianus' goddess is circular which is not a common earring found on coins. The wheel is a symbol associated with Fortuna.

Gemini Numismatic Auctions, LLC Auction III Lot 297

On this third type, the goddess resembles the one with the anguiped tympanum. Her hair is ornamented with poppies and there appears to be a horn above her ear. The control symbol is a branch.

Numismatica Ars Classica Auction 33 Lot 261

What appears to be a horn above the ear on worn dies is more clearly seen as hair twisted into the shape of a horn on better preserved coins. The control symbol is a quiver.

Moreover, the caduceus which Crawford associated with Proserpina and the underworld may have completely different associations if connected with the pirate war. If Cestianus' non-AED•CVR coins represent money minted during the pirate war, the caduceus which appears on the reverses of two issues is easily understood as a symbol of the trade and commerce that the war sought to restore. Pompey cleared the waters of the Mediterranean in an incredibly short time and opened the sea again to commerce represented by the caduceus on the reverse. The caduceus appeared later as a symbol of Pompey's success in the pirate war on the coin minted by Sicinius pictured previously. Since the non-AED•CVR coins have not been dated to 67 by other commentators, the association of the caduceus with the pirate war has not been made and most of Cestianus' types have proven to be difficult to interpret.

Gemini Numismatic Auctions, LLC Auction V Lot 235

The same goddess with the jug and torch reverse also appears here with a winged caduceus reverse. A dagger is the control mark on this obverse.

Although separate cases can be made to identify each of the obverse goddesses on Cestianus' coins as Fortuna, why are they depicted with different attributes? Can all of these deities really be Fortuna? There was no shortage of temples of Fortuna in Rome, each emphasizing a different aspect of the goddess. Vitruvius said that there was an area of the Quirinal near the Colline Gate known as the Tres Fortunae because it had three temples dedicated to Fortuna: the temple of Fortuna Publica Populi Romani Quiritium Primigenia, probably the temple vowed in 204, the temple of Fortuna Publica Citerior (meaning that it was nearer the city than the others), and the third dedicated to Fortuna, without specific mention of title.[27]

It is quite possible then that all of Cestianus' goddesses on the non-AED•CVR coins are Fortuna represented in the different aspects under which she was worshipped in Rome, especially the Tres Fortunae. Gabinius told the people that the most important reason to appoint Pompey to the command of the pirate war was because of his enjoyment of good Fortune in all his undertakings. This confidence in Pompey's good Fortune may have contributed to Cestianus' decision to continue using Fortuna on these coins minted for the pirate war.

The deity on the obverse of the seventh type is a beardless male with long flowing hair and no other attribute. The symbols behind the head are control marks and do not help identify the figure. Crawford suggested that he might be Mercury since a winged caduceus is on the reverse. Babelon identified him as Bonus Eventus, Good Outcome. Grueber noted that this figure is not the same as the one clearly identified as Bonus Eventus on coins by Lucius Scribonius Libo where the youth is beardless, but does not have long flowing hair.

Classical Numismatic Group, Inc. 72 Lot 1323

This obverse head on Scribonius Libo's coin is identified as Bonus Eventus by inscription. He is young and beardless, but does not have the hair falling down the neck as seen on the god on Cestianus' coin.

Classical Numismatic Group, Inc. Triton VI Lot 720

This male head on Cestianus' coin is probably the god Bonus Eventus. Various symbols are used behind the head as control marks but do not help to identify him. This coin has a ladder. A winged caduceus is on the reverse.

The best reason to identify Cestianus' deity as Bonus Eventus is the fact that the god is frequently coupled with Fortuna in dedicatory inscriptions. Also, Romans frequenting the Capitoline would have seen two statues by Praxiteles, one of Bonus Eventus and the other of Bona Fortuna. Praxiteles' statues were probably originally statues of Agathos Daimon and Agathe Tyche which the Romans identified with their own local gods.[28] We do not know what Praxiteles' statue of Bonus Eventus looked like, but Roman Imperial coins and gems from Galba onwards frequently have a beardless youth identified by inscription as Bonus Eventus. To identify Cestianus' beardless god as Bonus Eventus is preferable to Crawford's suggestion of Mercury who usually has easily recognizable attributes. Since Bonus Eventus and Fortuna were paired together, it is not surprising to see them share the same winged caduceus on the reverse. Both deities were responsible for Pompey's success against the pirates and the return of safe commerce.

Addendum

Persephone (Proserpina) was a popular deity in Sicily and the obverse of the Syracusan tetradrahm below minted by Agathokles between 317-289 gives us a fairly typical Greek depiction of the goddess. Her hair is wreathed with grain, long hair trails down her neck, and she wears a drop earring.

Classical Numismatic Group, Inc. Inventory no. 783861

Chapter 31

MANIUS AQUILLIUS 67 BCE

The moneyer Manius Aquillius, son of Manius, grandson of Manius, is unknown and hoard evidence is minimal. Aquillius did not appear in the Ossero and Tolfa hoards with Crepereius and, since Aquillius' issue from an estimated ninety-eight reverse dies is about four times as large as Crepereius',[1] it seems better placed in 67 when the pirate war was making greater demands on the treasury. The serrated flan suggests that he followed the practice of the other two mint magistrates before him. The only other mint magistrate of the period to serrate his flan was Hosidius Geta, who does not appear until the Licuriciu hoard. Hosidius serrated some of his flans and left others smooth like Egnatius had done earlier. It seems that Hosidius marks a transition back to the practice of not serrating flans. The practice was abandoned after Hosidius save for the one exception by Roscius Fabatus who imitated Papius' serrated coins. Therefore, I assign Aquillius to 67.

Classical Numismatic Group, Inc. Triton VIII Lot 881

On the reverse, the moneyer depicted his grandfather Manius Aquillius lifting up a fallen girl identified as Sicily by the inscription SICIL in the exergue.

Although our moneyer remains unknown in the annals of history, his family was famous and he celebrated one of the family's proudest moments, the victory achieved by his grandfather in the slave wars of Sicily. Our moneyer has very carefully identified his figures on the coin's reverse. Along the right side of the figure dressed in a military cloak and carrying a shield on his left arm is the inscription MN•AQVIL, identifying him as Manius Aquillius. Below the kneeling female figure are the letters SICIL for Sicilia, the personification of the island of Sicily. Along the left edge of the coin the moneyer has inscribed the letters MN•F•MN•N in order that one know that this moneyer is the grandson of the Manius Aquillius who restored peace and prosperity to the island of Sicily long tormented by a slave rebellion.

Events in Gaul precipitated the slave revolts in Sicily three years before Manius Aquillius came to the island. In 104, the consul Marius received command in Gaul against the Cimbri and Teutoni and the Senate granted him permission to summon troops from overseas. Marius sent to Nicomedes the king of Bithynia for soldiers, but he replied that he had none to send since most of his men had been seized by the tax farmers and were in slavery in the Roman provinces. The Senate then decreed that no citizens of allied states should be held in slavery in Roman provinces and that the praetors should see to their liberation.

The governor of Sicily, Publius Licinius Nerva, complying with the decree held investigations and in a few days had set about 800 slaves free. This raised the hopes of all the slaves that they too might soon be set free, but the men of wealth and power hastily convened a meeting with the governor and prevailed upon him to cease his investigations. Disappointed in their hopes, the slaves began to discuss revolt. A small band of 200 slaves who had fortified a strong position were quickly overcome by Licinius, but he failed to take adequate steps when another band of eighty raised a new revolt. Taking the governor's inaction for cowardice, the ranks of the rebel slaves quickly swelled to 800 and then 2,000. When Licinius sent Titinius against them with only 600 men, the rebels routed them and gained a good quantity of arms. Their numbers grew to 6,000. After electing a certain Salvius as their leader, they set off to besiege Morgantina. The Roman relief army was defeated and more arms captured. His army now having grown to 30,000, Salvius proclaimed himself king and called himself Tryphon. In another area, the Cilician slave Athenion had assembled a force of 10,000 men and laid siege to Lilybaeum, but soon abandoned the enterprise. Tryphon summoned Athenion to join him, as if giving orders to one of his own generals. To everyone's surprise Athenion came and united his force with Tryphon's. Tryphon then seized Triocala, fortifying it with a wall and a moat, and he began to build himself a palace assuming the trappings of a king.

The following year the Senate sent Lucius Licinius Lucullus to Sicily with an army of 17,000 men. He won a major victory near Scirthaea, slaughtering about 20,000 out of the 40,000 rebels. Lucullus waited nine days to follow up his victory with a siege of the demoralized survivors at Triocala, but retired after suffering some casualties and the rebels revived. He did nothing more to prosecute the war for the rest of his term and it was suspected that his inaction was purchased by bribes. Two years later Lucullus faced these charges in court and was driven into exile. During the term of Lucullus' successor Gaius Servilius, Tryphon died and Athenion took over the command. He besieged cities, overran the countryside, and gained control over vast areas. The praetor did nothing to stop him and Servilius too was later tried, condemned, and exiled.

To quote Diodorus Siculus, 'Confusion and an *Iliad* of woes held the whole of Sicily' when the consul Manius Aquillius was sent by the Senate in 101 to take over the mismanaged slave war. Diodorus said that Aquillius 'through his own valor overcame the rebels in a notable battle.' He met Athenion in single combat face to face and slew him, although suffering a wound to the head. He recovered from his injury and continued his campaign against the remaining 10,000 rebels, attacking and capturing the strongholds where they had taken refuge. Finally, only 1,000 remained and Aquillius intended to subdue them by force, but after an exchange of envoys, the slaves surrendered. They were spared immediate punishment for Aquillius had better plans for them. He carried them off to Rome with him when he returned in 99, intending to use them as entertainment in wild animal fights during the celebration of his victory. Aquillius celebrated an ovation, but his entertainment did not meet expectations for the slaves forestalled his plans, according to one story, by slaying each other at the public altars.[2]

Shortly after celebrating his ovation, Aquillius was brought up on charges of extortion by a certain Lucius Fufius who gained a reputation for his diligence in the prosecution of the case.[3] Witness after witness came forward with telling proof of Aquillius' guilt.[4] The mounting evidence might have convicted him except for the brilliant courtroom theatrics of his defense counsel Marcus Antonius, who packed the court with Aquillius' friends and supporters, all weeping and downcast. Gaius Marius himself, under whom Aquillius had served as legate in 103 and his colleague in the consulship of 101, was foremost among them, tearfully asking for acquittal. But most dramatically, Antonius called Aquillius to stand before the judges and tore open his tunic to reveal the scars from wounds he had received fighting for the Republic. In light of the excellent service he had done his country in suppressing the slave revolt, Aquillius was acquitted.[5]

Aquillius seems to have maintained his political base, for in 89 he was appointed the chief ambassador on a mission to Asia. The Senate had decided on the restorations of Nicomedes to his ancestral kingdom of Bithynia and Ariobarzanes to Cappadocia and ordered Lucius Cassius, in command of a small army around Pergamum, to cooperate with Aquillius. Similar orders were sent to Mithridates. But angered over the Roman interference in Cappadocia and the earlier loss of Phrygia, Mithridates refused to cooperate. Aquillius and Cassius carried out the restorations using forces collected elsewhere. Once the two kings were back in power, Aquillius began to urge them to make incursions into Mithridates' territory. They balked at starting such a momentous war, but special pressure was brought to bear on Nicomedes who had promised large bribes for his restoration, which were still owed, as well as large sums borrowed previously from Roman lenders. Nicomedes reluctantly attacked. Mithridates sent envoys to protest, but receiving no satisfaction from the Roman ambassadors bent on provoking an armed conflict, he seized Cappadocia. He then sent his envoy back to the Roman ambassadors blaming them for what had happened and announced that he would send envoys to the Senate in Rome to denounce them. They in turn ordered Mithridates to keep away from Bithynia and Cappadocia and sent away his envoy under guard.

Without any consultation of the Senate, the ambassadors undertook preparation for war. Things quickly went against the Romans. They were defeated in their first battle; Mithridates took Bithynia and invaded Phrygia, and even the Roman generals were captured. Mithridates was particularly spiteful against Aquillius.[6] Years before, Mithridates' father had dealt with Aquillius' father, the consul of 129, whom he had assisted in his war against Aristonicus. After offering the elder Aquillius a very large bribe, he had obtained Phrygia as a reward for his service. Aquillius, however, was tried for taking bribes and, although he escaped punishment, the Senate annulled his acts and took Phrygia away from Mithridates' father.[7] Now this Manius Aquillius, following in the footsteps of his father in taking bribes from Nicomedes for his restoration to the throne of Bithynia, had become the chief instigator of the current war. Mithridates intended to settle the score. After humiliating Aquillius by parading him around on an ass and proclaiming him as 'Maniac' to all spectators, Mithridates poured molten gold down his throat, a particular reproach to Roman bribetaking.[8]

Such was the ignoble end of our moneyer's grandfather. Cicero said of Aquillius that he had befouled the memory of his youth with the shame of his old age.[9] Our moneyer, of course, chose to focus our attention on the glory of his grandfather's youth and it was the perfect time to derive maximum benefit from the good service Aquillius had done in ending the slave war in Sicily. This coin was minted only four years after the end of the famous slave war led by Spartacus, still very fresh in the memory of the moneyer's contemporaries.

In its initial stages, Spartacus' revolt in 73 was similar to that in Sicily. About seventy slaves had escaped from the gladiator training school at Capua and had taken refuge on Mount Vesuvius. Their numbers grew and they began to plunder the surrounding countryside. The first Roman armies sent against them were of inferior troops and were quickly defeated by the gladiators who now armed themselves with the captured weapons. After two different armies commanded by praetors had suffered defeats, the Senate ordered the new consuls of 72 to deal with the escalating danger. Lucius Gellius Publicola succeeded in destroying the German contingent which had broken contact with Spartacus. The other consul, Gnaeus Cornelius Lentulus Clodianus, surrounded Spartacus' main body, but when his quarry turned on him and attacked, he was not only defeated, but suffered the loss of all his equipment. Spartacus then headed for the Alps. An army of 10,000 men under the command of Gaius Cassius Longinus, the governor of Cisalpine Gaul, stood in his way and was mauled. Cassius barely escaped alive. Although nothing now prevented their escape from Italy, the slaves had become overconfident in their successes and prolonged their stay in Italy to continue plundering.

The Senate, on the other hand, was finally fed up with the incompetence of its commanders and ordered the consuls to return to civilian life. Marcus Licinius Crassus was appointed proconsul in supreme command of the war. When his troops were beaten in an initial skirmish, throwing away their arms and running away in the face of the enemy, Crassus restored discipline by collecting 500 of their number and decimating them. Spartacus in the meantime slipped away to the sea. At the Straits, he contracted with some Cilicians to transport 2,000 men across to Sicily where he hoped to rekindle the slave wars extinguished by Aquillius. These hopes were frustrated by the Cilicians who sailed away taking only their bribes. Crassus continued to press Spartacus hard and, after some small successes, brought Spartacus to a decisive engagement. Spartacus, knowing that everything depended on that battle, is said to have drawn his sword and killed his horse when it was brought to him, saying that if they won, the Romans had plenty of good horses, and if they lost, he would not need a horse. He then made for Crassus, pressing through the crowds of men, but he failed to reach him. A javelin in the leg stopped his onslaught and he died fighting amidst great slaughter around him. Appian said that the numbers of dead were too many to count and Plutarch said that Spartacus' body was not found. About 6,000 men were captured alive, but Crassus had no intention of reserving them for wild beast fights as had Aquillius. He nailed each to a cross and lined the road from Capua to Rome with 6,000 crosses, a much more impressive monument to his victory. It was all over in only six months and Crassus returned to Rome to celebrate an ovation.

In light of the recent suppression of the slave revolt under Spartacus, our moneyer has taken the opportunity to remind the Romans of the debt they owed to his family, for the war against Spartacus might have been much worse had not his grandfather already extinguished the revolt in Sicily. However, the particular design he has used to commemorate his grandfather's achievement was deeply influenced by that prosecution for extortion which followed on victory's heels. Lucius Fufius was responsible for Aquillius' grandfather's prosecution in 98.[10] Our moneyer inherited a personal enmity for the Fufii and it seems more than coincidental that Aquillius chose to represent Virtus who had just appeared on Fufius Calenus' coin two years before. On the reverse, he has given us an allegorical representation showing Aquillius lifting up a fallen Sicily depicted as a helpless girl whom he has shielded with his military might. His military virtue is epitomized by the draped and helmeted bust of Virtue who is clearly identified with the inscription VIRTVS on the obverse. Our moneyer seems to refute those old charges of extortion by proclaiming Virtus as a part of his family tradition. It was the Virtus of his grandfather that lifted Sicily up, and it was his Virtus recognized by the Roman people that defended him before the court and saved him. In his prosecution of Aquillius on extortion charges, Lucius Fufius had painted a picture of a Sicily raped and plundered by a greedy proconsul. On this coin minted in 67, Aquillius' grandson offered a vindication of those charges showing that Aquillius and his Virtus lifted up a downtrodden Sicily and rescued her. And, on the basis of this coin, that is how we would remember it today if we could not check the historical record.

Classical Numismatic Group, Inc. Triton VIII Lot 880

This head of Virtus is smaller than the previous example and has much more hair falling beneath the crested helmet ornamented with a side feather.

Chapter 32

GAIUS HOSIDIUS GETA 66 BCE

The surviving records offer no prosopographical evidence for Gaius Hosidius Geta and hoard evidence is minimal. He was not in the Ossero and Tolfa hoards with Crepereius. The coin first appeared in the Licuriciu hoard with the coins of Manius Aquillius, Lucius Furius Brocchus, and Aemilius Paullus. On prosopographical evidence, I dated Paullus to 63 in *Roman Republican Moneyers and Their Coins 63 BC-49 BC* and his coin appears to be the terminus of the Licuriciu hoard. Hosidius issued coins on both serrated and unserrated flans, which suggests to me that he stands between those moneyers who issued only serrated coins and those who issued only unserrated coins. Furius and Aemilius Paullus issued no serrated coins and their coins do not appear in earlier hoards. Grueber had dated Hosidius and Aemilius Paullus as early as 71; Crawford dated Hosidius' coin to 68; Hersh and Walker dated him to 64. Hosidius follows Aquillius in my arrangement, which gives a date of 66 for his coin. We cannot find the name of the Hosidii in Rome before this moneyer inscribed it on his coins, but the family name does occur in inscriptions from Histonium, the chief town of the Frentani on the Adriatic coast of Italy.[1]

Hosidius issued only one coin type, but the engraving of the dies was rendered in two distinctly different styles. Approximately twenty dies were engraved with larger designs in low relief and struck on broader serrated flans. The coin's obverse depicts Diana clearly identified by the bow and quiver over her shoulder. Long strands of twisted or braided hair drawn from the front of her head and tied in the back sit like a crown on her neatly combed hair. Her hair, cut short at the back, ends on a line level with her drop earring. On smaller, unserrated flans we see busts of Diana with a small head in high relief. A diadem was added to the hair and long wavy strands fall down her neck. She has changed earrings, now wearing one in the shape of a cross, and on her neck is a double necklace with long pendants.

The reverse design depicts a boar hunt. On the wider serrated flan, the boar is rendered larger. Etched lines indicate the coarse hair of his hide and a spear is stuck in his back. His front feet are stretched forward as he charges to the right, while a barking dog less than half his size snaps at his side. On the smaller flan, the scene is the same, but the hair on the back of a somewhat smaller boar bristles and stands straight up. The scene might be any boar hunt were it not that the boar is rendered so obviously oversized. Long ago Longperier recognized the scene as representing the Calydonian boar hunt, the most famous boar hunt of all. He suggested that the design was simply a parlant for the moneyer's name Hosidius, deriving it from the Greek word *hus* for 'pig.' Grueber accepted his identification of the theme as the Calydonian boar hunt in Aetolia, but said the design merely complements Diana on the obverse. Since the types occurred on coins of Aetolia, Grueber instead suggested that an ancestor of the moneyer took part in the Roman conquest of the province and that his coin commemorated that event.[2] However, it is hard to detect military prowess in a scene that is purely one of hunting.

Classical Numismatic Group, Inc.73 Lot 791

The moneyer's name Geta is behind the head of Diana and III•VIR is on the right. The Calydonian boar wounded by a spear in his back and attacked by a dog is on the reverse of this large serrated flan.

The hunt for the Calydonian boar took place a generation before the Trojan War. There are references to the hunt in Homer, but no major literary work has survived that recounts the full story. However, one of the most famous depictions of the hunt is found on the Francois krater, a mixing bowl of Athenian workmanship (*ca.* 570) found in an Etruscan tomb at Chiusi. The boar, facing left, occupies the center of a narrow band at the top of the krater and hunters are attacking from both sides. His hair bristles and he is drawn huge in comparison to the dogs and hunters. One dog bites at his rear leg, another lies on his back dead, his feet in the air. The dogs are all named by inscriptions, as are the hunters. Peleus and Meleager attack frontally with their spears as the boar lunges forward. Behind them stands the girl Atalanta, painted with white limbs instead of the black used for the men. Behind her stands Melanion. Beneath the boar lies the unfortunate Ankaios, gored and killed by the beast. Kastor and Polydeukes attack from the rear and behind them are Akastos and Admetos.

This was no ordinary boar, no ordinary hunt. Ovid described the boar as larger than the bulls of Epirus, with blood and fire in his eyes. His neck was iron and his bristles stood like spears. His tusks were as large as those of the Indian elephant and lightning poured from his mouth and the grasses burned from his breath.[3] This huge and vicious boar was sent by Diana to ravage Oeneus' kingdom of Calydon, to avenge the neglect he had shown Diana when he offered all the other gods but her appropriate gifts for a successful year. Oeneus' son Meleager organized the hunt to save the kingdom. With the telling of the tale over the centuries, many different names are given for the hunters, but from the sixth century the girl Atalanta is constant and essential to the story. It was her weapon that drew the first blood, wounding the boar enough to allow the hunters to surround it. Meleager rushed in to deliver the fatal thrust of the spear. Somewhat smitten by the huntress, Meleager made her a present of the hide and the head, the trophies of the hunt. There was a general murmur of discontent that this prize should go to a girl. When his mother's two brothers snatched away her spoils, the blood within Meleager boiled and in a rage he killed his uncles. Upon the return of the hunters, Althaea's joy at their success quickly turned to grief over the death of her brothers. But when she learned that Meleager, not the boar, was the cause of their deaths, grief turned to hate and a yearning for revenge, even though it was against her own son. Years before when Althaea lay in childbirth, the Fates appeared telling her that her son would live only so long as the log then burning in the fire should last. Althaea had snatched it from the flames and had hidden it away all these years, but now in her grief and mad search for revenge, she returned it to the fire and so Meleager perished.[4]

Classical Numismatic Group, Inc. 61 Lot 1428

Hosidius' second type is on a smaller unserrated flan. It has a smaller Diana wearing a diadem with the braided hair still beneath. Note that the name and office are reversed. Also, the boar is smaller and leaner.

The story of the Calydonian boar hunt is a purely Greek legend about a hunt that took place in Aetolia. We have seen similar Greek themes on other moneyers' coins: Mamilius' Ulysses, Strabo's Europa, Poblicius' Nemean lion, and Cossutius' Bellerophon. We have seen how these scenes related to the mythological descent of the moneyers' families from heroes or gods and it is most likely that Hosidius is following in the same vein. Men from the Italian *municipia* who sought office in Rome were from wealthy and influential families in their own towns and the designs on their coinage reflected the traditions in which their families found pride and status in their own area.

Numismatica Ars Classica Auction 63 Lot 234

This rare variant on a serrated flan seems to mark the transition from the larger to the smaller size rendering.

A ready connection between the myth of the Calydonian boar and the area of Italy where Hosidii lived can be found if we continue to trace events following the death of Meleager. Althaea, having killed her own son, next turned her hand against herself and perished either from a self-inflicted knife wound between her thighs, in Ovid's version, or by hanging, according to Apollodorus. Oeneus later married Periboea and their union produced Tydeus. He too shared that hot blood that boiled in Meleager and was banished from the kingdom for a killing. He fled to Argos where he married Adrastus' daughter, Deipyle, and they bore Diomedes, one of the major Greek heroes of the Trojan War, the leader of the Argives.[5] Diomedes survived the war, but did not return to Argos. He had learned that his wife had been living a base life there with another woman. This love affair was the revenge Venus had on Diomedes for his being so rash as to wound her on the hand when she was shielding her son Aeneas during a battle. Diomedes sailed instead to Italy where he married the daughter of Daunus of Iapygia and established a new kingdom for himself. In Virgil's *Aeneid*, Turnus sent Venulus to Arpi, the city Diomedes was then building, to ask his help in expelling the Trojans from Italy. Diomedes refused saying that he had had enough of fighting Trojans.[6]

Italian traditions record that Diomedes was important in the local foundation myths of a number of cities in eastern Italy, including Histonium, which seems to have been the home of the Hosidii. Many Italians on the Adriatic coast of Italy traced their descent from Arkadian colonists among whom the story of the Calydonian boar hunt was very popular since it was their native myth. Histonium was just north of Arpi. The city of Arpi, founded by

Diomedes, used the boar on coins minted in the third century. Even among the Veneti on the most northern shores of the Adriatic Sea, there was a tradition of an apotheosis of Diomedes and they decreed divine honors to him. A white horse was sacrificed and two sacred precincts still existed in Strabo's time, one to Argive Hera and one to Aetolian Artemis.[7] It is surely not coincidental that in the Italian legends Diomedes' city of origin is given as Calydon, not Argos as in Homer. Ovid even called the area *Calydonia regna*.[8] Just how popular the Calydonian boar hunt was with the people of eastern Italy is evidenced by the fact that those famous boar's tusks that had caused so much grief in Arcadia had been deposited at Beneventum when Diomedes founded the city. He had supposedly received the tusks from his uncle Meleager. The tusks were tourist attractions for centuries and were seen by Procopius in the sixth century CE.[9]

It appears then that our moneyer Hosidius chose to depict a legend that was well known and important to the people on his coast of Italy. Quite possibly his family traced itself back to Diomedes, which would have made it one of the oldest and most respected families in the area. Such a pedigree goes back every bit as far as any blue-blooded Roman who traced his family line to the Trojans. Hosidius could have expected many Italian voters to recognize the reference and to see in his reference a man of kindred heritage and worthy of their support.

Classical Numismatic Group, Inc. Inventory number 895469

This is a bronze coin from Arpi with a boar reverse (*ca*. 325-275).

Whether Gaius Hosidius Geta won election to the quaestorship and admission to the Senate is not certain. No political activity of the Hosidii Getae has been preserved until the mention of a certain Hosidius Geta proscribed by the triumvirs in 43, which suggests that he had supported the losing side. Although no *praenomen* was given, this Hosidius was well enough known to have his name recorded by both Appian and Dio Cassius in their list of famous people who had suffered in the proscriptions.[10] Hosidius was saved by his son who pretended to burn his body in a fake funeral. Hosidius then concealed his identity by wearing a patch over his eye. When peace returned and he could remove his disguise, he found that he had lost the sight of that eye. Over time the family recovered its status. Under Claudius, the propraetor Gnaeus Hosidius Geta campaigned against the Moors in Mauretania in 42 CE. The next year he was awarded the ornaments of a triumph for his victory in Britain and when Claudius further rewarded him with a suffect consulship either in 43 or 45 CE, the family was finally ennobled.[11]

Numismatica Ars Classica Auction 63 Lot 233

This die variant does not have a spear in the boar's back.

Addendum

An interesting Geto-Dacian imitation of Geta's coin appeared in a Classical Numismatic Group auction.

Classical Numismatic Group, Inc. Auction 84, Lot 927

The catalog says, 'This piece, an ancient imitation of a Hosidius Geta denarius, was reportedly found with a Julius Caesar/Cassius mule imitation… Compared to the official issue, the lettering on this imitation is quite crude. In addition, the boar on the reverse is facing left, while on official issue it faces right.'

Chapter 33

QUINTUS POMPONIUS MUSA 65 BCE

The moneyer Quintus Pomponius Musa is unknown and none of his coins appear in any of the hoards before Ancona whose latest coin was Faustus Sulla's S•C issue of 54. With no prosopographical evidence on Musa and no hoard findings earlier than Ancona, the dating of his coins to the 60s had been done on stylistic grounds. Comparing Pomponius' coins to those of Marcus Plaetorius Cestianus, Grueber dated him to 67. Crawford dated Pomponius to 66 based on the stylistic similarity of his obverse head with the Apollo on Gaius Calpurnius Piso Frugi's coin that he had dated to 67. The discovery of the Mesagne hoard has upset this dating. None of Pomponius' coins were found among the 5940 denarii in the hoard. Since he used ten different types, it is usually assumed that Pomponius issued quite a large number of coins and his absence from the Mesagne hoard convinced Hersh and Walker that Pomponius must be dated after Mesagne's terminus of 58. They moved Pomponius Musa's date down to 56. This date has gained acceptance in many catalogs. The evidence of the Mesagne hoard is indeed compelling, but there were three other moneyers whose absence from the hoard suggested they be re-dated after 58 as well. Hersh and Walker noted the problems this evidence created. 'One difficulty certainly raised by our new arrangement is the squeezing of the issues of twenty-three other moneyers into the eight year period between 58 and 51. This would seem to be too many for such a short period.'[1]

In Hersh and Walker's arrangement, there are four moneyers for the year 57, four for 56, five for 55, and two for 54. In *Roman Republican Moneyers and Their Coins 63BC-49BC,* I decided not to treat Pomponius Musa as a moneyer of the 50s. The scanty appearance of his coins in any of the later hoards calls into question the assumption that his issue was large. Crawford estimated that no type had more than ten reverse dies and, judging from their infrequent appearance on the coin market, a smaller number of dies is likely. Rarity may explain Musa's absence from Mesagne as well as the later 972 coin Compito whose terminus was after 55. Moreover, I believe the fact that Musa developed a series of ten different types indicates that he was the primary moneyer for his year of office and I can find no room for him in the years 57, 56, 55, or 54 when we have more easily dateable moneyers minting rather large issues. In 56, the year to which Hersh and Walker assigned Pomponius Musa, the mint magistrate L. Marcius Philippus used an estimated 497 reverse dies.

Chapter 33

In the dating system that I have worked out, Pomponius Musa's presence is necessary in the pool of non-S•C moneyers between 81 and 64 in order to have enough mint magistrates to assign one to each year. This, of course, is not proof that he belongs here. But there is one very small aspect of this coin that does increase the likelihood that Pomponius did mint in the 60s. Pomponius placed an apex, which looks like an accent mark, over the V of his *cognomen* MVSA. Although Greek is written with accent marks, they are not used in Latin. The purpose of the apex was to mark a long vowel, not accent the syllable. Quintilian said the mark was not practical to use all the time, but was useful on words which were spelled alike, but of different meaning and pronunciation.[2] The apex began to appear on inscriptions after Sulla. Previously they had doubled the vowel to indicate length, but the apex placed over the single vowel became a shorthand alternative.[3] Pomponius Musa and Furius Brocchus are the only moneyers who used the apex on coinage. In Musa's case, his *cognomen* came from the Greek word *Mousa* whose dipthong *ou* was long by nature and accented in Greek with a circumflex. Musa's V with the apex was a Latin adaptation of the Greek word with pronunciation guide, so to speak. And one that nobody needed. But in the case of Furius Brocchus, the name of his *gens* was Latin, which the earlier moneyers Marcus Furius Philus (*ca.* 119) and Publius Furius Crassipes (*ca.* late 80s) both spelled FOVRIVS. The same spelling FOVRIVS commonly appears on dedicatory stone inscriptions. What prompted Furius Brocchus to alter the traditional spelling of his family name? The V with apex used by Furius Brocchus is more understandable if done by the same die engraver or done in imitation of Musa's orthography. This suggests that Pomponius minted before Furius, probably quite recently before Furius. It seems more likely that this unusual use of the apex by two different mint magistrates should occur closely in time rather than separated by eight to ten years. Moreover, we find that Faustus Sulla in 55 preferred to use the doubled vowel to indicate the long nature of the E in FEELIX rather than use E with the apex. Hoard evidence places Furius Brocchus firmly in the 60s since he appeared in the Licuriciu hoard whose latest coin was minted by Lepidus Paullus in 63. Since neither Pomponius nor Furius serrated their flans, it is likely that they followed Hosidius Geta who discontinued the practice during his moneyership in 66. On my timeline, Pomponius Musa comes before Furius Brocchus and is dated to 65.

Quintus Pomponius Musa inscribed his name on the reverse of nine different coins beside the representation of a Muse. Each Muse wears a long flowing tunic and Greek *peplum*, but the stance of each is varied since she is engaged in the activity for which she became best known in the ancient world.

Classical Numismatic Group, Inc. Triton VIII Lot 891

Calliope, the Muse of epic poetry, is depicted playing a lyre which is supported on a pedestal. The symbol of the lyre key behind the head on the obverse is an attribute for her special sphere of patronage.

Classical Numismatic Group, Inc. Triton VI Lot 725

Cleio, the Muse of history, holds an open scroll in her right hand and rests her left elbow on a pedestal. The scroll appears as her attribute on the obverse.

Classical Numismatic Group, Inc. Triton VI Lot 726

Melpomene, the Muse of tragedy, facing right holds out a tragic mask in her left hand and rests her right hand on a club stood upright on the ground. At her side she wears a sword. A scepter appears on the obverse as her attribute.

Each Muse's specialization in a particular art was a late development and the distinctions were not canonical. Originally in Greek myth, they were not so differentiated. In Hesiod's *Theogony*, written in the eighth century, the Muses were daughters of Jupiter and Mnemosyne (Memory). Jupiter laid with her for nine nights and in due course she bore nine daughters whom Hesiod described as 'all of the same mind,' whose chief care of heart was song, which brought to men a release from evils and a respite from troubles.[4] Many layers of myth had been added by the first century when Diodorus Siculus gave his audience a short summary of the basic facts about the Muses.

> The majority of myth writers, especially the most esteemed, say that they were daughters of Jupiter and Mnemosyne. But a few of the poets, among whom is Alcman, declare them to be daughters of Uranus and Ge 'Heaven and Earth.' Likewise they disagree even about their number, for some say there were three, others say nine. The number nine has won out, having been established by the most famous men, I mean Homer and Hesiod and other such poets....To each of them, men attribute a special disposition for pursuits related to the arts, for example, poetry, singing, pantomimic dancing, choral dancing, astronomy, and the other pursuits. Most myth writers say they are virgins since the excellence achieved by education seems to be uncorrupted. They are called Muses from the word *muein*, that is, from the teaching of noble and fitting subjects which are unknown to the uneducated. They say that men named them giving a literal meaning to the name of each Muse. Cleio is so named because when men are extolled in poetry the praise bestows great fame (*kleos*), Euterpe is named for delighting (*terpein*) her listeners with the benefits of education, Thaleia because those who are extolled in poetry live on and flourish (*thallein*) for many ages, Melpomene is named for the melodies (*melodia*) with which she stirs the souls of her listeners, Terpsichore because she delights (*terpein*) her listeners with the benefits of education, Erato because she makes those who are educated desirable and loveable (*eperastos*), Polymnia because with her great praise (*polle humnesis*) she makes famous those who have won immortal repute through their writings, Urania because she raises to the heavens (*ouranos*) those who have been instructed by her, for with lofty thoughts and ideas souls are elevated to heavenly heights, Calliope is named from her beautiful voice (*kale ops*), that is, with the beauty of her language she wins the approbation of her listeners.[5]

In the Greek world, statue groupings of the Muses were usually found in temples of Apollo. The head depicted on the obverses of all ten types of Musa's coins has been identified as Apollo. However, the standard identification of Apollo as the obverse of the nine Muses coins is questionable. Grueber noted the different form of the head on these coins. 'It is laureate, and the hair is rolled back, and there is an ornament near the ear...'[6] If we look closely at the hair styles on most of the Muses, we note the same rolled up hair. The obverse head on the nine types of the Muses is not Apollo but a Muse. The head of each Muse is not individualized, for all were sisters of one mind. What makes each distinct is the attribute placed behind her head.

Classical Numismatic Group, Inc. Triton XIII Lot 281

Erato, the Muse of erotic poetry, faces forward and plucks the lyre with her right hand. A flower is her attribute on the obverse. This is the rarest of the series and this coin is possibly the best example known.

Classical Numismatic Group, Inc. 63 Lot 1171

Terpsichore, the Muse of dance, holds her lyre in her left hand and in her right hand she holds the plectrum. On this obverse die, there is a flower on a stalk beside her head.

Classical Numismatic Group, Inc. Triton VIII Lot 898

On this die variant, Terpsichore has a tortoise behind her head.

In Diodorus' passage we see that the Muses Euterpe and Terpsichore were described in the same way, receiving no distinction in their patronage. A similar thing happens with the depictions of the Muses on these coins where Terpsichore and Erato both hold lyres in similar stances and share the same attribute of the flower on a stalk. This repetition is not surprising when we remember that originally they were not differentiated from one another, all being of the same mind as Hesiod said. Crawford said that the nine Muses were chosen as types because of the moneyer's *cognomen.* Although this could have been accomplished with just a single representation of one Muse and the name MVSA, our moneyer has been very clever in advertising his name. Each coin with its individualized Muse invites inspection and Pomponius' name is right there beside her even with a pronunciation guide.

Classical Numismatic Group, Inc. Triton VIII Lot 895

Euterpe, the Muse of lyric poetry, rests her left elbow on a pedestal and supports her head with her left hand. Her right hand holds two flutes, attributes which are depicted crisscrossed on the obverse.

Classical Numismatic Group, Inc. Triton IX Lot 1300

Urania, the Muse of astronomy, holds a rod in her right hand and points downward touching a globe which rests on a tripod. A star appears on the obverse as her attribute.

The apex was apparently only important to our moneyer in his own name for on his tenth type which depicted a figure identified as HERCVLES MVSARVM on the reverse there is no apex over the V of MVSARVM. The representation of this statue of Hercules also suggests that the thoughts behind Musa's types go beyond just a punning allusion to his name. The nine Muses and Hercules represent the statues that Marcus Fulvius Nobilior dedicated in the temple of Hercules. It is uncertain whether Fulvius Nobilior actually built the temple or restored it, but for all time thereafter it was known as the temple of Hercules of the Muses. Its location near the Circus Flaminius is shown on a fragment of the Forma Urbis. The statues of the Muses came from the Epirote city of Ambracia, which had once been the royal capital of Phyrrus. The city was filled with numerous and splendid works of art. Following a siege in 189, Ambracia was surrendered to the consul Fulvius Nobilior under terms of a treaty. Nobilior then proceeded to pack up the city's art treasures and ship them to Rome where he displayed 785 bronze and 230 marble statues in his triumph held on 23 December 187.[7]

Numismatica Ars Classica Auction 59 Lot 788

Thalia, the Muse of comedy, holds a comic mask in her right hand and rests her left elbow on a pedestal. On some coins she holds a shepherd's crook in her left hand. A sandal appears as her attribute on the obverse.

Classical Numismatic Group, Inc. Triton VI Lot 731

Polymnia, the Muse of rhetoric, stands facing forward, her right arm partially raised in gesture. On her head she wears a wreath, which also appears on the obverse as her attribute.

As noted earlier, statue groupings of the Muses were usually found in temples of Apollo and, in fact, one of Apollo's epithets was Musagetes, Leader of the Muses. Although Apollo does appear on the obverse of Musa's tenth type, he is not in his role as Leader of the Muses. That role has been usurped by Hercules Musarum on the reverse — a very strange role indeed for Hercules. The coin depicts a statue of Hercules standing naked save for his lion skin. He plays the lyre, having put down his club, which now rests against his leg. Hercules' career as a minstrel was quite limited. Traditions tell how as a teenager he was educated in the usual Greek arts. His music teacher was the famous Linus, who is sometimes called the son of the Muse Urania, sometimes the son of the Muse Calliope. Linus found Hercules' musical sensibilities lacking and on one occasion struck his pupil with rods. Hercules became enraged and smashed the lyre over his teacher's head killing him. Alarmed by his violent temper, Amphitryon sent him off into the country to watch over the herds of cattle. Hercules killed his first lion while guarding his herds and his subsequent career was filled with heroic deeds of strength and courage not music.[8] Even so, images of Hercules the musician (Heracles mousikos) had already appeared on Greek vases in the late sixth century depicting the hero, nude save for his lion skin, holding or playing a cithara, or sometimes a lyre, or even a flute. He is often standing on a podium with the goddess Athena near him, which suggests that he is involved in a musical contest. This image of Hercules seems to have lost popularity about the beginning of the fifth century, but was revived in the Hellenistic age and Roman period. The statue of Hercules that Nobilior brought to Rome was clearly in that tradition.

Numismatica Ars Classica Auction 46 Lot 387

Hercules of the Muses, identified by inscription, is on the reverse of Pomponius' tenth coin type. He is naked except for his lion skin. He plays a lyre while his iconic club rests against his left leg.

But to find Hercules in the role of leader of the Muses is indeed strange, especially since he reputedly killed the son of one of the Muses. How did Hercules acquire this role of leader of the Muses? Eumenius, a Roman writer of the early fourth century CE, said that while Fulvius Nobilior was in Greece he learned that Hercules was a Musagetes.[9] This implies that such a role was unknown to the Romans before Nobilior imported the cult to Rome. Eumenius' explanation has been accepted without much question. But two centuries earlier, a Greek author puzzled over the strange association the Romans had made between Hercules and the Muses. Plutarch asked, 'Why did Hercules and the Muses have an altar in common? Was it because Hercules taught Evander's people to read? They held literacy to be an honorable thing but until late the people only taught their family and friends.'[10]

Plutarch's question and less than enlightening answer show that the Greeks too were puzzled by the Roman temple of Hercules of the Muses. This calls into question whether the statue of Hercules of the Muses originally belonged with the nine Muses. The statue of Hercules playing the lyre may have been an unrelated piece of booty among the 1015 statues taken from Ambracia. Was it a sacred cult statue or simply the possession of a private individual? This was the very problem that the college of pontiffs had to determine in 187. Nobilior's personal enemy Marcus Aemilius Lepidus tried to deny Nobilior his triumph by introducing delegates of the Ambraciots into the Senate with accusations against Nobilior, claiming that despite having concluded a peace treaty, he had ravaged their countryside and terrorized their city and worst of all, he had stripped the city's temples of their ornaments and their cult statues, leaving only bare walls and doorposts for the people to worship. The Senate offered some relief to the Ambraciots, but referred the matter of the statues and artworks to the college of pontiffs to determine which were sacred and which profane.[11] The sacred statues were rededicated in temples in Rome and Italy. Dedicatory inscriptions have been found in Rome and Tusculum.[12]

Now in their deliberations, what were the pontiffs to make of the statue of Hercules holding a lyre? The lion skin and the club clearly identified the figure as Hercules. It would be natural to assign the statue to a temple of Hercules. But the lyre in his hands clearly defined a different and unusual side of his nature, but one already popular in Greek art. Moreover, the Hercules statue resembled the statues of the Muses Calliope, Erato, and Terpsichore which also stood in similar poses holding lyres. The pontiffs might well have assumed some sort of association between these statues.

Nobilior himself was likely to have promoted this pairing of the rough all-conquering strong man with the gentle and elegant patrons of the arts. Such a pairing reflected Nobilior's own nature. He was a rugged, conquering general, but was also a man of letters who knew the value of a literary record of his achievement. He took the poet Ennius along with him on his campaign to chronicle the events for posterity. Ennius wrote a play on the capture of Ambracia and Fulvius expected Ennius' Muse to immortalize his achievements. Cicero said that Nobilior even dedicated the spoils of the war to the Muses.[13] He also deposited into the safekeeping of Hercules and the Muses a copy of the Fasti which he himself had written.[14] And, finally, he entrusted into their safekeeping an ancient shrine of the native goddesses known as Camenae. These obscure Italian deities, whom Ennius invoked in his poem, had come to be identified with the Greek Muses and Nobilior's transfer of their shrine into the temple of Hercules of the Muses cemented the identification. Servius in his commentary on Virgil said that the shrine had originally been made by Numa. After it had been struck by lightning, it was moved into the temple of Honos and Virtus. Fulvius Nobilior transferred the shrine into the temple of Hercules, from whence it came to be called the temple of Hercules and the Muses.[15]

What has all of this to do with our unknown moneyer Quintus Pomponius Musa? The *gens* Pomponia was an old and established family that traced its line back to Pompo, a son of Numa. An earlier coin by the moneyer Lucius Pomponius Molo boasted this line of descent with a depiction of Numa Pompilius preparing to sacrifice a goat at an altar. Numa is clearly identified by the inscription NVMA POMPIL.

Classical Numismatic Group, Inc. 61 Lot 1297

Lucius Pomponius Molo (*ca.* 97) depicted Numa Pompilius about to sacrifice a goat. The Pomponia *gens* claimed descent from Numa through his son Pompo.

The *cognomen* Musa is not found in the family line until its appearance on these coins. Our moneyer's specific reference to the ten statues set up in the temple of HERCVLES MVSARVM suggests that the family did not use the *cognomen* Musa until some time after Fulvius Nobilior dedicated the statues in the temple of Hercules. None of the sources suggest that any Pomponius had a role in the events surrounding the dedication of the statues in the temple, but when Fulvius transferred Numa's shrine, he gave the Pomponii an opportunity to claim some credit.

When Fulvius Nobilior brought the statues of the Muses from Ambracia and recognized their kinship with the shrine of the Camenae by moving that shrine into the temple of Hercules, it became advantageous for a Pomponius to focus attention on a tradition that had previously been insignificant. They could claim that it was their ancestor Numa who had dedicated the first shrine to the Muses. To illustrate his point our moneyer has used the famous, easily recognizable statues of the Muses brought to Rome by Fulvius Nobilior, undercutting Nobilior's unique creation of the temple of

Hercules of the Muses and claiming for the Pomponii a share in renown earned by another.

Classical Numismatic Group, Inc. 61 Lot 1457

Chapter 34

LUCIUS FURIUS BROCCHUS 64 BCE

The moneyer Lucius Furius Brocchus is unknown. His coin appeared in the Licuriciu hoard in which the latest coin seems to be the joint issue by Paullus Lepidus and Scribonius Libo that I dated to 63 in *Roman Republican Moneyers and Their Coins 63 BC-49 BC*. In the previous chapter, I discussed how Furius' change in the usual spelling of the family name from FOVRIVS to FVRI, with an apex over the V to mark it as a long vowel, seemed imitative of Pomponius Musa, whom I dated to 65. The only year remaining for Furius then, in my arrangement, is the year 64.

Numismatica Ars Classica Auction 59 Lot 791

The moneyer inscribed his name L•FVRI CN•F over the curule chair that he placed between two *fasces*. Over the V he placed an apex to indicate that the vowel was long.

The *gens* Furia had many different branches with a number of prominent members who attained curule offices. Nothing is known of our moneyer's branch, the Brocchi, except a little piece of dirt preserved by Valerius Maximus. A certain Gnaeus Furius Brocchus was heavily censured for debauching his family.[1] Whether this Gnaeus was the father of the moneyer or another relative is unknown. We note only that our moneyer did not shrink from using his father's name Gnaeus on his coin, which suggests that the name carried no stigma at that time.

On the reverse, Brocchus depicted a curule chair between *fasces*. This was the third time that a curule chair appeared on a denarius. Publius Furius Crassipes was the first to use the type. Crassipes had put the head of Cybele on the obverse and on the reverse the curule chair inscribed with the moneyer's name P•FOVRIVS as a reference to his own curule aedileship. Plaetorius Cestianus copied Crassipes' design for his curule aedileship in 68. When Furius Brocchus reused the curule chair on his coin's reverse in 64, the look was similar, but the meaning was changed. Crassipes and Cestianus both were alluding to their own curule aedileships, but Furius Brocchus had not yet held curule office as was clearly shown by the inscription III VIR on the obverse, used here for only the second time. Furius' curule chair recalls the many curule offices held by other Furii.

Instead of Cybele for his obverse, Furius depicted Ceres wearing a wreath of grain. The reference to grain is further stressed with the barley-corn before her head and the wheat-ear behind. Grueber suggested that the coin was a reference to the office of plebeian aedile.[2] A coin by the plebeian aediles Marcus Fannius and Lucius Critonius (*ca.* 86) actually depicted those two plebeian aediles functioning as *curatores annonae,* 'curators of grain.' They used a bust of Ceres with the inscription AED•PL on the obverse and on the reverse they depicted themselves sitting on benches to distribute grain symbolized by a single ear of grain to the right.

Numismatica Ars Classica Auction 25 Lot 282

A grain wreathed Ceres similar to Furius Brocchus' Ceres is on the coin by the plebeian aediles Marcus Fannius and Lucius Critonius. The money was issued to buy grain represented by the ear of grain on the right.

Crawford said that Furius Brocchus perhaps intended to recall 'the *cura annonae* of an aedilician ancestor or indicate his own ambitions.'[3] Nothing in the surviving historical evidence records a special *cura annonae* held by a Furius, but the record may simply be lost. Let us note that even today the message most easily extracted from the coin is that the moneyer is making a reference to management of grain distribution. Grain flowed freely into Rome after the pirate war in 67 had reopened the lanes of commerce. It would appear that the grain crisis, which the Senate had been wrestling with since the passage of the *lex Terentia et Cassia* in 73, had come to an end following Pompey's successful campaign. Why then did Furius Brocchus think that grain was still an important issue to stress on his coinage in 64?

Classical Numismatic Group, Inc. 63 Lot 1165

Furius inscribed his *cognomen* BROCCHI beneath the head of Ceres on the obverse of his coin. She wears a grain wreath in her hair and a wheat-ear is behind her head, a barley-corn in front.

Furius Brocchus was minting at a time when social discontent and frustration were building. Conditions for many of the urban poor were reaching the point of desperation. Catiline wooed the mood of discontent attaching to himself men who had given up hope of any improvement in their condition without a violent revolution. He had begun in 64 to lay the foundations for the insurrection that was to burst forth in Cicero's consulship the next year.

In the long list of social causes that Cicero enumerated as underlying reasons for the support Catiline found for his conspiracy, grain was never mentioned. Yet, immediately following Cicero's revelation of the plot and the execution of five of the ringleaders in December 63, Cato proposed a grain measure. Plutarch said that Cato was alarmed at the potential for further unrest and persuaded the Senate to pass a bill to conciliate the poor and landless by including them in the distribution of grain. Cato's measure was presumably an extension of the program instituted under the *lex Terentia et Cassia* of 73. The cost of the program was an additional 7,500,000 denarii a year.[4] Furius Brocchus' coinage of 64 shows that Cato's legislation did not just appear out of nowhere. There must have been some kind of effort to expand the grain dole for the poorest citizens prior to the passage of Cato's measure and it would appear that our moneyer Furius Brocchus took note of the grain issue well before Cato's legislation. With this coin's design, our moneyer Furius Brocchus has pinned a badge on himself as one of the *populares* interested in promoting the issues of the plebs rather than the senatorial agenda. The coin is a declaration of his politics.

Introduction
1. Dio Cassius, 54.26.7.
2. Dio Cassius, 54.26.5.
3. Harold B. Mattingly, 'The Management of the Roman Republican Mint,' *AJJN* 29 (1982) p. 12.
4. Andrew Burnett, 'The Authority to Coin in the Late Republic and Early Empire,' *NC* (1977) p. 37.
5. Andrew Burnett, 'The Authority to Coin in the Late Republic and Early Empire,' *NC* (1977) p. 42.
6. M. H. Crawford, *Roman Republican Coinage*, vol. 2, pp. 608-9.
7. M. H. Crawford, *RRC*, p. 81.
8. Lily Ross Taylor, *The Voting Districts of the Roman Republic,* Rome (1960) p. 117.

Chapter 1 Aulus Postumius Albinus
1. H. A. Grueber, *Coins of the Roman Republic in the British Museum*, vol. 1, p. 319.
2. Plutarch, *Sulla,* 32.1.
3. Appian, *Civil War*, 1.94.
4. M. H. Crawford, *RRC*, vol. 1, p. 81.
5. Livy, 1.45.
6. Plutarch, *Roman Questions*, 4.
7. Dionysius of Halicarnassus, 6.12.6.
8. Velleius Paterculus, 2.15.3.
9. Livy, 40.50.6-7; 41.6.4.
10. Plutarch, *Sertorius,* 10.1.

Chapter 2 Gaius Marius Capito
1. M. H. Crawford, *RRC*, vol. 2, pp. 608-9.
2. Appian, *Civil War,* 1.98.
3. Plutarch, *Sulla,* 33.1.
4. Appian, *Civil War,* 1.100.
5. H. A. Grueber, *CRR*, vol.1, p. 353.
6. Appian, *Civil War*, 1.95.
7. Appian, *Civil War*, 1.96.
8. Appian, *Civil War*, 1.104.
9. Plutarch, *Sulla,* 33.4.
10. Appian, *Civil War*, 1.101.

Chapter 3 L. Vol Strabo
1. M. H. Crawford, *RRC*, vol.1, p. 82.
2. Ovid, *Metamorphoses*, 2.874-75.
3. M. H. Crawford, *RRC*, vol.1, p. 391.
4. Cicero, *In Verrem* II, 4.135.
5. Strabo, *Geography,* 6.3.3.
6. Suetonius, *Galba,* 2.
7. Livy, 1.49; Dionysius of Halicarnassus, 4.45.
8. Cicero, *In Verrem* II, 5.180.
9. Cicero, *In Pisonem,* 2.

Chapter 4 Lucius Procilius
1. Cicero, *Ad Quintum Fratrem*, 2.6.1.
2. L. R. Taylor, 'Magistrates of 55 B.C. in Cicero's Pro Plancio and Catullus 52,' *Athenaeum* n.s. 42 (1968) 19.
3. Cicero, *Ad Atticum*, 4.15.4; 4.16.5.
4. Livy, 32.30.10.
5. Cicero, *Pro Murena*, 41.
6. Cicero, *De Divinatione,* 1.4; Julius Obsequens, 55.
7. Livy, *Ep*. 63.
8. Hieronymus, *Ol*. 173.4.
9. Livy, *Ep*. 98.
10. Cicero, *De Legibus*, 2.2.5.

Chapter 5 Gaius Poblicius
1. M.H. Crawford, *RRC*, vol.1, p. 396.
2. Theocritus, *Idylls,* 25.
3. W. Llewellyn, *The Etruscan Lion*, Oxford (1969) p. 140.
4. H. A. Grueber, *CRR*, vol.1, p. 365.
5. Dionysius of Halicarnassus, 3.34ff.
6. Virgil, *Aeneid*, 7.670; Servius, *Commentary on Virgil's Aeneid,* 7.670.
7. Pausanius, *Description of Greece,* 2.15.2.
8. Pausanius, *Description of Greece*, 5.17.8.
9. Virgil, *Aeneid*, 6.776.
10. Pliny, *Naturalis Historia*, 3.23.

Chapter 6 Gaius Naevius Balbus
1. Livy, 45.13.10-11.
2. Sallust, *Hist.* ii, 34M.
3. M. H. Crawford, *RRC*, vol.1, p. 390.
4. M. H. Crawford, *RRC*, vol.1, p. 82, note 3.
5. H. A. Grueber, *CRR*, vol.1, p. 367.
6. Dionysius of Halicarnassus, 7.73.2.

Chapter 7 Lucius Papius
1. Lily Ross Taylor, *The Voting Districts of the Roman Republic,* Rome (1960) p. 190.
2. Dio Cassius, 37.9.5.
3. Dessau, 8893.
4. C. Hersh and A. Walker, 'The Mesagne Hoard,' *ANSMN* 29 (1984) p. 119.
5. M. H. Crawford, *RRC*, vol.1, p. 399.
6. Aelian, *On the Nature of Animals*, 4.27.
7. M. H. Crawford, *RRC*, vol.1, p. 399.
8. H. A. Grueber, *CRR*, vol.1, p. 372.

Chapter 8 Tiberius Claudius Nero
1. Appian, *Mithridatic War*, 95.
2. Plutarch, *Pompey,* 26.
3. Sallust, *Bellum Catilinae*, 50.4.

4. H. A. Grueber, *CRR*, vol.1, p. 381.
5. M. H. Crawford, *RRC*, vol.1, p. 398.
6. Plutarch, *Sertorius*, 11.
7. Plutarch, *Sertorius*, 20.

Chapter 9 Gaius Egnatius Maxsumus
1. M. H. Crawford, *RRC*, vol.1, p. 82.
2. H. A. Grueber, *CRR*, vol.1, p. 399.
3. Appian, *Civil War*, 1.41.
4. Appian, *Civil War*, 1.45.
5. Lily Ross Taylor, *The Voting Districts of the Roman Republic,* Rome (1960) p. 211.
6. Cicero, *Pro Cluentio*, 135.
7. Sallust, *Histories,* 1.55.
8. Sallust, *Histories,* 1.77.
9. Appian, *Civil War*, 1.97.
10. Lucretius, *De Rerum Natura*, 1.29-40.
11. Suetonius, *Tiberius,* 2.3; Valerius Maximus, 8.1; Livy, *Per.*19.
12. Livy, 24.16.
13. Hyginus, *Fabulae*, preface.

Chapter 10 Lucius Farsuleius Mensor
1. M. H. Crawford, *RRC,* vol.1, p. 82.
2. H. A. Grueber, *CRR*, vol.1, p. 402.
3. M. H. Crawford, *RRC*, vol.1, p. 406.
4. Sallust, *Histories,* 1.77.
5. Plutarch, *Pompey,* 16.
6. Plutarch, *Pompey*, 17.
7. Sallust, *Histories*, 2.98.

Chapter 11 Lucius Cassius Longinus
1. Asconius, ed. Clark, p. 82.
2. Asconius, ed. Clark, 59.18.
3. G.V. Sumner, *The Orators in Cicero's Brutus: Prosopography and Chronology*, Toronto (1973) p. 50.
4. Sydenham, *The Coinage of the Roman Republic* (1952) p. 131.
5. Sallust, *Histories,* 2.47.
6. Strabo, *Geography,* 8.6.23.
7. Dionysius of Halicarnassus, 6.17.3-4.
8. Dionysius of Halicarnassus, 6.94.3.
9. Dionysius of Halicarnassus, 6.87.
10. Dionysius of Halicarnassus, 6.89.3.
11. Livy, 3.55.13.
12. Velleius Paterculus, 2.30.4.
13. Sallust, *Histories*, 3.48.
14. Livy, 2.41ff; Dionysius of Halicarnassus, 8.77.2-80.
15. Livy, 2.42.1.
16. Livy, 2.41.10.

Chapter 12 Marcus Volteius

1. M. H. Crawford, *RRC*, vol.1, p. 40.
2. C. Hersh and A. Walker, 'The Mesagne Hoard,' *ANSMN* 29 (1984) table 2.
3. H. A. Grueber, *CRR*, vol.1, pp. 387-8.
4. Lucretius, *De Rerum Natura*, 2.600-39.
5. Ovid, *Fasti*, 4.210.
6. Cicero, *De Haruspicum Responso,* 24.
7. Livy, 29.10.4ff.
8. Ovid, *Fasti*, 4.251-4.
9. Ovid, *Fasti*, 4.259-60.
10. Livy, 29.11.
11. Ovid, *Fasti*, for the 4th; Livy 29.14 says the day before the Ides.
12. Livy, 34.54.
13. Ovid, *Fasti*, 4.326.
14. Livy, 30.39.8.
15. Ovid, *Fasti*, 4.393-4.
16. Ovid, *Fasti*, 4.493.
17. Ovid, *Fasti*, 4.562.
18. Ovid, *Fasti*, 4.497.
19. Ovid, *Fasti,* 4.682ff.
20. Livy, 25.12.9-10.
21. Servius, *Commentary on Virgil*, 3.332.
22. H. A. Grueber, *CRR*, vol.1, p. 389.
23. M. H. Crawford, *RRC*, vol.1, p. 402.
24. Dionysius of Halicarnassus, 7.71.2.
25. Livy, 6.42.12.
26. Dionysius of Halicarnassus, 7.72.
27. Cicero, *Brutus*, 72; *Tusculan Disputations,* 1.3.
28. Tacitus, *Histories,* 3.72.
29. Dionysius of Halicarnassus, 3.69.1-2.
30. Livy, 1.55.5-6.
31. Livy, 2.8.6-8; Dionysius of Halicarnassus, 5.35.3.
32. Dionysius of Halicarnassus, 4.61.4.
33. Dionysius of Halicarnassus, 4.61.3.
34. Dionysius of Halicarnassus, 7.73.1-4.
35. H. A. Grueber, *CRR*, vol.1, p. 388.
36. Pseudo Asconius, *In Verrem* I, Orelli p. 143.
37. Livy, 23.30.
38. George Duckworth, *The Nature of Roman Comedy*, Princeton (1971) p. 76.
39. Vitruvius, 1.7.1.
40. Ovid, *Fasti*, 6.209-12.
41. Diodorus Siculus, 4.12.
42. Pausanius, 8.24.5.
43. M. H. Crawford, *RRC*, vol.1, p. 402.
44. Sallust, *Histories,* ii.47.
45. Stewart Oost, 'Cyrene, 96-74 BC,' *Classical Philology* (1963) p. 20.
46. Pliny, *Naturalis Historia*, 19.40.
47. Appian, *Civil War,* 1.111.

Chapter 13 Lucius Rutilius Flaccus
1. M. H. Crawford, *RRC*, vol.1, p. 403.
2. Livy, *Ep*., 70.
3. Dio Cassius, frg. 28.97.
4. Quintilian, *Institutio Oratoria,* 11.1.12.
5. Appian, *Civil War,* 1.111.
6. Cicero, *Ad Atticum*, 12.20.

Chapter 14 Gnaeus Cornelius Lentulus Marcellinus
1. M. H. Crawford, *RRC*, vol.1, p. 84.
2. M. H. Crawford, *RRC*, vol.1, p. 82.
3. H. A. Grueber, *CRR*, vol.2, p. 358 footnote 1.
4. Plutarch, *Lucullus*, 29.
5. H. A. Grueber, *CRR*, vol.2, p. 359 footnote 1.
6. M. H. Crawford, *RRC*, vol.1, p. 82 footnote 3.
7. Sallust, 2.98.
8. Plutarch, *Lucullus*, 5.
9. Cicero, *De Imp. Pomp*., 58.
10. Appian, *Mithridatic War*, 95.
11. J. M. Reynolds, 'Cyrenaica, Pompey and Cn. Cornelius Lentulus Marcellinus,' *JRS* (1962) p. 97.
12. G.V. Sumner, *The Orators in Cicero's Brutus: Prosopography and Chronology*, Toronto (1973) pp. 133-4.
13. C. Hersh and A. Walker, 'The Mesagne Hoard,' *ANSMN* 29 (1984) chart 2.
14. H. A. Grueber, *CRR*, vol.2, p. 243.
15. M. H. Crawford*, RRC*, vol.1, p. 409.
16. Valerius Maximus, 7.3.1.
17. Appian, *Syrian Wars,* 51.
18. Cicero, *Ad Familares,* 1.1.
19. Cicero, *Ad Quintum Fratrem,* 2.4.5.
20. Valerius Maximus, 6.2.6.
21. Cicero, *Brutus,* 70.
22. Cicero, *Pro Balbo*, 6.16.

Chapter 15 Publius Satrienus
1. M. H. Crawford, *RRC*, vol.1, p. 404.
2. Cicero, *De Divinatione*, 1.20; Julius Obsequens, 61.
3. Livy, 22.12.
4. Cristina Mazzoni, *She-Wolf: The Story of a Roman Icon*, Cambridge University Press (2010) p. 22.
5. Otto J. Brendel, *Etruscan Art*, New York, Pelican Books (1978) pp. 250ff.

Chapter 16 Lucius Lucretius Trio
1. C. Hersh and A. Walker, 'The Mesagne Hoard,' *ANSMN* 29 (1984) chart 2.
2. H. A. Grueber, *CRR*, vol.1, p. 396.
3. H. A. Grueber, *CRR*, vol.1, p. 583.
4. Livy, 2.16.
5. Dionysius of Halicarnassus, 2.50.3; Varro, *De Ling Lat*., 5.74.

6. M. H. Crawford, *RRC*, vol.1, pp. 404-5.
7. H. A. Grueber, *CRR*, vol.1, p. 396.
8. Livy, 40.28.
9. Livy, 42.35.3; 42.56.1ff; Polybius, 27.7.1.
10. Appian, *Mithridatic War*, 92.
11. Appian, *Mithridatic War*, 77-8.

Chapter 17 Lucius Rustius

1. C. Hersh and A. Walker, 'The Mesagne Hoard,' *ANSMN* 29 (1984) table 2.
2. M. H. Crawford, *RRC*, vol.1, p. 404.
3. H. A. Grueber, *CRR*, vol.1, p. 398.
4. Horace, *Odes,* 1.35.1.
5. T. P. Wiseman, *New Men in the Roman Senate 139B.C.-14A.D.*, Oxford (1971) p. 257.
6. Strabo, *Geography,* 5.3.5.
7. Dionysius of Halicarnassus, 1.72.
8. Strabo, *Geography,* 5.3.6; Ovid, *Fasti*, 4.69.
9. Homer, *Odyssey*, 9.166ff.

Chapter 18 Gaius Postumius

1. M. H. Crawford, *RRC*, vol.1, p. 82.
2. G. V. Sumner, 'The Lex Annalis under Caesar,' *Phoenix* (1971) p. 254, note 26.
3. Cicero, *Brutus*, 269.
4. G.V. Sumner, *The Orators in Cicero's Brutus: Prosopography and Chronology*, Toronto (1973) p. 144.
5. Cicero, *Pro Murena*, 57.
6. G.V. Sumner, *The Orators in Cicero's Brutus: Prosopography and Chronology*, Toronto (1973) p. 144.
7. Plutarch, *Lucullus*, 24.
8. Plutarch, *Lucullus*, 8.4.

Chapter 19 Lucius Axius Naso

1 Valerius Maximus, 1.8.61.
2. M. H. Crawford, *RRC*, vol.1, p. 412.
3. Varro, *De Re Rustica,* 3.2.7 and 3.7.10.
4. Cicero, *Ad Atticum*, 1.12.1; 4.5.5; 10.15.4.
5. H. A. Grueber, *CRR*, vol.1, p. 419.
6. H. A. Grueber, *CRR*, vol.1, p. 419.
7. Pliny, *Naturalis Historia*, 8.76.
8. M. H. Crawford, *RRC*, vol.1, p. 412.
9. Homer, *Iliad*, 16.288.
10. Homer, *Iliad*, 21.136ff.
11. Plato, *Republic,* 327a, 328a, and 354a.
12. Museum of Fine Arts, Boston, catalog no. 1983.553.
13. Eberhard-Karls Universität, Tübingen, Germany, catalog no. S101347.
14. Plutarch, *Lucullus*, 29.8.
15. Plutarch, *Pompey*, 21.2-5.
16. Appian, *Civil War*, 1.121.

Chapter 20 Titus Vettius Sabinus

1. M. H. Crawford, *RRC*, vol.1, p. 86.
2. M. H. Crawford, *RRC*, vol.1, p. 414.
3. T. Robert S. Broughton, *The Magistrates of the Roman Republic*, vol.2, Additions and Corrections, p. 69.
4. Cicero, *In Verrem* II, 3.168.
5. Cicero, *Ad Familares*, 15.20.1.
6. Livy, 1.13.
7. M. H. Crawford, *RRC*, vol.1, p. 414.
8. Cicero, *In Verrem* II, 3.135 *coepit Scandilius recuperatores aut judicem postulare.*
9. Sallust, *Histories,* 3.19.
10. Asconius, 8C, ed. Clark.
11. Cicero, *In Verrem* II, 3.163.
12. Cicero, *In Verrem* II, 3.167.
13. Cicero, *In Verrem* II, 3.165; Plutarch, *Pompey,* 25.
14. Cicero, *In Verrem* II, 3.167.
15. Cicero, *In Verrem* II, 3.163-4.
16. Cicero, *In Verrem* II, 3.35.

Chapter 21 Gnaeus Pompeius Magnus

1. H. A. Grueber, *CRR*, vol.2, pp. 464-6.
2. Cicero, *Pro Murena*, 5.
3. Licinianus, 39 Bonn.
4. C. F. Hill, *Historical Roman Coins*, London (1909) pp. 96-7.
5. Cicero, *Pro Balbo*, 16.
6. M. H. Crawford, *CRR*, vol.1, p. 83.
7. M. H. Crawford, *CRR*, vol.1, p. 413.
8. Plutarch, *Pompey*, 12.
9. Plutarch, *Pompey*, 13.
10. Plutarch, *Pompey*, 14.
11. Plutarch, *Pompey*, 21.
12. Polybius, 1.39-40.

Chapter 22 Lucius Cossutius Sabula

1. Dio Cassius, 38.5.1.
2. Vitruvius, 7.15.
3. Suetonius, *Caesar*, 1.
4. Apollodorus, *Library,* 2.4.2.
5. Ovid, *Metamorphoses,* 4.753ff.
6. Pindar, *Oly*., 13.84ff.
7. Pausanius, 9.31.3; Strabo, *Geography,* 4.195.
8. Homer, *Iliad*, 6.179; Hesiod, *Theogony*, 319.
9. H. A. Grueber, *CRR*, vol.1, p. 405.
10. M. H. Crawford, *RRC*, vol.1, p. 408.
11. Pausanius, 2.3.5.
12. Pliny, *Naturalis Historia,* 31.48.

Chapter 23 Publius Cornelius Lentulus Spinther

1. *Inscr. Ital.* 13.1.131.
2. G.V. Sumner, *The Orators in Cicero's Brutus: Prosopography and Chronology*, Toronto (1973) p. 143.
3. Cicero, *De Officiis*, 2.57-9.
4. H. A. Grueber, *CRR*, vol.1, p. 406.
5. Harold Mattingly, *Roman Coins*, London (1977) p. 76.
6. Plutarch, *Sertorius*, 22.
7. M. H. Crawford, *RRC*, vol.1, p. 409.
8. Dio Cassius, 38.5.1.
9. Broughton, *MRR,* 3.93; see also Broughton, *CQ* 7 (1957) pp. 82-5; Cicero, *Ad Familiares,* 1.9.13.
10. Cicero, *Pro Sestio*, 72.
11. Cicero, *Pro Sestio*, 107.
12. Cicero, *Pro Sestio*, 117.
13. Dio Cassius, 39.12-16; Cicero, *Ad Familiares,* 1.1.
14. Cicero, *Ad Familiares*, 1.9.2.
15. Cicero, *Ad Atticum*, 5.21.4.
16. Caesar, *De Bello Civile*, 1.15.3.
17. Caesar, *De Bello Civile*, 1.22.3.
18. Cicero, *Ad Atticum*, 7.23.1.
19. Cicero, *Ad Atticum*, 9.11.7.
20. Cicero, *Ad Atticum*, 9.13.7.
21. Cicero, *Ad Familiares,* 12.14.3; 9.18.2.
22. Cicero, *Brutus*, 268.

Chapter 24 Lucius Plaetorius

1. Cicero, *Pro Cluentio*, 165.
2. Livy, 5.47.4ff.
3. Livy, 7.28.3ff.
4. H. A. Grueber, *CRR*, vol.1, p. 404.
5. M. H. Crawford, *RRC*, vol.1, p. 408.
6. Imhoof- Blumer, *Nomisma* (1910) p. 40.
7. H. A. Grueber, *CRR*, vol.1, p. 404.
8. Cicero, *In Verrem* II, 1.31.

Chapter 25 Quintus Fufius Calenus

1. H. A. Grueber, *CRR,* vol.1, p. 415.
2. Cicero, *De Divinatione*, 1.59.
3. Plutarch, *Caesar,* 5.2.
4. Plutarch, *Caesar,* 6.3-4.
5. Cicero, *Philippics*, 8.19.
6. Cicero, *Ad Atticum*, 1.14.5; 1.16.2; 1.18.1.
7. Dio Cassius, 38.8.1.
8. Cicero, *Ad Atticum*, 2.18.1.
9. Caesar, *Bellum Gallicum*, 8.39.4.
10. Cicero, *Ad Atticum*, 9.5.1.
11. Caesar, *Bellum Civile*, 1.87.4; 3.8.2ff.

12. Caesar, *Bellum Civile*, 3.14; 3.26.
13. Caesar, *Bellum Civile*, 3.55.
14. Cicero, *Ad Atticum*, 11.8.2.
15. Dio Cassius, 42.55.4.
16. Appian, *Civil War*, 5.51, 5.54, and 5.59; Dio 48.20.3.

Chapter 26 Cordius
1. Livy, 2.12.13.
2. M. H. Crawford, *RRC*, vol.1, p. 413.
3. Cicero, *Pro Sulla*, 24.
4. *ILLRP,* 414.

Chapter 27 Quintus Pomponius Rufus
1. M. H. Crawford, *RRC,* vol.1, p. 82.
2. H. A. Grueber, *CRR*, vol.1, p. 407.
3. Livy, *Epitome* for 70-68 BCE.
4. Pliny, *Naturalis Historia,* 33.57.
5. Dio Cassius, 37.44.
6. Pliny, *Naturalis Historia*, 19.23.
7. Tacitus, *Histories*, 4.53.
8. Livy, 1.55.5-6.
9. Tacitus, *Histories,* 3.72.

Chapter 28 Publius Sulpicius Galba
1. Cicero, *Ad Atticum*, 1.1.1.
2. Cicero, *In Verrem* II, 1.18.
3. H. A. Grueber, *CRR*, vol.1, p. 433.
4. Livy, 1.20.5-7.
5. Cicero, *De Har. Resp*., 12.
6. Livy, 10.9.2.
7. Macrobius, *Saturnalia,* 3.13.10-12.
8. Cicero, *De Har. Resp*., 12.
9. Cicero, *In Verrem* II, 3.122.

Chapter 29 Quintus Crepereius Rocus
1. M. H. Crawford, *RRC*, vol.1, p. 411.
2. H. A. Grueber, *CRR,* vol.1, p. 408.
3. Cicero, *In Verrem* II, 1.30.
4. Barbara Levick and Shelagh Jameson, 'C. Crepereius Gallus and His Gens,' *JRS* 54 (1964) p.100.
5. Barbara Levick and Shelagh Jameson, 'C. Crepereius Gallus and His Gens,' *JRS* 54 (1964) p.107.

Chapter 30 Marcus Plaetorius Cestianus
1. Cicero, *Pro Cluentio*, 146.
2. Cicero, *Pro Cluentio*, 125.
3. H. A. Grueber, *CCR*, vol.1, p. 435.
4. M. H. Crawford, *RRC*, vol.1, p. 437.

5. P. G. P. Meyboom, *The Nile Mosaic of Palestrina: Early Evidence of Egyptian Religion in Italy*, Leiden (1995) p. 160.
6. Dessau, 6206.
7. *CIL*, xiv 2891, 3091, 3095; Dessau, 3420.
8. Cicero, *De Divinatione*, 2.85-7.
9. Dessau, 3684.
10. Cicero, *De Legibus*, 2.28.
11. Plutarch, *Fortuna of the Romans*, 4.
12. *CIL*, xiv 2867.
13. Livy, 29.36.
14. Livy, 34.53.7.
15. H. A. Grueber, *CRR*, vol.1, p. 435.
16. Cicero, *Ad Familiares*, 1.8.1.
17. Plutarch, *Pompey,* 24.
18. Dio Cassius, 36.27.4-6.
19. Plutarch, *Pompey,* 25; Appian, *Mithridatic Wars,* 94.
20. Pliny, *Naturalis Historia*, 7.93.
21. Plutarch, *Pompey,* 26.
22. H. A. Grueber, *CRR*, vol.1, p. 434.
23. Pausanius, 8.29.3.
24. Diodorus Siculus, 4.21.6.
25. M. H. Crawford, *RRC*, vol.1, p. 418.
26. Pausanius, 9.16.2.
27. Vitruvius, 3.2.2.
28. Pliny, *Naturalis Historia,* 36.23.

Chapter 31 Manius Aquillius
1. M. H. Crawford, *RRC,* vol.1, p. 412.
2. Diodorus Siculus, 36.3-6.
3. Cicero, *Brutus,* 222.
4. Cicero, *Pro Flacco,* 39.
5. Cicero, *De Oratore,* 2.195.
6. Appian, *Mithridatic War,* 12-20.
7. Appian, *Mithridatic War,* 57.
8. Appian, *Mithridatic War,* 21.
9. Cicero, *Pro Scauro,* 3.2.
10. Cicero, *Brutus,* 222.

Chapter 32 Gaius Hosidius Geta
1. *CIL* ix, 2847=*ILS* 971.
2. H. A. Grueber, *CRR*, vol.1, p. 419.
3. Ovid, *Metamorphoses*, 8.260ff.
4. Ovid, *Metamorphoses*, 8.515-46.
5. Apollodorus, *Library,* 1.8.5.
6. Virgil, *Aeneid* 8.9; Servius, *Commentary on Virgil's Aeneid,* 8.9.
7. Strabo, *Geography,* 5.1.9.
8. Ovid, *Metamorphoses*, 14.512; see also Virgil, *Aeneid,* 11.270.
9. Procopius, 5.15.8.

10. Dio Cassius, 47.10.6; Appian, *Civil War*, 4.41.
11. Dio Cassius, 60.9.1.

Chapter 33 Quintus Pomponius Musa
1. C. Hersh and A. Walker 'The Mesagne Hoard,' *ANSMN* 29 (1984) p. 131.
2. Quintilian, 1.7.2.
3. Quintilian, 1.4.10.
4. Hesiod, *Theogony,* 55-61.
5. Diodorus Siculus, 4.7.1ff.
6. H. A. Grueber, *CRR*, vol.1, p. 442.
7. Livy, 39.5.15.
8. Apollodorus, *Library*, 2.9.
9. Eumenius, *Latin Panegyrics,* 9.7.3 Baehrens.
10. Plutarch, *Roman Questions*, 59.
11. Livy, 38.3-9; Polybius, 21.30.
12. *CIL,* vi 1307.
13. Cicero, *Pro Archia*, 27.
14. Macrobius, *Saturnalia*, 1.2.16.
15. Servius, *Commentary on Virgil's Aeneid,* 1.8; cf. Livy, 1.21.

Chapter 34 Lucius Furius Brocchus
1. Valerius Maximus, 6.1.13.
2. H. A. Grueber, *CRR*, vol.1, p. 486.
3. M. H. Crawford, *RRC*, vol.1, p. 440.
4. Plutarch, *Cato the Younger*, 26.1; *Caesar,* 8.